IN THE KITCHEN
WITH
STEFANO FAITA

IN THE KITCHEN
WITH STEFANO FAITA

OVER 250 SIMPLE AND DELICIOUS EVERYDAY RECIPES

PENGUIN
an imprint of Penguin Canada

Published by the Penguin Group
Penguin Group (Canada), 90 Eglinton Avenue East, Suite 700,
Toronto, Ontario, Canada   M4P 2Y3

Penguin Group (USA) Inc., 375 Hudson Street, New York, New York 10014, U.S.A.

Penguin Books Ltd, 80 Strand, London WC2R 0RL, England

Penguin Ireland, 25 St Stephen's Green, Dublin 2, Ireland (a division of Penguin Books Ltd)

Penguin Group (Australia), 707 Collins Street, Melbourne, Victoria 3008, Australia
(a division of Pearson Australia Group Pty Ltd)

Penguin Books India Pvt Ltd, 11 Community Centre, Panchsheel Park,
New Delhi – 110 017, India

Penguin Group (NZ), 67 Apollo Drive, Rosedale, Auckland 0632, New Zealand
(a division of Pearson New Zealand Ltd)

Penguin Books (South Africa) (Pty) Ltd, 24 Sturdee Avenue, Rosebank,
Johannesburg 2196, South Africa

Penguin Books Ltd, Registered Offices: 80 Strand, London WC2R 0RL, England

First published 2013

1 2 3 4 5 6 7 8 9 10

Copyright © Canadian Broadcasting Corporation/Stefano Faita Inc., 2013

Food photography: Leila Ashtari
Other photography: Darren Goldstein, Vanessa Heins, Tim Leyes

Manufactured in the U.S.A.

LIBRARY AND ARCHIVES CANADA CATALOGUING IN PUBLICATION
Faita, Stefano, author
In the kitchen with Stefano Faita : over 250 simple and delicious everyday recipes / Stefano Faita.
Includes index.

ISBN 978-0-14-318878-0 (pbk.)

1. Cooking. 2. Cookbooks. I. Title.

TX714.F345 2013   641.5   C2013-904044-7

Visit the Penguin Canada website at www.penguin.ca

Special and corporate bulk purchase rates available; please see
www.penguin.ca/corporatesales or call 1-800-810-3104, ext. 2477.

ALWAYS LEARNING

PEARSON

To all the viewers who spend time
with me In the Kitchen.

CONTENTS

INTRODUCTION

Hello, fellow cooks!

Thanks so much for giving this cookbook a place in your kitchen. It's exciting to think that these recipes will help you put dinner on the table each night, entertain friends on weekends or simply make something delicious that makes you proud.

It's an honour to be in your homes on television every afternoon. When we shoot *In the Kitchen with Stefano Faita* in CBC's Toronto studios in front of a live audience, I get an amazing opportunity to talk to you, one-on-one. You ask me food questions and personal questions, but the thing I get asked the most is, "How did *In the Kitchen* come to be?"

Well, it all started with my family's store in Montréal. We own a shop called Dante's, in Little Italy. It carries housewares and hunting supplies. It has been written up in magazines and seen on TV shows, becoming a popular stop for locals and tourists. I've worked there since I was a kid. We also own the Mezza Luna cooking school on the same street. My mom, Elena, is pretty well known in food circles and does guest spots on various TV shows. I would go to cooking classes and TV tapings with her, and at a young age I was bitten by the cooking bug, too. Once, when my mom was unable to appear on a local food show, I took her place—that was the start of my being on TV.

I had a "real job" as a graphic designer for a while—and I wasn't bad at it, either—but I soon discovered that looking at a computer screen all day wasn't for me. So I took a big leap. I wrote a cookbook, in French. It came pretty naturally to me, this food thing, and it shocked me how much people responded to my recipes. I even won a couple of awards for my book. Then TV came calling … literally.

About four years ago, while working at Dante's, I got a call from Krista Look, an executive producer with CBC Television in Toronto. She had come across my French cookbook and had seen some interviews I'd done and said she had a vision for a TV show that would bring my food to people across the country. That was cool.

Krista came to Montréal and we talked for ages over espressos and panini. She knew she couldn't promise me anything, but she said she would keep me posted as she pitched her concept to the "big cheeses" in Toronto. And she did. It takes a long time to get a show concept off the ground in this business, but she did whatever she had to do to get us on the air—making demo reels, writing pitches, talking to anyone who would listen about this crazy guy in Montréal who could cook.

Two years passed and I started work on two TV shows in Québec. I was getting pretty well known in French Canada. I was happy. I was busy. But I was always hopeful that I would get a chance to share my food with English-speaking Canada, too. The shot came—Krista and I were asked to shoot a pilot for the show. We did. Then we waited. Six months later, I was flown to Toronto to receive the news in person: *In the Kitchen with Stefano Faita* was a go.

Two seasons and 155 episodes later, this book is our answer to the second most asked question during those audience breaks in the studio: "When are you coming out with an English cookbook?"

In these pages are more than 250 recipes that I have developed with our fantastic *In the Kitchen* food team. Every one of them is a fan favourite from the series, and I love that now they're all in one place for you to enjoy.

When we started writing this book together and choosing the recipes, Krista and I were sure to include all the things that viewers like about our TV show—all the ingredient substitutions and suggestions about how and when to serve each dish. If you've seen me cook on TV, you know precision isn't my strongest suit. I add an extra drizzle of olive oil or a shaving of Parmesan to almost every dish, which makes it tougher to nail down a recipe, but our team made sure the recipes in this book are rock-solid. I would make any one of them for my family or friends.

But I hope you experiment with them, like I do—make them your own, adjust them to your taste. Please don't just look longingly at the beautiful photographs, thinking the dishes are too complicated to try. Get in the kitchen, roll up your sleeves, put on some music and pour a glass of wine—we'll cook our way through this book together.

Bon appétit, guys!

STEFANO

BREAKFAST & BRUNCH

Very Berry Smoothie

There's nothing better than a smoothie to put fuel in your engine and kick-start your day in a healthy way. Packed with yogurt, sweet berries and a hint of maple syrup, this is a rich smoothie that's a definite keeper. **MAKES 4 SERVINGS**

TIP For an extra-healthy kick, add 2 tbsp (30 mL) ground flaxseeds, flax oil or wheat germ. And feel free to substitute regular yogurt for the Greek-style variety.

1 cup (250 mL) Greek-style plain yogurt
½ cup (125 mL) blueberries
½ cup (125 mL) halved strawberries
½ cup (125 mL) raspberries
1 mango, peeled and diced (or 1 cup/ 250 mL frozen mango pieces)

2 tbsp (30 mL) maple syrup
½ cup (125 mL) soy milk
2 to 3 ice cubes

Place all ingredients in a blender. Purée until smooth.

Coconut Mango Smoothie

This creamy smoothie has an exotic flavour twist that will charm its way into your family's morning routine. It has the goodness of coconut water and mango, with no added sugar. Just throw all the ingredients in a blender, give it a whizz and voilà—breakfast is served! **MAKES 2 SERVINGS**

1 cup (250 mL) coconut water

¾ cup (175 mL) Greek-style vanilla yogurt

½ cup (125 mL) mango purée or juice

About ½ cup (125 mL) crushed ice

1 small banana

Pineapple wedge, for garnish

TIP If you find this smoothie a bit sweet for your taste, replace the vanilla yogurt with plain yogurt. Don't have mango purée or juice? Just add 1 peeled ripe mango.

Place coconut water, yogurt, mango purée, ice and banana in a blender. Purée until smooth. Pour into glasses and garnish with pineapple.

. . . .

Here's how to extract coconut water from a fresh coconut:

Bake the coconut in a 400°F (200°C) oven for 15 to 20 minutes. The coconut shell will crack and be much easier to work with. Let cool completely.

With a clean screwdriver or metal skewer, pierce a hole through two of the soft eyes of the coconut. Drain coconut water through one hole. Strain before using.

To crack the coconut, break apart with a hammer. Dislodge meat from shell with a paring knife.

Coconut Cranberry Granola Bars

It's easy to buy granola bars, but believe it or not, it's equally easy to make your own. This recipe is quick and tasty, and you'll feel good knowing it includes only healthful ingredients. Make a big batch for the whole week . . . if they last that long! MAKES 9 BARS

2 cups (500 mL) quick-cooking rolled oats

1 ½ cups (375 mL) slivered almonds

½ cup (125 mL) honey

¼ cup (60 mL) packed brown sugar

3 tbsp (45 mL) sunflower oil

2 tsp (10 mL) vanilla extract

½ tsp (2 mL) salt

1 cup (250 mL) shredded coconut, toasted

⅔ cup (150 mL) dried cranberries

½ cup (125 mL) unsalted roasted sunflower seeds

¼ cup (60 mL) ground flaxseeds

¼ cup (60 mL) wheat germ

TIP Use this recipe as a base and feel free to change it up—substitute dried raisins for cranberries, or maple syrup for honey. Add a handful of chopped dried apricots for some extra chew, or dark chocolate chips.

Preheat oven to 350°F (180°C). Grease an 8-inch (2 L) square cake pan.

Spread oats and almonds on a baking sheet. Bake, stirring occasionally to evenly toast, until almonds are lightly golden brown and fragrant, 10 to 15 minutes. Set aside to cool.

In a small saucepan, combine honey, brown sugar, sunflower oil, vanilla and salt. Heat over medium-low heat, stirring occasionally, until sugar dissolves.

Meanwhile, in a large bowl, combine coconut, cranberries, sunflower seeds, flaxseeds and wheat germ. Stir in toasted oats and almonds. Pour in the honey mixture. Mix with your hands until thoroughly combined.

Transfer granola mixture to cake pan, pressing firmly to an even thickness. Bake until golden brown, about 25 minutes. Let cool completely before removing from pan. Cut into 9 bars.

Fruit Salad with Fresh Coconut and Mint

It's easy to fall into a rut, making fruit salad with the same ingredients all the time. I wanted to change it up a little, adding some tropical flavours to the mix (and a bit of rum). Suddenly, fruit salad is exciting again! **MAKES 6 TO 8 SERVINGS**

½ medium watermelon

1 cantaloupe, cut in half, seeds removed

1 small pineapple, peeled and cubed

2 bunches seedless green grapes, removed from stem

Juice of 2 lemons

½ cup (125 mL) dark rum

About ⅓ cup (75 mL) freshly grated coconut

2 tbsp (30 mL) chopped fresh mint

Using a melon baller, scoop balls from watermelon and cantaloupe. (Alternatively, dice the melons.) Place in a large bowl. Add pineapple, grapes, lemon juice and rum. Toss to combine. Let stand in fridge for at least 30 minutes. Before serving, toss salad with coconut and mint.

Citrus Carpaccio

This is probably one of the easiest recipes in this book, guys. It's full of colour, texture and flavour. Just pick the juiciest fruits you can find and you have a brunch dish that everyone will enjoy! **MAKES 4 SERVINGS**

1 large orange

1 ruby red grapefruit

½ cup (125 mL) honey

1 tsp (5 mL) fennel seeds

1 cinnamon stick

½ vanilla bean

2 tbsp (30 mL) chopped raw pistachio nuts, for garnish

Mint leaves, for garnish

Peel orange and grapefruit. Cut into thin crosswise slices and remove any seeds. Arrange slices on a platter.

In a small saucepan, combine honey, fennel seeds, cinnamon stick and vanilla bean. Heat over low heat until honey is thin, syrupy and fragrant, about 5 minutes.

Strain honey syrup and drizzle over fruit slices. Garnish with pistachios and mint leaves.

Breakfast Yogurt Parfaits

This pretty parfait has a little bit of everything—yogurt, fruit and an easy granola topping. I love to serve it in little jars for a grab-and-go breakfast. No kid can resist this morning treat when it looks so colourful and fun! **MAKES 4 SERVINGS**

EASY GRANOLA TOPPING

¼ cup (60 mL) chopped hazelnuts

2 tbsp (30 mL) ground flaxseeds

2 tbsp (30 mL) wheat germ

2 tbsp (30 mL) unsweetened shredded coconut

2 tbsp (30 mL) brown sugar, or to taste

2 tbsp (30 mL) large-flake rolled oats

1 tsp (5 mL) cinnamon

2 tbsp (30 mL) flax oil

1 tsp (5 mL) vanilla extract

YOGURT PARFAITS

1 cup (250 mL) blueberries

4 cups (1 L) Greek-style or drained plain yogurt

About ¼ cup (60 mL) honey

1 cup (250 mL) chopped mango

1 cup (250 mL) chopped kiwifruit

1 cup (250 mL) chopped strawberries

TIP Get creative here. Shake up the selection of fruit or use different nuts in the granola. Serve the parfaits in a small mason jar: the screw-on lid makes it portable to take to work or school.

To make the granola topping: In a small bowl, combine hazelnuts, flax meal, wheat germ, coconut, brown sugar, oats and cinnamon. Sprinkle with flax oil and vanilla. Toss to combine.

To make the yogurt parfaits: In 4 parfait glasses or pint (500 mL) mason jars, layer blueberries, one-quarter of the yogurt, a drizzle of honey (about 1 tsp/5 mL), mango, one-quarter of the yogurt, a drizzle of honey, kiwi, one-quarter of the yogurt, a drizzle of honey, strawberries and remaining yogurt. Top with granola topping.

Creamy Oatmeal with Banana-Nut Topping

I eat oatmeal for breakfast at least twice a week. It's nourishing, and it keeps me satisfied for a good part of the day. On top of all that, I like that you can get creative, adding the flavours you love. So here's the ultimate oatmeal recipe for you to enjoy twice a week, too! **MAKES 4 SERVINGS**

BANANA-NUT TOPPING

½ cup (125 mL) slivered almonds, toasted

3 tbsp (45 mL) crushed dried banana chips

2 to 3 tbsp (30 to 45 mL) brown sugar

2 tbsp (30 mL) butter, melted

CREAMY OATMEAL

1 cup (250 mL) water

2 cups (500 mL) milk

1 cup (250 mL) steel-cut rolled oats

Pinch of salt

2 tbsp (30 mL) maple syrup, or to taste

1 tsp (5 mL) vanilla extract

¼ tsp (1 mL) nutmeg

2 bananas, mashed

1 cup (250 mL) plain yogurt, for topping

To make the banana-nut topping: In a small bowl, combine slivered almonds, banana chips, brown sugar and melted butter. Stir until well combined.

To make the oatmeal: In a medium saucepan, bring water to a boil over medium-high heat. Add milk. When mixture returns to a simmer, stir in oats and salt. Cover and simmer over low heat, stirring occasionally. If you like your oatmeal with a little texture, simmer for 15 minutes. If you like it creamier, simmer for 20 minutes. Remove from heat and let stand, covered, for 5 minutes. Stir in maple syrup, vanilla, nutmeg and mashed banana. Serve oatmeal topped with a dollop of yogurt and a sprinkle of banana-nut topping.

Easy Scrambled Eggs

Everyone needs a good scrambled-egg recipe in their repertoire, and this one can be yours. Whether you're making them for a quick weekday breakfast or a leisurely weekend brunch, these delicious eggs, with a hit of Parmesan and fresh herbs, will please everyone at the table. **MAKES 4 SERVINGS**

8 large eggs

2 tbsp (30 mL) grated Parmesan cheese

2 tbsp (30 mL) whipping cream (35%)

1 tbsp (15 mL) chopped fresh parsley

1 tbsp (15 mL) chopped fresh chives

Salt and freshly ground pepper

1 tbsp (15 mL) butter

1 tbsp (15 mL) olive oil

In large bowl, lightly whisk eggs. Whisk in Parmesan, cream, parsley, chives, and salt and pepper to taste.

Melt butter with oil in a large skillet over medium-low heat. Pour egg mixture into skillet. Cook, stirring constantly, until eggs are softly set but still creamy, 5 to 7 minutes. Serve immediately.

Stefano's Big Western Sandwich

This light, airy omelette, full of sweet peppers, ham and Parmesan cheese, is served up on some thick Texas toast with a layer of rich avocado spread. Go big or go home, I say! MAKES 4 TO 8 SERVINGS

8 large eggs

½ cup (125 mL) milk or cream

2 tbsp (30 mL) chopped fresh basil

1 tbsp (15 mL) grated Parmesan cheese

Salt and freshly ground pepper

4 tbsp (60 mL) olive oil

1 small onion, finely chopped

½ sweet red pepper, diced

½ sweet green pepper, diced

1 garlic clove, minced

3 thick slices ham, diced

Pinch of hot pepper flakes (optional)

8 slices whole wheat Texas-style bread, toasted

1 avocado, mashed

4 small handfuls spinach leaves

4 thick slices aged Cheddar cheese

2 tomatoes, thickly sliced

Preheat oven to 400°F (200°C) or preheat broiler.

In a large bowl, beat eggs. Whisk in milk, basil, Parmesan, and salt and pepper to taste. Set aside.

Heat a 10-inch (25 cm) ovenproof nonstick skillet over medium heat. Add 2 tbsp (30 mL) of the oil. When oil is hot, add onions and peppers. Cook until vegetables are soft, 2 to 3 minutes. Add garlic, ham and hot pepper flakes, if desired. Stir to combine and cook for 1 to 2 minutes more.

If pan looks dry, add 1 to 2 tbsp (15 to 30 mL) olive oil. Add egg mixture to pan. When eggs start to set around the edges, after about 5 minutes, transfer to oven. Cook until eggs are set. Cut Western omelette into wedges.

Assemble sandwiches with toasted bread, mashed avocado, spinach, Western omelette, cheese and tomato slices.

Baked Eggs with Cheddar

These easy-to-assemble all-in-one packages bring a hearty bun, Cheddar cheese and a baked egg together for a crowd-pleasing breakfast combination. I like to use brioche buns, but you can use pretty much anything—soft dinner rolls, even a slice of white bread trimmed and pressed into the muffin cup. Make a batch and serve a bunch! **MAKES 8 SERVINGS**

8 small buns

½ cup (125 mL) shredded Cheddar cheese

8 large eggs

8 tsp (40 mL) butter

Salt and freshly ground pepper

1 to 2 tbsp (15 to 30 mL) chopped fresh chives, for garnish

Paprika, for garnish

TIP Substitute any cheese you have on hand in these baked eggs—mozzarella or fontina cheese will be equally delicious. Add a few pieces of ham or some veggies to the bun for an all-in-one breakfast.

Preheat broiler. Slice tops off buns. Toast bun tops under broiler until golden brown, about 1 minute, if desired.

Preheat oven to 350°F (180°C). Lightly grease 8 cups in a muffin pan.

Pull out some of the bread from each of the buns, leaving a ½-inch (1 cm) shell intact. (Use bread to make bread crumbs, stuffing or bread pudding.) Place each bun in a muffin cup. Sprinkle 1 tbsp (15 mL) cheese inside each bun.

Crack an egg into a small ramekin or measuring cup and carefully slide into each bun. Top each egg with 1 tsp (5 mL) butter and season with salt and pepper.

Bake until eggs are set to your liking, 20 to 30 minutes. Garnish with chives and a pinch of paprika. Top with bun tops, if desired.

Broccoli and Cheese Party Quiche

This is definitely one of my favourite go-to entertaining recipes. Nothing says "feeding a crowd" more than a big deep-dish quiche, and this one has the tastiest combination of rich, creamy eggs, flaky pastry and flavourful ingredients. Just whisk everything together in a bowl, pour and bake. Brunch is served!

MAKES 8 TO 12 SERVINGS

PASTRY

2 cups (500 mL) all-purpose flour

1 tsp (5 mL) sugar

1 tsp (5 mL) salt

¾ cup (175 mL) cold unsalted butter, cut in small cubes

¼ cup (60 mL) milk

1 egg yolk

QUICHE

2 bunches broccoli, cut in small florets

10 large eggs

5 large egg yolks

4 cups (1 L) half-and-half cream (10%)

4 green onions, chopped

2 tbsp (30 mL) chopped fresh parsley

Pinch of nutmeg

Salt and freshly ground pepper

3 cups (750 mL) shredded Gruyère cheese (12 oz/340 g)

To make the pastry: In a large bowl, mix together flour, sugar and salt. Cut butter into flour mixture with your fingertips or a pastry blender until mixture resembles coarse meal. Beat together milk and egg yolk. Stir into flour mixture just until dough comes together. Form dough into a ball and flatten into a disc. Wrap in plastic wrap and refrigerate for at least 1 hour.

Set a rack in bottom third of oven and preheat oven to 375°F (190°C).

To make the quiche: Blanch broccoli florets in a pot of boiling salted water until tender-crisp, about 1 ½ minutes. Drain, rinse under cold water and pat dry. Set aside.

Dust work surface and pastry dough with flour. Roll out pastry to fit a 13- × 9- × 3-inch (3 L) baking dish. Fit pastry into baking dish. Trim edges. Put pastry in fridge while making the filling.

In a large bowl, whisk eggs and egg yolks until combined. Whisk in cream. Stir in green onions, parsley, nutmeg, and salt and pepper to taste.

Arrange cheese and broccoli florets in pastry shell. Pour egg mixture over top.

Bake quiche until set, with just a little bit of jiggle in centre, 1 hour 45 minutes to 2 hours. If pastry and quiche start to brown too quickly, loosely cover quiche with foil. (Alternatively, cover quiche with foil from the beginning and uncover for the last 20 minutes.) Let quiche stand for 10 minutes before cutting.

TIP Make this quiche with cauliflower in place of broccoli. While you're at it, why not add strips of smoked salmon for ribbons of flavour and colour throughout.

Apple and Cheddar French Toast

Everyone loves French toast, and the amazing flavour combination of apple and Cheddar cheese will make all your guests extra-happy at brunch. Not only does it taste incredible, but prep is a snap. You can make everything in advance and just reheat when you are ready to serve. I like to use Fuji apples, but you can substitute Cortland or Granny Smith for a more tart option. **MAKES 4 SERVINGS**

3 to 4 tbsp (45 to 60 mL) butter

2 apples, peeled and diced

½ tsp (2 mL) cinnamon

2 eggs

¾ cup (175 mL) milk

1 loaf day-old brioche bread

½ cup (125 mL) shredded aged Cheddar cheese

Icing sugar and maple syrup, for serving

TIP Replace the apples with pears and change up the cheese, if you like. Instead of stuffing the cheese inside, place only fruit in the sandwich and top with a dollop of a lighter cheese, such as ricotta.

In a small skillet over medium heat, melt 1 to 2 tbsp (15 to 30 mL) butter. Add apples, sprinkle with cinnamon and cook, stirring frequently, until apples are tender and golden, 5 to 7 minutes. Set aside.

Beat eggs with milk in a shallow bowl. Set aside.

Cut bread into 8 thick slices. Spoon apples evenly over 4 of the bread slices. Sprinkle evenly with Cheddar. Top with remaining bread slices. Dip each sandwich into egg mixture until evenly soaked.

Heat griddle to medium. (Alternatively, cook French toast in batches in a large skillet.) Add remaining 2 tbsp (30 mL) butter. When butter has melted, add French toast sandwiches. Cook until golden brown and crisp on both sides and cheese is melted, 3 to 4 minutes per side.

If needed, keep French toast warm in a 250°F (120°C) oven. Serve with a dusting of icing sugar and a drizzle of maple syrup.

Oven-Puffed Pancake

Here's a quick way to make a pancake without heating up the griddle. This light, family-sized pancake puffs up high as it cooks in the oven with impressive results every time. It will make the kids (and adults) excited to eat breakfast!

MAKES 4 TO 6 SERVINGS

3 large eggs

1 cup (250 mL) all-purpose flour

2 tbsp (30 mL) sugar

¼ tsp (1 mL) salt

2 cups (500 mL) milk

1 tsp (5 mL) grated orange zest

4 tbsp (60 mL) butter

4 cups (1 L) chopped mixed fruit, such as strawberries, blueberries, pineapple, kiwifruit, oranges

1 tbsp (15 mL) honey

½ cup (125 mL) whipping cream (35%)

Icing sugar, for dusting

Preheat oven to 400°F (200°C).

In a large bowl, whisk together eggs, flour, sugar and salt. Add milk and whisk until smooth. Stir in orange zest.

Heat an 8-inch (20 cm) cast-iron or ovenproof skillet over medium-high heat. When hot, add butter. When butter has just melted and is sizzling, add batter to pan.

Transfer to oven. Bake until set, golden brown and puffed, about 40 minutes.

While the pancake is baking, toss fruit with honey and whip the cream.

Cut pancake into wedges and serve with mixed fruit and whipped cream. Dust with icing sugar.

Ricotta Pancakes with Orange Butter Sauce

I make pancakes every Saturday for my daughter Emilia, and these are her favourite. They're a perfect texture, somewhere between fluffy and dense, with a rich, buttery orange-infused sauce that will knock your socks off! This sauce is heavenly over other pancakes, waffles or French toast as well as ice cream, cake or dessert crêpes. **MAKES 8 PANCAKES**

ORANGE BUTTER SAUCE

½ cup (125 mL) unsalted butter, at room temperature

½ cup (125 mL) sugar

Grated zest of 2 oranges

1 ¼ cups (300 mL) freshly squeezed orange juice

Healthy splash of orange liqueur (optional)

3 oranges, segmented, for garnish

RICOTTA PANCAKES

4 large eggs

1 cup (250 mL) milk

¼ cup (60 mL) sugar

1 tsp (5 mL) vanilla extract

1 cup (250 mL) all-purpose flour

1 tsp (5 mL) baking powder

Pinch of cinnamon

Pinch of salt

1 cup (250 mL) ricotta cheese

1 tbsp (15 mL) butter or vegetable oil

Orange Butter Sauce or maple syrup

Whipped cream or drained plain yogurt

Icing sugar, for dusting (optional)

To make the orange butter sauce: In a small saucepan or skillet over medium heat, combine butter, sugar and orange zest. When butter has melted and sugar has dissolved, add orange juice. Bring to a boil and reduce until syrupy, 5 to 10 minutes.

Remove from heat and add orange liqueur, if desired. Return sauce to heat. Flambé sauce, igniting with a long match. (Have the lid handy to extinguish the flame if needed.) Let sauce reduce for 3 to 5 minutes more. Set aside and keep warm. Before serving, transfer sauce to a serving dish and garnish with orange segments.

To make the ricotta pancakes: Separate eggs, transferring whites to a medium bowl and yolks to a large bowl.

Beat egg whites to stiff peaks. Set aside.

Add milk, sugar and vanilla to egg yolks; whisk to combine. Whisk in flour, baking powder, cinnamon and salt. Add ricotta and mix until smooth.

Fold egg whites into ricotta mixture. Let batter stand in fridge for 20 minutes.

Heat a large griddle or nonstick skillet over medium heat. Brush griddle or pan with butter. For each pancake, scoop about ⅓ cup (75 mL) batter onto griddle, spreading batter slightly until pancake is about the size of a CD. Cook pancakes until edges are golden brown and bubbles start to form on surface, 1½ to 2 minutes. Flip and cook until set in centre, about 1 minute more.

Serve pancakes with Orange Butter Sauce and a dollop of whipped cream. Dust with icing sugar, if desired.

Stefano's Waffles with Two Toppings

Waffles are the ultimate weekend treat, and these ones are simply irresistible. Serve with fresh macerated berries and a dollop of sweet, creamy mascarpone topping, or go the savoury route with the bacon-and-egg topping. Either way, make a big batch—you'll definitely be asked for seconds! **MAKES 10 TO 12 WAFFLES**

WAFFLES

3 cups (750 mL) all-purpose flour

3 tbsp (45 mL) sugar

4 tsp (20 mL) baking powder

½ tsp (2 mL) baking soda

½ tsp (2 mL) salt

3 large eggs, at room temperature

2 ½ cups (625 mL) whole milk, at room temperature

½ cup (125 mL) butter, melted

BERRY AND MASCARPONE TOPPING

1 cup (250 mL) mixed berries, such as raspberries, blueberries, blackberries, strawberries

2 tsp (10 mL) sugar

2 tsp (10 mL) orange liqueur or orange juice

½ cup (125 mL) Greek-style plain yogurt

½ cup (125 mL) mascarpone cheese

¼ cup (60 mL) honey, plus more for drizzling

SAVOURY TOPPING

1 slice Cheddar cheese per waffle

2 slices bacon per waffle, cooked until crispy

1 fried egg per waffle

Chopped fresh chives

Maple syrup (optional)

TIP Mix up your savoury toppings, replacing the bacon with ham or the Cheddar with Emmental.

To make the waffles: In a large bowl, stir together flour, sugar, baking powder, baking soda and salt.

In another bowl, beat eggs. Whisk in milk and butter. Pour wet ingredients into dry and whisk just to combine. Let batter rest for 5 to 10 minutes before using. (Meanwhile, prepare your desired topping.)

Preheat waffle iron according to manufacturer's instructions.

Ladle enough batter into waffle iron to cover about two-thirds of the grid surface. Close lid. Cook until steam stops emerging from waffle iron and waffles are golden brown and crisp, about 4 minutes. Keep waffles warm on the middle rack of a 250°F (120°C) oven. Repeat with remaining batter.

To make the berry and mascarpone topping: Place berries in a bowl. Sprinkle with sugar and orange liqueur. Toss to combine. Set aside.

In a small bowl, combine yogurt, mascarpone and ¼ cup (60 mL) honey. Stir to blend. Top each waffle with a little of the berry mixture, a dollop of the mascarpone topping and a drizzle of honey.

To make the savoury topping: Preheat broiler.

Put a slice of cheese on each waffle and broil just until cheese melts, 1 to 2 minutes. Top each waffle with bacon slices, a fried egg, a sprinkle of chives and a drizzle of maple syrup, if desired.

Pineapple Bourbon Glazed Ham Steaks

Add this amazing meaty dish to any hearty breakfast. The classic combination of ham and pineapple is amped up with a sweet bourbon glaze. You can usually find a big ham steak at the meat counter, or just ask your butcher to cut a few thick slices for you. MAKES 8 TO 10 SERVINGS

¼ cup (60 mL) brown sugar

2 tbsp (30 mL) butter

2 tbsp (30 mL) bourbon or whisky

2 tbsp (30 mL) pineapple juice

Salt and lots of freshly cracked pepper

4 ham steaks (½ to 1 inch/1 to 2.5 cm thick)

4 fresh pineapple rings

To make the glaze: In a small saucepan, combine brown sugar, butter, bourbon, pineapple juice, salt and pepper. Bring to a boil over medium heat, stirring occasionally. Remove from heat.

Preheat grill to medium-high. Brush grill with oil.

Grill ham steaks and pineapple rings just until grill-marked, 3 to 4 minutes per side. Remove pineapple from grill. Brush ham steaks with glaze and cook for another 1 to 2 minutes per side.

Peameal Bacon Roast

This easy bacon roast is the perfect accompaniment to any breakfast buffet. After a couple of hours in the oven, the meat is tender and the sweet, tangy glaze turns dark and crispy. Slice it at the table for an impressive touch to your spread.

MAKES 8 TO 12 SERVINGS

3 tbsp (45 mL) balsamic vinegar
3 tbsp (45 mL) honey
3 tbsp (45 mL) olive oil
1 piece peameal bacon (4 lb/1.8 kg)

Preheat oven to 375°F (190°C). Line a roasting pan with foil.

Combine balsamic vinegar, honey and olive oil.

Score fat of peameal bacon in a diamond pattern, making cuts about 1 inch (2.5 cm) apart. Transfer bacon to roasting pan and drizzle with balsamic glaze.

Roast, basting occasionally, until internal temperature reaches 160°F (70°C), 1 hour 45 minutes to 2 hours. Tent with foil and let stand for 15 minutes before slicing.

TIP A little serving tip for you: present this peameal roast on a big wooden board as part of a buffet, surrounding the bacon with a selection of mustards and pickles.

Maple Sausage Patties

These patties give you all the flavour of a tasty sausage made from scratch without all the effort. They're the perfect combination of fresh ground pork and spices, with a bit of maple sweetness—the perfect side dish for a stack of pancakes, French toast or waffles. MAKES 8 PATTIES (3 OZ/85 G EACH)

¼ tsp (1 mL) dried rosemary

¼ tsp (1 mL) dried thyme

¼ tsp (1 mL) dried sage

1 tsp (5 mL) ground fennel

1 ½ lb (675 g) ground pork

¼ tsp (1 mL) nutmeg, or to taste

Pinch of cayenne pepper, or to taste

1 tbsp (15 mL) maple syrup, plus more for brushing

1 large egg, lightly beaten

Salt and white pepper

1 to 2 tbsp (15 to 30 mL) vegetable oil

TIP I use dried herbs in this recipe, but by all means use ¾ tsp (4 mL) of each chopped fresh herb if you have them. Make these patties with a mix of meats, like pork and veal.

Using a mortar and pestle or a spice grinder, grind rosemary, thyme and sage to a powder. Stir in fennel.

In a large bowl, combine ground pork, ground herbs, nutmeg, cayenne, 1 tbsp (15 mL) maple syrup and egg. Season with salt and white pepper. Mix with your hands to combine.

Divide mixture into 8 even portions and shape into thin oval patties.

Heat grill or griddle over medium to medium-high heat. Brush with oil. When oil is hot, add patties in batches if necessary so you don't crowd the pan. Cook patties until golden brown on each side and meat is cooked through, about 2 minutes per side. Remove patties from pan and brush with maple syrup to finish.

Toad in the Hole

Sausages baked in a Yorkshire pudding batter . . . WOW! This super-simple recipe will become one of your family's favourites. Just remember, the key to getting super-puffed results is to have a piping-hot pan before pouring the batter over the sausages. Pop it in the oven and watch it grow in size and deliciousness! Serve with mashed potatoes and cooked peas. **MAKES 4 TO 5 SERVINGS**

BATTER

4 large eggs

1 ½ cups (375 mL) milk

1 ¼ cups (300 mL) all-purpose flour, sifted

1 tsp (5 mL) chopped fresh rosemary

Pinch of salt

ONION GRAVY

2 tbsp (30 mL) butter

1 large onion, sliced

1 leek (white part only), sliced

2 tbsp (30 mL) all-purpose flour

½ cup (125 mL) red wine

1 ¼ cups (300 mL) good-quality beef stock

Worcestershire sauce

Salt and freshly ground pepper

TO ASSEMBLE

¼ cup (60 mL) peanut oil

4 to 5 small pork sausages
   (or 2 large sausages cut in half crosswise)

3 or 4 sprigs thyme

3 or 4 small sprigs rosemary

1 small bunch cherry tomatoes
   on the vine, stems removed

To make the batter: In a medium bowl, whisk eggs. Whisk in milk. Gradually whisk in flour until smooth. Add rosemary. Season with salt. Cover and let batter rest in fridge for 30 minutes to 1 hour before using. Transfer to large measuring cup so batter is easy to pour.

While batter rests, make the onion gravy: Melt butter in a medium saucepan over medium heat. Add onions and leek; cook, stirring occasionally, until golden brown and caramelized, 15 to 20 minutes. Sprinkle with flour. Cook, stirring constantly, for 2 minutes. Whisk in red wine. Stir in beef stock. Season with Worcestershire sauce, salt and pepper. Bring to a boil, then reduce heat to a simmer. Cook, stirring occasionally, until gravy thickens, 10 to 15 minutes. Taste and adjust seasoning.

continued . . .

Preheat oven to 500°F (260°C).

To assemble the toad in the hole: In a large, heavy ovenproof skillet, heat peanut oil over medium heat. When oil is hot, add sausages. Brown sausages, turning and cooking until almost cooked through, 10 to 15 minutes.

Increase heat to high. Add thyme sprigs, rosemary sprigs and cherry tomatoes. Whisk batter and pour into skillet. Transfer to oven. Bake until golden, puffed and set, 20 to 25 minutes. (Do not open the oven or you risk the toad in the hole collapsing.) Serve immediately with Onion Gravy.

Cajun Home Fries

These southern-inspired skillet-fried potatoes are a comforting part of any breakfast. Cook up an extra-big batch of potatoes and use the leftovers the next day to make these rustic home fries. The peppers, onions and Cajun seasoning will make these potatoes a hit any day of the week. MAKES 6 TO 8 SERVINGS

3 large russet potatoes

2 tbsp (30 mL) olive oil

1 small onion, finely chopped

1 garlic clove, chopped

½ sweet red pepper, diced

½ sweet green pepper, diced

3 tbsp (45 mL) butter

1 tbsp (15 mL) chopped fresh thyme

1 tsp (5 mL) Cajun seasoning, or to taste

Salt and freshly ground pepper

2 tbsp (30 mL) chopped
   fresh Italian parsley

Preheat oven to 350°F (180°C).

Pierce potatoes with a fork. Bake until tender, about 1 hour. Let cool completely. (This step can be done the day before.) Dice potatoes, leaving the skin on. Set aside.

Heat a large cast-iron or nonstick skillet over medium heat. Add olive oil. When oil is hot, add onions, garlic and peppers. Cook, stirring frequently, until veggies have softened, 3 to 5 minutes. Add butter, potatoes, thyme, Cajun seasoning, and salt and pepper to taste. Cook, stirring occasionally, until potatoes are golden brown, 10 to 12 minutes. Serve sprinkled with parsley.

Banana Pecan Bread Pudding

I'm just going to say it: this is probably the best bread pudding you will ever make. This decadent dish, made with bananas, pecans and dates, is an over-the-top sweet, crunchy brunch treat. Trust me, it will be hard to eat just one piece!

MAKES 6 TO 8 SERVINGS

4 large eggs

½ cup (125 mL) sugar

1 ¼ cups (300 mL) milk

1 ¼ cups (300 mL) whipping cream (35%)

2 tbsp (30 mL) dark rum

2 tsp (10 mL) vanilla extract

¼ tsp (1 mL) freshly grated nutmeg

6 cups (1.5 L) day-old egg bread cut in 1-inch (2.5 cm) pieces

2 large ripe bananas, chopped

½ cup (125 mL) chopped dates

½ cup (125 mL) chopped pecans

Maple syrup, plain yogurt and berries, for serving (optional)

TIP Day-old bread is always best to use in a bread pudding, but in a pinch you can lightly toast fresh bread instead, just enough to dry the edges. You can replace the nutmeg with a little cinnamon and the dates with some raisins that have been soaked in lukewarm water for 20 minutes.

Preheat oven to 350°F (180°C). Butter a 9-inch (2.5 L) square baking dish.

In a medium bowl, whisk eggs with sugar until combined. Whisk in milk and cream. Add rum, vanilla and nutmeg. Whisk to combine.

In a large bowl, combine bread pieces, bananas, dates and pecans. Pour custard mixture over bread and stir to evenly combine. Let stand for 10 to 15 minutes so that bread absorbs the custard.

Transfer bread mixture to prepared baking dish. Bake until custard is set and top of bread pudding springs back lightly when touched, 45 minutes to 1 hour. Serve with maple syrup, yogurt and berries, if desired.

Chocolate Hazelnut Crêpes

I love making crêpes. You can serve them with a sweet or a savoury filling, and they're perfect at breakfast, lunch or dinner. This sweet crêpe recipe, inspired by a French street treat, has a delicious combination of chocolate, hazelnuts and whipped cream. You can taste the love in this dish! **MAKES 4 SERVINGS**

CRÊPES

3 large eggs, at room temperature

1 ¾ cups (425 mL) all-purpose flour

2 cups (500 mL) milk, at room temperature

2 tbsp (30 mL) vegetable oil or melted butter, plus more for brushing pan

1 tsp (5 mL) grated orange zest

Pinch of sugar

Pinch of salt

TO ASSEMBLE

½ cup (125 mL) whipping cream (35%)

1 tbsp (15 mL) icing sugar

Orange liqueur

½ cup (125 mL) chocolate hazelnut spread, or to taste

2 tbsp (30 mL) chopped hazelnuts

Fresh raspberries and icing sugar, for garnish

To make the crêpe batter: Place eggs, flour, milk, vegetable oil, orange zest, sugar and salt in a blender. Pulse until smooth. (Alternatively, whisk batter by hand.) Let batter rest in fridge for 30 minutes.

Heat an 8-inch (20 cm) crêpe pan or nonstick skillet over medium heat. When pan is hot, lightly brush with vegetable oil.

Check the consistency of the batter. It should be the consistency of whipping cream. Thin the batter with 1 to 2 tbsp (15 to 30 mL) water, if needed. Pour about ¼ cup (60 mL) batter into the pan, swirling the pan so only a thin layer of batter covers the bottom, and pouring any excess batter back into the bowl.

Cook crêpe until set and lightly golden brown, 1 to 2 minutes. Flip and cook until lightly golden brown, about 1 minute more. Repeat with remaining batter, stacking cooked crêpes on a plate.

To assemble, whip cream to stiff peaks. Stir in icing sugar and orange liqueur to taste.

Spread about 2 tbsp (30 mL) chocolate hazelnut spread over each crêpe. Fold crêpes in quarters. Arrange 2 crêpes on each plate. Top with the orange-flavoured whipped cream and hazelnuts. Garnish with raspberries and dust with icing sugar, if desired.

TIP When making crêpes, using a pan that has a low edge will help you flip them more easily. The first crêpe of the batch rarely works out. Use this one experiment to find the right temperature for your pan.

Cinnamon Swirl Scones

Just imagine . . . a cinnamon bun combined with a scone. (It blows my mind, too!) These quick-bread scones, with a ribbon of butter, brown sugar and cinnamon woven throughout, are a real crowd-pleaser. Take my advice: make a double batch! **MAKES 12 TO 15 SCONES**

2 cups (500 mL) all-purpose flour

4 tsp (20 mL) baking powder

1 tbsp (15 mL) white sugar

½ tsp (2 mL) salt

4 tbsp (60 mL) cold unsalted butter, cut in cubes

1 to 1 ¼ cups (250 to 300 mL) whipping cream (35%)

1 tsp (5 mL) vanilla extract

2 tbsp (30 mL) unsalted butter, melted

½ cup (125 mL) brown sugar

2 tsp (10 mL) cinnamon

Brown sugar or maple sugar, for finishing (optional)

ICING

2 cups (500 mL) icing sugar

½ cup (125 mL) whipping cream (35%)

1 tbsp (15 mL) maple syrup

TIP Make these scones even more decadent by adding some raisins or semisweet chocolate chips to the filling. Yummy!

Preheat oven to 425°F (220°C). Line a baking sheet with parchment paper.

In a large bowl, combine flour, baking powder, white sugar and salt. Stir with a whisk to thoroughly combine. Rub butter into flour mixture with your fingertips until mixture resembles coarse crumbs. (Some bigger clumps are okay.)

Combine 1 cup (250 mL) cream and vanilla. Stir into flour mixture with a wooden spoon just until dough starts to come together. Add ¼ cup (60 mL) more cream if dough feels dry.

Lightly flour work surface. Turn out dough and knead a few times, just until dough comes together. Do not overwork the dough or the scones will be tough.

If dough is sticking, lightly dust dough and/or work surface. Roll out dough to a 14- × 7-inch (35 × 18 cm) rectangle about ½ inch (1 cm) thick. Brush with melted butter. Sprinkle with brown sugar and cinnamon.

Roll up from a long side into a log. Cut into 1-inch (2.5 cm) pieces. Arrange cut side up and evenly spaced apart on prepared baking sheet. Bake until golden brown, about 15 minutes.

Meanwhile, make the icing: Stir together icing sugar, cream and maple syrup. Adjust consistency with more icing sugar or cream, if needed.

Drizzle scones with icing and sprinkle with brown sugar or maple sugar, if desired.

Blueberry Muffins

In my home province of Québec, blueberry season is a magical time. Baskets of flavourful wild blueberries fill the farmer's markets, and I love dreaming up ways to use them. Whenever blueberries are in season where you live, freeze some and use them to make these muffins year-round. Crack one open and spread with a bit of butter while it's still hot. Yum! **MAKES 6 TO 8 MUFFINS**

1 ¼ cups (300 mL) + 1 tbsp (15 mL) all-purpose flour

1 ½ tsp (7 mL) baking powder

½ tsp (2 mL) baking soda

¼ tsp (1 mL) cinnamon

Pinch of salt

¼ cup (60 mL) unsalted butter, at room temperature

½ cup (125 mL) sugar

1 large egg

¾ cup (175 mL) Greek-style plain yogurt

1 tsp (5 mL) vanilla extract

Grated zest of ½ orange

¾ cup (175 mL) fresh or frozen blueberries

Preheat oven to 375°F (190°C). Grease and flour 6 to 8 muffin cups or line with paper liners.

In a medium bowl, stir together 1 ¼ cups (300 mL) flour, baking powder, baking soda, cinnamon and salt. Set aside.

In a large bowl, beat butter with sugar until well combined. Add egg and beat until smooth. Add yogurt, vanilla and orange zest; stir until well combined. Stir in flour mixture just until combined. Do not over-mix.

Toss blueberries with remaining 1 tbsp (15 mL) flour. Gently fold blueberries into muffin batter.

Spoon batter into muffin cups. Bake until golden brown and a tester comes out clean, 18 to 20 minutes.

TIP Take this recipe in a sweeter direction, adding some white chocolate chips. Or make them nutty, throwing in some sliced almonds. Make a bigger batch, so you can freeze them for a later date. To freeze, let cool completely. Package individually so you can take out as many as you need at a time. Seal airtight and freeze for up to 1 month.

SNACKS & APPETIZERS

Party Snack Mix

I love having friends over to watch the big game, and funny thing, when you're a good cook, no one seems to turn down the invitation! This snack mix is a must at any casual get-together. Just pair it with a cold beer and you've got a winning combination. MAKES 8 ½ CUPS (2.125 L)

1 cup (250 mL) raw cashews

1 cup (250 mL) raw almonds

1 cup (250 mL) raw hazelnuts

1 cup (250 mL) raw pistachio nuts

1 cup (250 mL) shredded wheat cereal

1 cup (250 mL) toasted oat cereal

½ cup (125 mL) sunflower seeds

⅓ cup (75 mL) olive oil

1 tsp (5 mL) sea salt

½ tsp (2 mL) smoked paprika

Freshly ground pepper

1 cup (250 mL) pretzel sticks

1 cup (250 mL) mini cheese crackers

TIP Make a sweet 'n' savoury party mix by adding dried fruit, such as cranberries, or mini milk chocolate chips.

Preheat oven to 350°F (180°C).

In a large bowl, combine cashews, almonds, hazelnuts, pistachios, shredded wheat cereal, oat cereal and sunflower seeds.

In a small bowl, stir together oil, salt, smoked paprika and pepper to taste. Add spice mixture to nut mixture and toss until thoroughly combined. Spread evenly on a baking sheet.

Bake, stirring occasionally, until nuts and cereals are evenly toasted, about 15 minutes.

Add pretzel sticks and mini cheese crackers to baked mixture. Toss to combine. Let cool completely. Store in airtight containers.

Sweet 'n' Spicy Candied Peanuts

I take after my dad when it comes to my love of peanuts. These addictive slightly sweet, slightly spicy nuts are so easy to make and have only a few ingredients. It's a quick way to make ordinary peanuts extraordinary! MAKES 2 CUPS (500 ML)

1 cup (250 mL) sugar

3 tbsp (45 mL) water

2 cups (500 mL) unsalted peanuts

2 tsp (10 mL) kosher salt

1 tsp (5 mL) smoked salt

Pinch of cinnamon

Pinch of cayenne pepper,
   or to taste

Combine sugar and water in a medium saucepan. Cook over medium heat until sugar melts and starts to boil, 3 to 5 minutes. Add peanuts, kosher salt, smoked salt, cinnamon and cayenne. Cook, stirring occasionally, until sugar crystallizes. (It will get sandy in texture.)

Transfer to a baking sheet and let cool completely. Store in an airtight container.

Warm Mixed Olives with Orange and Rosemary

"Easy, easy, easy" is the only way to describe this recipe. Just start with store-bought olives and warm them with a mix of orange, garlic and rosemary. These fragrant, flavourful olives are perfect as a savoury snack or as a finger-food at your next dinner party—they'll definitely keep your guests wanting more. MAKES 2 CUPS (500 ML)

3 tbsp (45 mL) hot pepper oil or
    extra-virgin olive oil

1 garlic clove, cut in half or chopped

2 strips of orange peel, each
    about 2 inches (5 cm) long

2 sprigs rosemary

2 cups (500 mL) mixed olives

Heat hot pepper oil in a large skillet over medium heat. Add garlic, orange peel and rosemary sprigs and let infuse into oil until fragrant, 3 to 5 minutes. Add olives and cook, stirring occasionally, until heated through and fragrant, about 5 minutes. Serve warm or make ahead and reheat before serving.

Endive with Smoked Salmon

I have been making this appetizer for years—it's one of my favourites. The bitterness of the endive is a perfect match for the sweetness of the smoked salmon and the cream cheese topping. Serve these perfect bites at any special gathering—they'll bring a bit of sunshine to your table. For a cocktail party, serve on a big platter. For a dinner party starter, serve 2 or 3 pieces per person. **MAKES 16 PIECES**

½ cup (125 mL) cream cheese, at room temperature

1 tbsp (15 mL) chopped green onion

1 tbsp (15 mL) chopped fresh dill

1 tbsp (15 mL) lemon juice

Salt and freshly ground pepper

16 Belgian endive leaves (about 2 heads)

5 oz (140 g) thinly sliced smoked salmon

1 to 2 tbsp (15 to 30 mL) minced fresh chives, for garnish

Whip the cream cheese until smooth. Beat in green onion, dill, lemon juice, and salt and pepper to taste.

Spoon about ½ tbsp (20 mL) cream cheese mixture into each endive leaf. Lay a slice of salmon on top. Garnish with chives.

TIP Change up the fresh herb flavour of the creamy cheese mixture by adding some chopped tarragon. Swapping in slightly sweet mascarpone cheese for the cream cheese will make this app taste completely different.

Blueberry and Peach Salsa with Brie

Nothing says summer like the fresh, flavourful combination of blueberries and peaches. Top a couple of these warm, creamy wheels of Brie cheese with this sweet and slightly spicy fruit salsa and you've got an instant hit at any party. MAKES 4 TO 6 SERVINGS

1 cup (250 mL) fresh blueberries

1 ripe peach, diced

½ to 1 jalapeño pepper, diced

Juice of 1 lime

1 tbsp (15 mL) chopped fresh mint

1 tbsp (15 mL) honey

1 tsp (5 mL) grated fresh ginger

Salt and freshly ground pepper

1 Brie wheel (about 5 inches/12 cm)

Baguette slices

TIP Use plums instead of peaches if that's what you have on hand. For more intense heat in the salsa, replace the jalapeño with a more potent bird's eye chili.

Preheat oven to 350°F (180°C). Line a baking sheet with parchment paper.

Combine blueberries, peach, jalapeño, lime juice, mint, honey, ginger, and salt and pepper to taste. Taste and adjust seasoning. Let salsa stand for 15 minutes at room temperature to let flavours marry.

Place Brie on baking sheet and heat in oven until warm and slightly softened, 2 to 5 minutes. Be careful—if left in the oven too long, the Brie will melt and start to ooze.

Transfer warm Brie to a serving plate. Top with salsa and serve with baguette slices.

Guacamole

This classic Mexican-inspired dip made with creamy avocado, tangy lemon and fresh cilantro is one of the few dishes that pleases almost every palate. Keep this easy, no-fail guacamole recipe for your next potluck or whip it up as a quick-and-easy snack. **MAKES 6 TO 8 SERVINGS**

2 ripe avocados

Juice of ½ lemon

2 tbsp (30 mL) extra-virgin olive oil

½ tsp (2 mL) ground cumin

¼ tsp (1 mL) ground coriander

Salt and freshly ground pepper

Cut each avocado in half and remove pit. Scoop avocado flesh into a medium bowl. Add lemon juice, olive oil, cumin and coriander. Mash with a fork or potato masher until smooth. Season with salt and pepper. Taste and adjust seasoning.

Hummus with Roasted Garlic

Hummus is a permanent fixture in my fridge at home—I'm sure you always have a tub of it on hand, too. It's the perfect between-meal snack for hungry kids and a great dip to serve with veggies any time of day. You'll be shocked how easy it is to make a big batch from scratch, and I guarantee that this recipe tastes better than any hummus you can buy at the store. MAKES ABOUT 3 CUPS (750 ML)

ROASTED GARLIC

1 small head garlic

1 tsp (5 mL) olive oil

Salt and freshly ground pepper

HUMMUS

1 can (19 oz/540 mL) chickpeas, drained and rinsed

¼ cup (60 mL) water

Juice of 2 lemons

½ cup (125 mL) tahini

Pinch of ground cumin

Pinch of cayenne pepper

¼ cup (60 mL) extra-virgin olive oil

Pita or flatbread wedges and vegetable sticks, for serving

To roast the garlic: Preheat oven to 375°F (190°C). Cut just the very tip off the head of garlic. Drizzle garlic with olive oil and season with salt and pepper. Wrap in foil. Bake until garlic is very soft, 40 to 45 minutes. Unwrap. When cool enough to handle, squeeze garlic out of skins.

To make the hummus: Combine chickpeas, water and lemon juice in a food processor. Process until smooth. Add roasted garlic, tahini, cumin, cayenne, and salt and pepper to taste. Pulse until smooth. While machine is running, slowly pour olive oil through the feed tube. Process until well combined. Serve with pita wedges and vegetable sticks.

Baked Spinach and Artichoke Dip

You know that dip you order at the pub, that decadent, ooey-gooey appetizer that's packed with spinach and artichokes? This is my version and you're going to love it! It's loaded with cream cheese, Parmesan, garlic and veggies. Serve it up with some toasted baguette slices for a special treat. MAKES 8 SERVINGS

1 tbsp (15 mL) butter

1 tbsp (15 mL) olive oil

5 oz (140 g) baby spinach

8 oz (225 g) cream cheese, at room temperature

½ cup (125 mL) mayonnaise

½ cup (125 mL) sour cream

Juice of 1 lemon

1 can (14 oz/398 mL) artichokes (packed in oil or water), drained and chopped

1 cup (250 mL) grated Parmesan cheese, plus more for garnish

2 to 3 garlic cloves, finely chopped

Pinch of cayenne pepper

Salt and freshly ground pepper

1 tbsp (15 mL) chopped fresh parsley, for garnish

1 baguette, sliced, toasted and brushed with olive oil

Preheat oven to 375°F (190°C). Butter a small baking dish with 1 tbsp (15 mL) butter.

Heat olive oil in a large sauté pan over medium heat. When olive oil is hot, add spinach and cook, stirring frequently, until it just begins to wilt. Let cool. Chop and squeeze dry with your hands.

In a large bowl, combine cream cheese, mayonnaise, sour cream and lemon juice. Beat with an electric mixer until smooth. Stir in spinach, artichokes, 1 cup (250 mL) Parmesan, garlic, cayenne, and salt and pepper to taste.

Transfer dip to prepared baking dish. Sprinkle with additional Parmesan. Bake until bubbly and lightly golden brown on top, 15 to 20 minutes. Garnish with chopped parsley and serve with toasted baguette slices.

TIP Assemble this dish ahead of time and bake it when you need it. Take it to a potluck and bake on the spot!

Spicy Mayo Dip

Spiced with cayenne pepper and smoked paprika, this dip is perfect with fries and onion rings or as a spread for sandwiches. MAKES ABOUT ½ CUP (125 ML)

½ cup (125 mL) mayonnaise

1 tbsp (15 mL) chopped fresh chives

2 tsp (10 mL) hot or sweet smoked paprika

1 tsp (5 mL) cayenne pepper, or to taste

Salt and freshly ground pepper

In a small bowl, combine mayonnaise, chives, smoked paprika, cayenne, and salt and pepper to taste. Stir until well combined.

· ·

Sea Salt and Rosemary Flatbread

I know, I know . . . making crackers at home sounds crazy, but this quick and easy flatbread will make you a believer. These crackers taste as delicious as the expensive ones you see at the grocery store, but you can make them for a fraction of the price. Serve them with some cured meats or your favourite cheese. MAKES 14 TO 16 FLATBREADS

1 cup (250 mL) all-purpose flour

Pinch of salt

2 tbsp (30 mL) extra-virgin olive oil, plus more for brushing

½ small onion, finely minced in food processor

2 to 3 tbsp (30 to 45 mL) water

Crushed dried rosemary

Sea salt

Set racks in top and bottom thirds of oven and preheat oven to 350°F (180°C). Brush 2 or 3 baking sheets with extra-virgin olive oil.

In a medium bowl, stir together flour and salt. Add olive oil. Mix with your fingertips until combined. Add minced onion and 2 tbsp (30 mL) water. Stir and knead until dough comes together in a ball, adding more water if needed.

Divide dough into 14 to 16 pieces. On a lightly floured surface, roll out each piece as thinly as possible. Transfer to prepared baking sheets. Brush flatbreads with olive oil and sprinkle with rosemary and sea salt to taste.

Bake, rotating and switching baking sheets halfway, until crisp and lightly golden brown, 10 to 12 minutes. Let cool on racks.

Blue Cheese and Caramelized Onion Flatbread

This flatbread appetizer is topped with amazing flavours and textures—sweet caramelized onions, tangy blue cheese, fresh arugula and roasted hazelnuts. It's a fancier alternative to pizza. And, like pizza, you can bake it in the oven or serve it hot off the grill. **MAKES 10 TO 12 SERVINGS**

CARAMELIZED ONIONS

¼ cup (60 mL) olive oil

2 ¼ lb (1 kg) cooking onions, thinly sliced (about 5 onions)

FLATBREAD

1 lb (450 g) pizza dough

Olive oil, for brushing dough

10 to 12 oz (280 to 340 g) blue cheese, crumbled

About 2 tbsp (30 mL) coarsely chopped roasted hazelnuts

Salt and freshly ground pepper

2 handfuls baby arugula

Extra-virgin olive oil or hot pepper oil, for finishing

TIP This is great to serve with cocktails. Make more caramelized onions than you need for the recipe—they're a sweet treat on a cheese plate or in a sandwich.

To make the caramelized onions: heat oil in a large, heavy skillet over medium to medium-low heat. Add onions and cook, stirring frequently, until dark golden brown, about 1 hour. (If onions start to stick to the pan or cook too quickly, reduce the heat and add a little water.)

Preheat a cast-iron griddle or grill to high and brush with oil.

To make the flatbread: Divide pizza dough in half. Dust work surface with flour. Roll out each piece of dough into a rustic oval about ¼ inch (5 mm) thick.

Brush dough with olive oil and place on griddle or grill. Cover and cook until dough is golden brown on the bottom, 2 to 3 minutes. Flip the flatbreads. Sprinkle with caramelized onions, cheese and hazelnuts. Season with salt and pepper. Cover and cook until cheese has melted and dough is cooked through, crispy and golden brown.

Top flatbreads with arugula and drizzle with olive oil or hot pepper oil. Cut each flatbread into 5 or 6 slices.

Easy Pretzels

I remember going to baseball games with my dad when I was a kid, and I used to love the big, warm pretzels we would buy up in the stands. Well, you can't always get to the stadium, so here's the recipe to make them at home. Serve them old-school with some yellow mustard, and play ball! MAKES 15 SERVINGS

1 tbsp (15 mL) active dry yeast

1 ⅓ cups (325 mL) warm water

2 ¾ to 3 cups (675 to 750 mL) all-purpose flour

1 tbsp (15 mL) sugar

1 tsp (5 mL) salt

1 egg beaten with 1 tbsp (15 mL) water, for egg wash

Coarse salt, for finishing

Set racks in top and bottom thirds of oven and preheat oven to 425°F (220°C). Line 2 baking sheets with parchment paper.

In a small bowl, stir yeast into warm water. Let stand for 5 minutes or until foamy.

Combine 2 ¾ cups (675 mL) flour, sugar and salt in a large bowl. Add yeast mixture and stir or mix with your hands until a dough forms, adding a little more flour if needed.

Sprinkle work surface with flour and knead dough until smooth and elastic, 2 to 3 minutes.

Divide dough into 12 equal pieces. Roll each piece into a 15-inch (38 cm) rope. Shape into a pretzel knot, pressing ends to seal. (You could also just make pretzel sticks, if you like.) Brush each pretzel with egg wash and sprinkle with coarse salt to taste.

Bake, rotating and switching baking sheets halfway, until golden brown, 15 to 20 minutes. Serve warm with mustard, if desired.

Stefano's Bread Buns

Use these homemade buns to make the perfect sandwich every time! To speed up the bread-making process, this recipe uses quick-rising, or instant, yeast so you don't have to wait as long for the dough to rise. **MAKES 6 BUNS**

1 package (2 ¼ tsp/8 g) quick-rising (instant) dry yeast

1 ½ cups (375 mL) warm milk

3 cups (750 mL) all-purpose flour

½ cup (125 mL) whole wheat flour

3 tbsp (45 mL) olive oil

1 tbsp (15 mL) sugar

1 tsp (5 mL) salt

1 tbsp (15 mL) butter, melted

Salt, sesame seeds or dried rosemary, for topping

In a large bowl, add yeast to warm milk. Stir to dissolve. Add all-purpose flour, whole wheat flour, olive oil, sugar and salt. Stir to combine.

On a lightly floured work surface, knead dough until smooth and elastic, 5 to 10 minutes.

Put the ball of dough in an oiled bowl and cover with plastic wrap. Let rise in a warm place until it doubles in volume, about 45 minutes.

Meanwhile, preheat oven to 400°F (200°C). Line a baking sheet with parchment paper.

Punch down dough. Divide into 6 equal pieces. Shape each piece into a large oval bun. Arrange buns on baking sheet. Score top of each bun with a sharp knife. Cover with a kitchen towel and let rise again until doubled in size, 15 to 20 minutes.

Brush buns with melted butter and sprinkle with desired topping. Bake until golden brown, 15 to 20 minutes. Cool on racks.

Lime-Flavoured Tortilla Chips

Here's a quick and easy way to transform store-bought tortilla chips into something a little more special. You'll have leftover zingy, flavourful lime salt—add it to fish or chicken dishes, soups and salads. **MAKES 6 TO 8 SERVINGS**

LIME SALT

Grated zest of 4 limes

¾ cup (175 mL) sea salt

LIME-FLAVOURED TORTILLA CHIPS

8 cups (2 L) unsalted tortilla chips

1 tbsp (15 mL) lime juice

1 tsp (5 mL) lime salt, or to taste

For the lime salt, preheat oven to 325°F (160°C). Line a small baking sheet with parchment paper.

Stir together lime zest and salt until well combined. Sprinkle evenly on prepared baking sheet. Bake, stirring halfway through baking time, until zest is dry but not browning, 10 to 15 minutes. Let cool completely. Store in an airtight container.

For the lime-flavoured tortilla chips, preheat oven to 350°F (180°C).

Spread tortilla chips evenly on large baking sheet. Sprinkle with lime juice. Bake until heated through, crisp and golden, 5 to 7 minutes. Immediately sprinkle with lime salt. Serve chips warm.

Pigs in a Blanket

Sausage rolls are always a big hit at a party, and my take on this classic appetizer wraps meaty sausage in flaky puff pastry. You can use any sausage you like, from chorizo to kielbasa. Just be sure to serve them warm with loads of homemade Sweet Tomato Ketchup and tasty honey mustard for dipping! **MAKES 20 MINI SAUSAGE ROLLS**

7 sausages, such as Oktoberfest, Italian, chorizo, or smoked kielbasa

¾ cup (175 mL) grainy Dijon mustard

3 tbsp (45 mL) liquid honey

2 sheets pre-rolled puff pastry (10 inches/ 25 cm square), thawed if frozen

1 egg beaten with 1 tbsp (15 mL) water, for egg wash

Handful poppy seeds and/or sesame seeds, for finishing

If sausages are raw, cook them and let cool before rolling in pastry.

Preheat oven to 400°F (200°C). Line a baking sheet with parchment paper.

Cut each sausage into 3 pieces and set aside. (You'll have 21 pieces but you only need 20. The extra piece can be the cook's treat, or serve a pig without its blanket.)

Stir together mustard and honey. Transfer ¼ cup (60 mL) to a small bowl for brushing the pigs in blankets and set aside. Reserve remaining honey mustard for serving.

Dust work surface lightly with flour. Cut each pastry sheet into 10 5- × 2-inch (12 × 5 cm) pieces. Brush a little honey mustard on each rectangle of pastry. Add a piece of sausage and roll up. Brush pastry with egg wash. Transfer seam side down to prepared baking sheet. Sprinkle with poppy seeds and/or sesame seeds.

Bake until pastry is golden brown, about 20 minutes. Serve warm with reserved honey mustard and Sweet Tomato Ketchup (page 353).

TIP Change up the sausage in your blankets and change up the flavour. Make a few different types of pigs as a nice surprise for your guests!

Tomato and Goat Cheese Bruschetta

We Italians know bruschetta well—it's a staple at every dinner party. Shake up your bruschetta toppings and try my favourite flavour combination, fresh tomato and tangy goat cheese. You'll discover why this appetizer is an Italian classic and a fixture on my dinner table! **MAKES 12 SERVINGS**

About 1 cup (250 mL) goat cheese

About ½ cup (125 mL) extra-virgin olive oil

Salt and freshly ground pepper

½ small onion

1 tomato (or 3 Campari tomatoes)

1 sweet banana pepper

Handful of basil leaves

½ baguette

1 large garlic clove

Preheat broiler to high.

In a medium bowl, mash goat cheese with a fork until smooth and creamy. Drizzle in a little olive oil to taste, and season with salt and pepper. Stir to combine. Set aside.

Very thinly slice onion, tomato, banana pepper and basil. Set aside.

Cut baguette into 12 slices and brush both sides of each slice generously with olive oil. Arrange on a baking sheet and toast under broiler, turning once, until golden brown, 1 to 2 minutes per side. Rub warm toast with garlic clove.

Spread a little of the goat cheese mixture onto each slice of toasted baguette. Garnish with onion, tomato, pepper and basil. Drizzle a little olive oil over each bruschetta. Serve.

Open-Faced Prosciutto and Fig Sandwich

This recipe may seem almost too simple, but just wait until you give this snack a try. The tastes and textures will blow your mind! The salty prosciutto, sweet figs and creamy ricotta satisfy all your cravings in one bite, but it's that final drizzle of honey that truly brings it all together. **MAKES 2 SERVINGS**

1 Stefano's Bread Bun sprinkled with
   rosemary (page 62)
⅓ cup (75 mL) ricotta cheese, drained
6 thin slices prosciutto

Handful of arugula leaves
2 fresh or dried figs, quartered
Honey, for drizzling
Olive oil, for drizzling

Slice bun in half horizontally. Top each half with ricotta, prosciutto, arugula and figs. Drizzle with honey and olive oil.

Prosciutto, Pear and Arugula Rolls

Even if you're not a great cook, you'll have no trouble assembling this easy, crowd-pleasing appetizer. When I have guests over, these super-tasty rolls are often a go-to. There's something about the perfectly balanced combination of salty prosciutto, sweet pear and fresh, peppery arugula that keeps everybody asking for more. **MAKES 16 TO 18 SERVINGS**

TIP The flavour of plums or peaches can be just as nice as pear in these rolls. You can also wrap your fruit and arugula with bresaola instead of prosciutto.

4 oz (115 g) cream cheese, at room temperature

5 oz (140 g) Gorgonzola cheese, crumbled

16 to 18 thin slices prosciutto

2 handfuls of arugula

1 ripe pear, such as Bartlett, cut into 16 to 18 slices

Handful of chopped walnuts, toasted (optional)

Balsamic glaze or aged balsamic vinegar, for drizzling

Stir together cream cheese and Gorgonzola until well combined. Spoon a dollop of cheese mixture on each slice of prosciutto. Top with a few arugula leaves, a slice of pear and chopped walnuts, if desired. Roll up. Secure with toothpicks, if desired. Just before serving, drizzle with balsamic glaze.

Crab Cakes with Roasted Red Pepper Mayonnaise

These lightly spiced cakes are crispy on the outside and moist and tender on the inside. You can serve them as a main (say 2 crab cakes per person) or as a starter. They don't have to cost a fortune to make, either—you can use fresh, frozen or canned crabmeat, whichever you prefer. **MAKES 6 SERVINGS**

ROASTED PEPPER MAYONNAISE

3 to 4 jarred roasted red peppers, drained

1 garlic clove

1 cup (250 mL) mayonnaise

1 tsp (5 mL) smoked paprika

Salt and freshly ground pepper

CRAB CAKES

2 cups (500 mL) lump crabmeat, drained well and patted dry

3 tbsp (45 mL) mayonnaise

1 tbsp (15 mL) grainy mustard

2 tbsp (30 mL) chopped fresh parsley

2 tbsp (30 mL) chopped fresh chives

2 tsp (10 mL) grated lemon zest

1 tsp (5 mL) hot pepper sauce, or to taste

1 tsp (5 mL) Worcestershire sauce

1 or 2 large eggs, beaten

¾ to 1 cup (175 to 250 mL) fresh bread crumbs

Sea salt and freshly cracked black pepper

Panko bread crumbs, for breading

¼ cup (60 mL) peanut oil

1 tbsp (15 mL) finely chopped fresh chives, for garnish

Micro greens and sweet red pepper slices, for garnish

To make the roasted red pepper mayonnaise: In a food processor, combine roasted red peppers, garlic, mayonnaise, smoked paprika, and salt and pepper to taste. Process until smooth. Set aside.

To make the crab cakes: In a medium bowl, combine crabmeat, mayonnaise, mustard, parsley, chives, lemon zest, hot sauce, Worcestershire sauce, 1 egg, ¾ cup (175 mL) bread crumbs, and sea salt and pepper to taste. Mix gently. If needed, add remaining egg and bread crumbs to bind the crab cakes.

Form crab mixture into 6 patties and dredge each in panko crumbs.

Heat oil in a large nonstick skillet over medium heat. When oil is hot, add crab cakes in batches. Fry until just heated through and golden brown on each side, 3 to 5 minutes per side. Drain briefly on paper towels. Serve crab cakes with Roasted Pepper Mayonnaise. Garnish with chives, micro greens and slices of red pepper, if desired.

TIP If you have trouble finding lump crabmeat, make this recipe with canned salmon or tuna.

Shrimp Kabobs with Roasted Red Pepper Dip

These flame-grilled kabobs are one of the tastiest, fastest appetizers around. Serve them at your next barbecue party for an impressive dish that's easy to pass around. The Spanish-inspired roasted red pepper dip, made with almonds and paprika, is a nice change from seafood sauce. **MAKES 6 SERVINGS**

ROASTED RED PEPPER DIP

½ cup (125 mL) whole raw almonds (about 3 oz/85 g), toasted

1 cup (250 mL) jarred roasted red peppers, drained

2 tsp (10 mL) sherry vinegar

1 large garlic clove

¼ tsp (1 mL) smoked paprika (hot or sweet)

3 to 4 tbsp (50 to 60 mL) extra-virgin olive oil

Salt and freshly ground pepper

SHRIMP KABOBS

18 jumbo shrimp (about 1 ½ lb/675 g), peeled and deveined

4 garlic cloves, chopped

½ cup (125 mL) extra-virgin olive oil

¼ cup (60 mL) finely chopped fresh Italian parsley

Salt and freshly ground pepper

Lemon wedges and chopped parsley or sprigs, for garnish

Soak 6 bamboo or wooden skewers in water for at least 30 minutes to help prevent them from burning on the grill (or use metal skewers).

To make the roasted red pepper dip: In a food processor, pulse almonds until very finely chopped. Add roasted peppers, vinegar, garlic and smoked paprika. Process until coarsely puréed. While machine is running, slowly pour 3 tbsp (50 mL) olive oil through feed tube and process until purée thickens slightly. Add more oil if needed. Season with salt and pepper. Transfer to a small bowl. Set aside.

To make the shrimp kabobs: Preheat grill to medium-high. Brush grill with oil.

In a large bowl, combine shrimp, garlic, olive oil and finely chopped parsley. Season with salt and pepper, and toss shrimp to evenly coat. Thread 3 shrimp onto each skewer, piercing the head and tail end of each shrimp. Brush shrimp with any of the remaining oil mixture.

Add shrimp skewers to grill. Cook, turning once, until shrimp turn pink, start to curl and are just cooked through, about 5 minutes total. Transfer shrimp to a serving platter. Garnish with parsley and lemon wedges. Serve with Roasted Red Pepper Dip.

Mini Meatball Sliders

Who doesn't like a good burger? These perfect mini meatball morsels bring the flavours of your favourite burger into an addictive two-bite package. Serve them as an appetizer at your next casual dinner party. No one will turn these down! MAKES **8 TO 10** SERVINGS

CREAMY RED PEPPER SAUCE

1 tbsp (15 mL) olive oil

½ onion, chopped

2 sweet red peppers, diced

½ cup (125 mL) vegetable stock

1 tbsp (15 mL) butter

Pinch of hot pepper flakes

Salt and freshly ground pepper

3 tbsp (45 mL) whipping cream (35%)

MINI MEATBALLS

3 ½ oz (100 g) ground veal

3 ½ oz (100 g) ground turkey

3 ½ oz (100 g) ground pork

3 ½ oz (100 g) capocollo, finely diced

2 oz (55 g) Pecorino Romano cheese, grated

1 small garlic clove, minced

1 tbsp (15 mL) chopped fresh Italian parsley

1 large egg, beaten

2 tbsp to ¼ cup (30 to 60 mL) fresh bread crumbs

Salt and freshly ground pepper

2 tbsp (30 mL) olive oil

TO ASSEMBLE

8 to 10 mini burger buns

8 to 10 small slices mozzarella cheese

Basil leaves, for garnish

To make the creamy red pepper sauce: Heat olive oil in a medium saucepan over medium heat. When oil is hot, add onions and cook until softened, 2 to 3 minutes. Stir in red peppers and continue to cook until peppers have softened slightly, 3 to 4 minutes.

Add stock. Bring to a boil, then reduce heat to a simmer. Cover and simmer until peppers are very tender, 8 to 10 minutes. Stir in butter and hot pepper flakes. Season with salt and pepper.

Transfer to blender and purée. Stir in cream. Set aside.

To make the mini meatballs: In a large bowl, combine veal, turkey, pork, capocollo, Pecorino Romano, garlic, parsley, egg and 2 tbsp (30 mL) bread crumbs. Season with salt and pepper. Mix with your hands to combine. If mixture is too moist, add 1 to 2 tbsp (15 to 30 mL) more bread crumbs.

Shape mixture into 8 to 10 meatballs (depending on number of buns). Flatten meatballs slightly so they will sit nicely in the buns without rolling.

Heat olive oil in a large skillet over medium to medium-high heat. When oil is hot, add meatballs in batches if necessary to avoid crowding the pan. Cook meatballs, turning to brown all sides, until well browned and meat is no longer pink inside, 10 to 15 minutes depending on size of meatballs.

To assemble the sliders, toast buns under broiler, if desired. Fill each bun with a slice of mozzarella, a meatball, some basil leaves and a spoonful of Creamy Red Pepper Sauce. Serve.

TIP Use the meatballs in a tomato sauce. The red pepper sauce can be tossed with pasta.

Garlic Chicken Wings

The most popular snack at any playoff party is definitely wings—there's something about watching the big game with friends that just begs for a big platter of this saucy finger food. These garlicky wings are insanely good. Just remember to put out a big stack of napkins—they're as messy as they are delicious!

MAKES 4 TO 6 SERVINGS

2 ¼ lb (1 kg) chicken wings

¼ cup (60 mL) maple syrup

¼ cup (60 mL) olive oil

Juice of 1 lime

2 garlic cloves, minced

2 tbsp (30 mL) chopped fresh cilantro

2 tbsp (30 mL) grated fresh ginger

1 tbsp (15 mL) Dijon mustard

1 tsp (5 mL) chopped peperoncino or your favourite hot chili, or to taste

1 tsp (5 mL) smoked paprika

1 tsp (5 mL) salt

1 tsp (5 mL) freshly ground pepper

Cut wings in half at the joint and remove wing tip, if desired.

In a large bowl or resealable plastic bag, combine maple syrup, olive oil, lime juice, garlic, cilantro, ginger, mustard, peperoncino, smoked paprika, salt and pepper. Add wings and toss to coat. Cover. Marinate in the fridge for at least 3 hours or up to 24 hours.

Preheat oven to 400°F (200°C). Line a baking sheet with foil.

Transfer wings to prepared baking sheet (discard any remaining marinade). Bake for 20 minutes. Flip and bake until wings are golden brown, juices run clean and meat is no longer pink, about 20 minutes more.

Serve with a blue cheese dip and veggie sticks, if desired. For a quick blue cheese dip, crumble your favourite blue cheese into sour cream and season with salt and pepper.

TIP Feel free to substitute honey for maple syrup here, and sweet paprika instead of smoked (or leave out the paprika altogether).

Stefano's Nachos Supreme

This is the only nacho recipe you will ever need, perfect for a family game night. There's something for everyone in here—seasoned ground sirloin, hearty beans, fresh veggies and loads of Monterey Jack cheese. The key is to build these nachos layer by layer, so that you get a bit of each tasty ingredient in every bite.

MAKES 6 TO 8 SERVINGS

2 tbsp (30 mL) olive oil

½ lb (225 g) ground sirloin

Salt and freshly ground pepper

1 jalapeño pepper, diced

2 garlic cloves, chopped

1 tsp (5 mL) dried oregano

1 tsp (5 mL) ground cumin

3 tbsp (45 mL) tomato purée (passata) or tomato sauce

2 tbsp (30 mL) tequila

Grated zest and juice of 1 lime

½ cup (125 mL) canned kidney beans, drained and rinsed

¾ bag (1 lb/450 g) tortilla chips, preferably artisanal

2 cups (500 mL) shredded Monterey Jack cheese

1 to 2 plum tomatoes, diced

3 tbsp (45 mL) finely chopped red onion

2 tbsp (30 mL) sliced pitted black olives

3 tbsp (45 mL) diced Cubanelle pepper or banana pepper

1 to 2 tbsp (15 to 30 mL) chopped fresh cilantro, for garnish

½ cup (125 mL) sour cream, for serving

½ cup (125 mL) salsa, for serving

Heat a large skillet over medium heat. Add olive oil. When olive oil is hot, add ground beef. Season with salt and pepper. Cook, stirring frequently, until meat starts to brown, 4 to 5 minutes. Add jalapeño, garlic, oregano and cumin; cook until veggies are soft, 2 to 3 minutes. Stir in tomato purée and cook for 1 minute. Stir in tequila and lime zest and juice. Stir in beans and cook, stirring occasionally, until they are heated through and pan is dry, about 5 minutes. Remove from heat.

Preheat broiler.

On a baking sheet or large pizza pan, layer tortilla chips, beef mixture, cheese, tomatoes, onions, olives and peppers. Broil until cheese melts. Garnish with cilantro. Serve with sour cream and salsa.

Grilled Vegetable Pizza

I get asked all the time, "Stef, what's your favourite food?" The answer is always pizza. The secret to a great pizza is the crust. Use my dough recipe and you'll get a delicious pizza base every time. Making it on the grill, like this delicious vegetable pizza, infuses the crust with a smokiness that takes my favourite food over the top! MAKES 1½ LB (675 G) DOUGH, ENOUGH FOR TWO 10-INCH (25 CM) ROUND PIZZAS OR ONE 24- × 18-INCH (60 × 45 CM) PARTY PIZZA

PIZZA DOUGH

2 ½ cups (625 mL) all-purpose flour

½ cup (125 mL) semolina

1 tbsp (15 mL) salt

1 tbsp (15 mL) sugar

2 tsp (10 mL) active dry yeast

1 cup (250 mL) warm water

PIZZA TOPPINGS

1 small eggplant, thinly sliced lengthwise

1 medium zucchini, thinly sliced lengthwise

1 portobello mushroom, thinly sliced

1 sweet red pepper, cut in half

2 tbsp (30 mL) olive oil, plus more for vegetables

1 to 1 ¼ cups (250 to 300 mL) tomato sauce or tomato purée (passata)

¾ cup (175 mL) shredded fontina or mozzarella cheese

¾ cup (175 mL) grated Parmesan or pecorino cheese

3 tbsp (45 mL) canned diced tomatoes, drained (optional)

½ tsp (2 mL) dried oregano

To make the pizza dough: In a large bowl, stir together flour, semolina and salt. In a small bowl, dissolve sugar and yeast in warm water. Let sit until foamy, 5 to 10 minutes.

Add yeast mixture to flour mixture. Stir or work with your hands until dough starts to form into a ball. On a lightly floured work surface, knead dough until smooth and elastic, 7 to 8 minutes, adding more flour if dough is sticky.

Put the ball of dough in an oiled bowl and cover with plastic wrap. Let rise in a warm place until it doubles in volume, 30 to 40 minutes.

While the dough is rising, preheat grill to high. (Alternatively, use a grill pan to grill the veggies.)

Toss eggplant, zucchini, mushroom and red pepper halves with enough olive oil to coat. Grill vegetables, turning once, until lightly charred on both sides, 5 to 10 minutes. Let cool. Cut veggies into bite-size pieces.

Set rack on lowest level of oven and preheat oven to 425°F (220°C).

Punch down dough. Cut in half. On a lightly floured work surface, roll out each piece to form a 10-inch (25 cm) round. Alternatively, make one party-size pizza (about 24 × 18 inches/60 × 45 cm). Place pizza base on a greased pizza pan or baking sheet.

Top pizza with tomato sauce, both cheeses, diced tomatoes and grilled veggies. Sprinkle with oregano and drizzle with 2 tbsp (30 mL) olive oil.

Bake pizza until crust is golden brown and crisp, 15 to 20 minutes.

TIP You can use whichever vegetables you like on this pizza. Just make sure they are pre-cooked or grilled. Adjust the amounts of cheese, or swap in whichever cheese you wish.

Thai Chicken Satay with Spicy Peanut Sauce

Chicken appetizers are always a hit, but when they're infused with the flavours of coconut and ginger, then grilled to perfection, you know you have a winner on your hands. These Thai-inspired skewers are easy for your guests to eat, and the spicy peanut sauce is an irresistible accompaniment. MAKES 15 SKEWERS

SPICY PEANUT SAUCE

Juice of 1 lime

1 cup (250 mL) finely chopped toasted peanuts

1 cup (250 mL) coconut milk

2 tbsp (30 mL) Thai red curry paste, or to taste

1 tbsp (15 mL) brown sugar

CHICKEN SATAY SKEWERS

3 boneless, skinless chicken breasts

¼ cup (60 mL) coconut milk

2 tbsp (30 mL) chopped fresh cilantro

1 tbsp (15 mL) chopped fresh ginger

2 tsp (10 mL) turmeric

2 tsp (10 mL) fish sauce, or to taste

Chopped peanuts, fresh cilantro leaves and lime wedges, for garnish

Soak 15 bamboo skewers in water for at least 30 minutes to help prevent them from burning on the grill.

To make the spicy peanut sauce: In a small saucepan, combine lime juice, peanuts, coconut milk, curry paste and brown sugar. Whisk to combine. Bring to a boil, reduce heat and simmer until slightly thickened, about 5 minutes. Set aside.

To make the chicken satay skewers: Slice each chicken breast lengthwise into 5 strips. Set aside.

In a large bowl, combine coconut milk, cilantro, ginger, turmeric and fish sauce. Add chicken to marinade and toss to combine. Cover and let chicken marinate in the fridge for 10 to 15 minutes or up to 1 day. Thread chicken onto skewers.

Preheat grill to medium-high.

Brush grill well with oil. Reduce heat to medium. Add skewers and grill, turning as needed, until chicken is cooked all the way through but still juicy, 5 to 8 minutes. Serve chicken skewers with Spicy Peanut Sauce. Garnish with chopped peanuts, cilantro leaves and lime wedges.

TIP Adjust the level of spice in the peanut sauce by using more or less Thai red curry paste.

Curry Lamb Pockets with Faita's Raita

Here's an easy way to bring the rich, exotic flavours of Indian food to your table. Just fill pizza dough rounds with a hearty combination of ground lamb, curry and fresh cilantro. It's a compact, easy-to-eat pocket that's made even more delicious when topped off with my cool cucumber dip. **MAKES 8 SERVINGS**

FAITA'S RAITA

1 ½ cups (375 mL) plain yogurt

½ cup (125 mL) diced cucumber

1 tbsp (15 mL) chopped fresh mint

Pinch of ground coriander

Salt and freshly ground pepper

CURRY LAMB POCKETS

1 tbsp (15 mL) vegetable oil

1 lb (450 g) ground lamb

Salt and freshly ground pepper

¼ cup (60 mL) Indian curry paste (mild or medium)

2 tbsp (30 mL) tomato paste

3 tbsp (45 mL) water

2 tbsp (30 mL) chopped fresh cilantro

1 lb (450 g) pizza dough

Butter, for finishing

Sesame seeds, for garnish

TIP You can easily make this recipe with ground beef, pork or chicken if you prefer. The cilantro can also be replaced with parsley. Make lots of raita—it's a delicious dip for veggies and great in sandwiches.

To make Faita's Raita: In a bowl, combine yogurt, cucumber, mint, coriander, and salt and pepper to taste. Taste and adjust seasoning. Refrigerate until needed.

To make the curry lamb pockets: In a large skillet over medium heat, heat oil. When oil is hot, add ground lamb. Season with salt and pepper. Cook, stirring, until meat is browned, 8 to 10 minutes. Stir in curry paste. Fry for 2 minutes. Stir in tomato paste, water and cilantro. Continue to cook, stirring frequently, until pan is dry, 4 to 5 minutes. Remove from heat and let cool completely.

Divide pizza dough into 8 equal pieces. Roll out each piece of dough into a ball. On a lightly floured work surface, pat or roll each ball into a 3-inch (8 cm) circle. Divide filling among circles, leaving a 1-inch (2.5 cm) border along the edges. Bring sides of dough up over filling and pinch ends together to seal. Roll out each pocket into a 6- × 3-inch (15 × 8 cm) oval about ½ inch (1 cm) thick.

Preheat grill to high.

Grill lamb pockets, turning once, until dough starts to bubble and lightly brown on each side, 2 to 3 minutes per side. Remove from grill. Brush with butter and sprinkle with sesame seeds. Serve with Faita's Raita.

STEFANO'S PASTA FAVOURITES

Pasta Fagioli

A classic peasant dish that is now served in many restaurants, this soup combines two important ingredients in Italian cuisine: pasta and beans. It's a hearty dish with intense flavour that will warm you up on a cold day. MAKES 4 TO 6 SERVINGS

1 ¼ cups (300 mL) dried borlotti beans

4 cups (1 L) tomato purée (passata)

½ cup (125 mL) olive oil

2 sprigs rosemary

2 large garlic cloves, minced

Salt and freshly ground pepper

¾ cup (175 mL) short pasta, such as tubetti

2 tbsp (30 mL) chopped fresh Italian parsley

1 tbsp (15 mL) chopped fresh basil, for garnish

Freshly grated Parmesan cheese and extra-virgin olive oil, for garnish

Toasted baguette slices

TIP Borlotti beans have a great texture, but not every grocery store has them. Replace them with regular white kidney beans, if you like. For a lighter take on this soup, you can make it without the pasta.

Soak beans in water to cover for 12 hours. Drain and rinse. Place in a large saucepan and cover with 5 cups (1.5 L) water. Bring to a boil over high heat. Reduce heat and simmer until beans are tender, 45 minutes to 1 hour. Drain beans, reserving the cooking liquid.

In a blender, combine 1 cup (250 mL) cooked beans, 1 cup (250 mL) cooking liquid and 2 cups (500 mL) tomato purée. Blend until smooth. Set aside.

Heat olive oil in a large pot over medium heat. When oil is hot, add rosemary sprigs. Let the rosemary infuse the oil for 1 to 2 minutes, then remove. Add the garlic and cook, stirring, for 1 minute. Add the puréed bean and tomato mixture, the remaining beans, 2 cups (500 mL) remaining cooking liquid and remaining 2 cups (500 mL) tomato purée. Season with salt and pepper. Bring to a boil, reduce heat and simmer, covered and stirring occasionally, for 10 to 15 minutes. If soup becomes too thick, thin with water. If soup is too thin, remove lid and continue to cook down until it reaches desired consistency.

Bring to a boil once again and stir in pasta. Cook until pasta is al dente, about 10 minutes. Stir in parsley. Taste and adjust seasoning.

Serve soup garnished with fresh basil, Parmesan and a drizzle of olive oil. Serve with toasted baguette slices.

Pasta with Basil Pesto

Nothing smells better than fresh basil, especially when it's mixed with toasted nuts and Parmigiano-Reggiano. Not only is this recipe tasty, but it's really easy to make any night of the week. **MAKES 4 TO 6 SERVINGS**

1 lb (450 g) pasta, such as trofie, fusilli or farfalle

Freshly grated Parmesan cheese, for serving

BASIL PESTO

2 cups (500 mL) packed fresh basil leaves (from about 1 large bunch)

2 garlic cloves

½ cup (125 mL) extra-virgin olive oil

3 tbsp (45 mL) pine nuts, toasted

2 tbsp (30 mL) freshly grated Parmesan cheese

2 tbsp (30 mL) grated pecorino cheese

Bring a large pot of water to a boil. Generously salt. Add pasta and cook until al dente.

Meanwhile, make the basil pesto: In a food processor, combine basil, garlic, olive oil, pine nuts, Parmesan and pecorino. Pulse to combine, adding more olive oil if needed to make a smooth paste. (Alternatively, use a mortar and pestle.)

Drain pasta, reserving 3 tbsp (45 mL) pasta water.

Transfer pesto to a large bowl and add 2 to 3 tbsp (30 to 45 mL) pasta water to loosen. Add the pasta and toss to combine. Serve with grated Parmesan.

Cherry Tomato and Feta Penne

Using the freshest ingredients in this recipe—tomatoes, basil, olives and feta cheese—will give you the best results. The prep is so simple—just build the salad and add the warm pasta. It doesn't get any easier than this! MAKES 4 TO 6 SERVINGS

1 lb (450 g) penne rigate

1 garlic clove, finely chopped

12 basil leaves, chopped

¾ cup (175 mL) extra-virgin olive oil

2 ½ cups (625 mL) cherry tomatoes, halved

1 ½ cups (375 mL) pitted black olives, sliced

10 oz (280 g) feta cheese, crumbled

Bring a large pot of water to a boil. Generously salt. Add pasta and cook until al dente.

Meanwhile, in a small bowl, stir together garlic, basil and olive oil. Set aside.

In a large bowl, stir together cherry tomatoes and olives. Set aside.

Drain pasta and add to tomato mixture. Add olive oil mixture and toss to combine. Stir in feta. Serve hot or cold.

Chicken Penne with Roasted Peppers and Mascarpone

Here's a great way to bring chicken and pasta together. The combination of ingredients in this recipe is just perfect—the mascarpone cheese gives you that slightly sweet creamy sauce, and the roasted peppers infuse it with a smoky flavour.

MAKES 2 SERVINGS

½ lb (225 g) penne rigate

2 tbsp (30 mL) olive oil

2 oz (55 g) pancetta or bacon, diced

1 boneless, skinless chicken
     breast, sliced crosswise

Salt and freshly ground pepper

2 green onions, chopped

2 roasted red peppers, sliced

4 or 5 basil leaves, chopped

Handful of fresh Italian parsley, chopped

3 tbsp (45 mL) mascarpone cheese

2 tbsp (30 mL) freshly grated
     Parmesan cheese

Bring a large pot of water to a boil. Generously salt. Add pasta and cook until al dente.

Meanwhile, heat olive oil in a large skillet over medium heat. When oil is hot, add pancetta and cook until it just starts to crisp. Remove from pan and set aside. Add chicken to pan, season with salt and pepper, and cook, stirring frequently, until golden brown and cooked through, 4 to 5 minutes. Return pancetta to pan along with green onions. Cook for 1 minute. Add roasted peppers, basil, parsley and mascarpone. Cook, stirring, for another 2 minutes.

Drain pasta and add to skillet. Add Parmesan and toss to combine. Serve.

TIP You can substitute ½ cup (125 mL) whipping cream for the mascarpone cheese. Just let it reduce slowly until it thickens. Sausage meat (taken out of its casing) is a great protein option for this dish.

Stefano's Pasta Primavera

This dish has everything—amazing fresh veggies, herbs and, of course, Parmesan cheese. I was inspired to put a sprinkling of pine nuts in for a bit of added texture. Save this recipe for your next Meatless Monday. **MAKES 4 TO 6 SERVINGS**

1 lb (450 g) farfalle

½ small head broccoli, cut into small florets

1 carrot, sliced

1 small bunch asparagus, trimmed and cut in thirds

¼ cup (60 mL) olive oil

2 garlic cloves, cut in half or smashed

2 green onions, chopped

1 small sweet yellow pepper, sliced

½ small green zucchini, sliced

½ small yellow zucchini, sliced

Pinch of hot pepper flakes (optional)

Salt and freshly ground pepper

2 tbsp (30 mL) chopped fresh basil

Freshly grated Parmesan cheese, to taste

¼ cup (60 mL) toasted pine nuts

Bring a large pot of water to a boil. Generously salt. Add pasta and cook for about 6 minutes. Add broccoli, carrots and asparagus. Cook until pasta is al dente and vegetables are tender.

Meanwhile, in a large skillet, heat olive oil over medium heat. When oil is hot, add garlic. Cook, stirring frequently, until garlic infuses oil, about 2 minutes. Add green onions, yellow pepper and zucchini. Season with hot pepper flakes, if desired, and salt and pepper. Cook, stirring occasionally, until vegetables are tender-crisp, about 5 minutes.

Drain pasta and veggies, reserving some of the pasta water. Add pasta and veggies to skillet. Stir to combine, adding some of the pasta water, if needed, to loosen the pasta from the pan. Add basil, Parmesan and pine nuts. Toss to combine. Serve.

Stefano's Pasta Puttanesca

If there is a pasta dish that exudes intense flavour, it is definitely this one. The best part is, you probably have all the ingredients in your fridge or pantry right now. Why not go make it? MAKES 6 SERVINGS

1 lb (450 g) tortiglioni, penne or spaghetti

½ cup (125 mL) extra-virgin olive oil

4 to 5 anchovies

2 garlic cloves, minced

1 tbsp (15 mL) chopped drained hot peppers packed in oil

1 ½ cups (375 mL) pitted black olives, whole or chopped

2 tbsp (30 mL) capers

1 tsp (5 mL) dried oregano

1 can (14 oz/398 mL) diced tomatoes, preferably San Marzano

Salt and freshly ground pepper

⅓ cup (75 mL) chopped baby arugula, parsley or basil

Bring a large pot of water to a boil. Generously salt. Add pasta and cook until al dente.

Meanwhile, heat olive oil in a large skillet over medium heat. Add anchovies and mash into a paste with a fork. Add garlic and hot peppers and cook, stirring, for 1 minute. Add olives, capers and oregano. Cook for another 1 to 2 minutes.

Add tomatoes. Bring to a boil, reduce heat and simmer until slightly thickened, 7 to 10 minutes.

Drain pasta, reserving some of the pasta water. Add pasta to sauce and toss to combine, adding a little pasta water, if needed, to loosen the sauce. Season with salt and pepper and stir in arugula. Serve.

TIP A traditional puttanesca sauce does not include the arugula, so feel free to prepare it either way. It's a good idea to make more than you need for dinner, because leftovers will make an even more delicious lunch the next day.

Penne alla Vodka

This classic restaurant-style pasta may sound fancy, but it takes only minutes to prepare at home. The vodka adds a surprising zing to the rich, creamy tomato sauce. Give it a try! **MAKES 4 TO 6 SERVINGS**

1 lb (450 g) penne

1 cup (250 mL) frozen peas (optional)

2 tbsp (30 mL) olive oil

1 tbsp (15 mL) butter

2 garlic cloves, smashed

1 tsp (5 mL) dried oregano

Hot pepper flakes

¼ cup (60 mL) vodka

1 ¾ cups (425 mL) tomato purée (passata)

½ to 1 cup (125 to 250 mL) whipping cream (35%)

Freshly grated Parmesan cheese, to taste

¼ cup (60 mL) halved cherry tomatoes, for garnish

1 tbsp (15 mL) chopped fresh parsley, for garnish

Bring a large pot of water to a boil. Generously salt. Add pasta and cook until al dente. If using peas, just before draining the pasta, add the peas; they will cook with the residual heat.

Meanwhile, in a large skillet over medium heat, heat olive oil with butter. Add garlic and cook, stirring frequently, until it softens and turns lightly golden, 1 to 2 minutes. Add oregano and hot pepper flakes to taste. Remove pan from heat and add vodka. Return pan to heat and let vodka reduce for 1 to 2 minutes. Add tomato purée and bring to a boil. Stir in cream, reduce heat and simmer until sauce thickens, 5 to 10 minutes.

Drain pasta, reserving some of the pasta water. Add pasta to sauce and toss to combine. Add a little pasta water to loosen the sauce, if needed. Stir in Parmesan. Serve garnished with cherry tomatoes and chopped parsley, if desired.

Penne Arrabbiata

Penne arrabbiata means "angry pasta" in Italian, but I'll leave it to you to control how "angry" this spicy tomato sauce gets. I dare you to turn up the heat!

MAKES 4 TO 6 SERVINGS

2 tbsp (30 mL) extra-virgin olive oil

1 garlic clove, chopped

5 oz (140 g) pancetta, cut into strips

2 cups (500 mL) fresh or bottled tomato purée (passata)

2 tbsp (30 mL) minced hot peppers, or to taste

Salt

1 lb (450 g) penne

10 basil leaves

1 tbsp (15 mL) chopped fresh Italian parsley, for garnish

Olive oil and freshly grated Parmesan or Pecorino Romano cheese, for serving

In a large skillet over medium heat, heat olive oil. When oil is hot, add garlic. When garlic begins to soften, add pancetta strips and fry until lightly golden, 1 to 2 minutes.

Add tomato purée, hot peppers and a little salt to taste. Bring to a boil, reduce heat and simmer until tomatoes have reduced and thickened slightly, about 15 minutes.

Meanwhile, cook pasta in a large pot of boiling salted water until al dente.

Drain pasta. Add fresh herbs and pasta to sauce and toss to combine. Serve topped with a drizzle of olive oil and freshly grated Parmesan.

TIP Make this spicy sauce as hot as you want by adjusting the amount of hot peppers you use. You can also replace the pancetta with bacon.

Spaghetti with Tomato Sauce and Pancetta

The is the perfect tomato sauce for my chicken parmigiana—or keep it simple and toss it with some spaghetti for an easy weeknight dinner. **MAKES 4 TO 6 SERVINGS**

3 tbsp (45 mL) olive oil

2 thick slices pancetta (about 3 ½ oz/100 g total), diced

1 small onion, chopped

2 cloves garlic, chopped or smashed

2 ¾ cups (675 mL) tomato purée (passata)

Salt and freshly ground pepper

Handful of basil leaves

1 lb (450 g) spaghetti

Freshly grated pecorino or Parmesan cheese, to finish

In a medium saucepan, heat olive oil and pancetta over medium heat. Cook, stirring occasionally, until pancetta is golden brown, 3 to 5 minutes. Add onions and garlic. Cook, stirring frequently, until onion has softened, about 3 minutes.

Add tomato purée and season with salt and pepper. Bring to a boil. Reduce heat and simmer for 20 to 30 minutes, until desired thickness. Stir in basil leaves.

Meanwhile, bring a large pot of water to a boil. Generously salt. Add pasta and cook until al dente.

Drain and toss with half the sauce. (Reserve remaining sauce for Stefano's Chicken Parmigiana or other uses.) Serve spaghetti sprinkled with freshly grated pecorino.

Mom's Spaghetti and Meatballs

My mom taught me a lot in the kitchen, but to this day I haven't been able to top her famous meatballs. Just because I like you, I am sharing the two-for-one recipe for her meatballs and the sauce they are cooked in. It's your lucky day!

MAKES 4 SERVINGS

TOMATO SAUCE

2 tbsp (30 mL) olive oil

½ onion, finely chopped

1 garlic clove, finely chopped

8 cups (2 L) tomato sauce or
    tomato purée (passata)

Salt and freshly ground pepper

4 to 6 basil leaves, chopped

MEATBALLS

5 oz (140 g) ground veal

5 oz (140 g) ground beef

5 oz (140 g) ground pork

½ cup (125 mL) fresh or dry bread crumbs

½ cup (125 mL) grated Parmesan cheese

¼ cup (60 mL) finely chopped
    fresh Italian parsley

¼ cup (60 mL) milk

2 large eggs

Pinch of dried oregano

TO ASSEMBLE

1 lb (450 g) spaghetti

Freshly grated Parmesan
    cheese, for serving

To make the tomato sauce: Heat olive oil in a large saucepan over medium heat. Add onions and garlic. Sauté until softened and lightly golden, 3 to 5 minutes. Add tomato sauce and bring to a boil. Season with salt and pepper. Reduce heat to low and let sauce simmer until slightly thickened, about 30 minutes.

While sauce is simmering, make the meatballs: In a large bowl, combine ground meats, bread crumbs, Parmesan, parsley, milk, eggs and oregano. Season with salt and pepper. Mix with your hands until combined. Coat your hands with olive oil and roll meat mixture into balls about the size of a golf ball. You should have about 16 meatballs.

Add meatballs to the simmering tomato sauce. Cook until meatballs are no longer pink in the centre and sauce has thickened, about 30 minutes. Stir in fresh basil.

While the meatballs are cooking in the sauce, cook spaghetti in a large pot of boiling salted water until al dente.

Drain spaghetti and toss with tomato sauce and meatballs. Serve topped with freshly grated Parmesan.

(photo on next page)

TIP I like using spaghetti for this recipe, but any long or short pasta will do just fine. Make a lot of meatballs—they can be served on their own with a nice salad or even in a bun for lunch.

Garlic and Olive Oil Spaghetti

This dish is simplicity at its best—proof that, with a few good-quality ingredients, you can make an incredibly delicious dinner, fast! **MAKES 4 TO 6 SERVINGS**

1 lb (450 g) spaghetti

⅓ to ½ cup (75 to 125 mL)
   extra-virgin olive oil

4 garlic cloves, finely chopped

1 tbsp (15 mL) chopped hot peppers packed
   in oil (or hot pepper flakes, to taste)

Salt and freshly ground pepper

2 tbsp (30 mL) chopped fresh
   Italian parsley

Freshly grated Parmesan
   cheese, to taste

TIP This recipe is fast and made in one pan. If you prefer very spicy, add more hot peppers. For even more flavour, add some chopped anchovies to the pan before adding the pasta.

Bring a large pot of water to a boil. Generously salt. Add pasta and cook until al dente.

Meanwhile, heat a large skillet over medium heat. Add a generous amount of olive oil. When oil is hot, add garlic and hot peppers. Cook, stirring frequently, until garlic softens, 1 to 2 minutes.

Drain pasta, reserving some of the pasta water. Add pasta to sauce and toss to coat. If needed, add a little pasta water to loosen the pasta. Season with salt and pepper. Add parsley and toss. Serve topped with freshly grated Parmesan.

Creamy Mediterranean Spaghetti

Have you ever eaten a pasta dish made with yogurt? Well, here's your chance. And guess what? It rocks! I hope you'll be inspired to try different flavour combinations with yogurt as the creamy base. MAKES 4 SERVINGS

1 lb (450 g) spaghetti

¼ cup (60 mL) olive oil

2 garlic cloves, finely chopped

3 zucchinis, julienned

¼ cup (60 mL) pitted black olives, sliced

1 tbsp (15 mL) coarsely chopped sun-dried tomatoes

½ cup (125 mL) Greek-style plain yogurt

2 tbsp (30 mL) chopped fresh basil

2 tbsp (30 mL) chopped fresh marjoram

2 tbsp (30 mL) chopped fresh Italian parsley

2 tbsp (30 mL) grated Parmesan cheese

Salt and freshly ground pepper

Bring a large pot of water to a boil. Generously salt. Add pasta and cook until al dente.

In a large heavy skillet, heat olive oil over medium heat. Add garlic and cook for 2 minutes. Add zucchinis, olives and sun-dried tomatoes. Cook for 4 or 5 minutes. Keep warm.

In a large bowl, combine yogurt with basil, marjoram and parsley.

Drain pasta. Add pasta to yogurt mixture, then add zucchini mixture, Parmesan, and salt and pepper to taste. Toss to combine. Serve.

TIP If you'd like a decadent result, replace the yogurt with mascarpone cheese.

Pasta Dough

Nothing beats the taste of fresh, homemade pasta, and it's a lot easier to make than you might think. MAKES ENOUGH PASTA FOR 6 TO 8 SERVINGS

3 cups (750 mL) super-fine semolina

4 eggs

2 tbsp (30 mL) olive oil

1 to 2 tbsp (15 to 30 mL) water, if needed

Mound semolina on work surface and form a well in the centre. Add eggs and oil to the well. Using a fork or your fingertips, mix together eggs and oil. Begin to incorporate semolina from the sides of the well. When dough starts to come together and looks shaggy, start kneading. Knead dough until smooth and elastic, 5 to 10 minutes. If dough feels dry, add a little water. Wrap dough in plastic wrap and let rest for 30 minutes.

On a lightly floured work surface, or using a pasta machine, roll and shape pasta to make lasagna sheets, noodles or stuffed pasta.

Creamy Mixed Mushroom Lasagna

Layer upon layer of pasta, béchamel sauce, mushrooms and cheese. Need I say more? **MAKES 8 TO 12 SERVINGS**

BÉCHAMEL SAUCE

⅓ cup (75 mL) unsalted butter

6 tbsp (90 mL) all-purpose flour

5 cups (1.25 L) milk

Salt and freshly ground pepper

LASAGNA

2 oz (55 g) dried porcini mushrooms

4 tbsp (60 mL) extra-virgin olive oil

4 tbsp (60 mL) butter

1 medium onion, chopped

2 garlic cloves, minced

2 lb (900 g) mixed fresh mushrooms, such as cremini, shiitake and oyster

2 tbsp (30 mL) chopped fresh thyme

2 tbsp (30 mL) chopped fresh sage

1 tbsp (15 mL) chopped fresh rosemary

6 tbsp (90 mL) white wine

10 fresh lasagna sheets (page 108 or store-bought)

¾ cup (175 mL) shredded Asiago cheese

¾ cup (175 mL) grated Parmesan cheese

2 tbsp (30 mL) chopped fresh parsley

To make the béchamel sauce: Melt butter in a large saucepan over medium heat. Add flour and stir to combine to make a roux. Cook, stirring constantly, for 2 or 3 minutes, without browning flour. Gradually whisk in milk, smoothly blending the roux into the milk. Bring to a boil, whisking constantly. Reduce heat and simmer, whisking frequently, until sauce thickens, about 10 minutes. Season with salt and pepper. Set aside.

To make the lasagna: In a small bowl, soak dried mushrooms in warm water for 20 minutes. Drain. Chop and set aside.

Heat 2 large skillets over medium heat. (Alternatively, use 1 skillet and cook half the ingredients at a time.) Add 2 tbsp (30 mL) olive oil and 2 tbsp (30 mL) butter to each pan. Divide onions and garlic between the pans. Cook, stirring frequently, until they begin to soften, 2 to 3 minutes. Increase heat to medium-high. Divide fresh mushrooms, thyme, sage and rosemary between the pans. Sauté mushrooms until golden brown, 8 to 10 minutes. Add reserved dried mushrooms and continue to cook for 2 minutes. Deglaze pans with white wine and cook until most of the wine has evaporated. Season with salt and pepper.

Preheat oven to 375°F (190°C). Butter a 12- × 8-inch (3 L) baking dish.

continued...

In a large saucepan of boiling salted water, cook 3 or 4 lasagna sheets at a time until al dente. (Do not overcook the lasagna sheets.) Immediately plunge them into a bowl of cold water to stop the cooking process, then drain in a single layer on a clean kitchen towel.

To assemble the lasagna, spread a few spoonfuls of béchamel to lightly cover the bottom of the baking dish. Arrange 2 lasagna sheets in bottom of baking dish. Top with about a quarter of the mushroom mixture, a quarter of the béchamel sauce, 2 tbsp (30 mL) Asiago and 2 tbsp (30 mL) Parmesan. Repeat layers three times, adding the cheese every other layer. Finish with the remaining lasagna sheets, remaining ½ cup (125 mL) Asiago and remaining ½ cup (125 mL) Parmesan. Add more cheese if you like it extra cheesy.

Bake lasagna until filling is hot and bubbling and cheese is golden brown, 30 to 35 minutes. Let lasagna rest for 10 minutes before cutting. Sprinkle with parsley and serve.

Spinach and Ricotta Lazy Lasagna

This quick and easy version of lasagna is a great way to use up leftover pasta. Make it any night of the week and you'll have a hearty, creamy pasta dish everyone will love. **MAKES 4 SERVINGS**

1 tbsp (15 mL) olive oil

1 garlic clove, chopped

5 oz (140 g) baby spinach

Salt and freshly ground pepper

1 large egg

1 cup (250 mL) ricotta cheese

½ cup (125 mL) grated Parmesan cheese

Pinch of freshly grated nutmeg

1 ¼ to 1 ½ cups (300 to 375 mL) tomato purée (passata) or tomato sauce

2 heaping cups (550 mL) leftover cooked short pasta, such as penne, tossed in butter

1 cup (250 mL) shredded mozzarella cheese

Preheat oven to 400°F (200°C). Grease an 8-inch (2 L) square baking dish with butter or olive oil.

Heat a large skillet over medium heat. Add olive oil. When oil is hot, add garlic. Stir and cook until garlic is soft but not colouring, 1 to 2 minutes. Add spinach, season with salt and pepper, and cook until spinach is just wilted. Remove from pan and let cool. Squeeze out any excess moisture.

In a medium bowl, beat egg. Add spinach, ricotta, ¼ cup (60 mL) Parmesan and nutmeg.

Layer evenly in the baking dish: ¼ cup (60 mL) tomato purée, 1 cup (250 mL) pasta, ½ cup (125 mL) tomato purée, ½ cup (125 mL) mozzarella cheese, all of the spinach and ricotta filling, remaining pasta, ½ cup (125 mL) more tomato purée, remaining mozzarella and remaining Parmesan. If you prefer your lazy lasagna more saucy, add ¼ cup (60 mL) more tomato purée.

Cover with foil. Bake until cheese is melted and pasta is thoroughly heated through, 25 to 30 minutes. Remove foil and bake until cheese is golden brown, about 10 minutes.

Lasagna Bolognese

I . . . love . . . lasagna. It's my go-to meal for feeding a crowd and always has everyone asking for seconds. This rich, meaty lasagna is a classic. Just try it— you'll be addicted! **MAKES 8 TO 10 SERVINGS**

BOLOGNESE SAUCE

¼ cup (60 mL) olive oil

3 tbsp (45 mL) butter

2 small onions, chopped

4 carrots, diced

4 celery stalks, diced

2 lb (900 g) ground beef

Salt and freshly ground pepper

1 heaping tbsp (18 mL) finely chopped fresh rosemary

1 heaping tbsp (18 mL) finely chopped fresh thyme

2 tsp (10 mL) hot pepper flakes, or to taste

2 cans (14 oz/398 mL each) diced tomatoes

2 cans (14 oz/398 mL each) puréed tomatoes

TO ASSEMBLE

10 to 12 fresh lasagna sheets (page 108 or store-bought)

1 ½ cups (375 mL) grated Parmesan cheese

1 ball (12 oz/340 g) mozzarella cheese, grated

1 to 2 tbsp (15 to 30 mL) butter (optional)

Handful of chopped fresh Italian parsley, for garnish

TIP Instead of mozzarella, you can use whatever good melting cheese you have on hand. Once assembled, you can freeze this lasagna. Cook from frozen, uncovered, in a 300°F (150°C) oven for 1 hour. This Bolognese sauce is also great paired with other pastas.

To make the Bolognese sauce: In a large saucepan, heat oil with butter over medium heat. When oil is hot, add onions and cook, stirring occasionally, until softened, about 5 minutes. Add carrots and celery; continue to cook until they begin to soften, about 5 minutes.

Increase heat to medium-high. Add ground beef and season with salt and pepper. Cook, stirring to break up the meat, until meat browns, 12 to 15 minutes. Add rosemary, thyme, hot pepper flakes, diced tomatoes and puréed tomatoes. Bring to a boil, reduce heat and simmer, uncovered, for 40 to 45 minutes.

Preheat oven to 375°F (190°C).

To assemble the lasagna, in a large saucepan of boiling salted water, cook 3 or 4 lasagna sheets at time until al dente. (Do not overcook the lasagna sheets.) Immediately plunge them into a bowl of cold water to stop the cooking process, then drain in a single layer on a clean kitchen towel. Trim sheets as needed to fit a 13- × 9-inch (3 L) baking dish.

Cover the bottom of the baking dish with a little Bolognese sauce. Top with a layer of lasagna sheets. Cover with about one-fifth of the Bolognese sauce. Sprinkle with a little Parmesan and mozzarella. Dot with a few teaspoons of butter, if desired. Repeat to make 5 to 6 layers, finishing with remaining sauce and then remaining cheese.

Cover with foil. Bake for 30 minutes. Remove foil and bake until filling is bubbling, cheese is melted and top of lasagna is golden brown, about 30 minutes more. Let lasagna rest for 15 minutes before cutting. Sprinkle with parsley and serve.

Farfalle with Cauliflower and Herb Pesto

Cauliflower may be one of the unsung heroes of the veggie world, but dishes like this tasty bow-tie pasta may put it on top. In this recipe, you also get my make-ahead pesto—keep it on hand to use in other pastas or on a pizza for a quick, flavour-packed weeknight meal. MAKES 4 TO 6 SERVINGS

Leaves from 3 or 4 sprigs thyme

Leaves from 3 or 4 sprigs marjoram

Handful of fresh Italian parsley leaves

3 ½ oz (100 g) grated Pecorino Romano cheese

¼ cup (60 mL) hazelnuts, toasted and skins removed

¼ cup (60 mL) extra-virgin olive oil

Pinch of freshly grated nutmeg

Salt and freshly ground pepper

1 small cauliflower (about ½ lb/225 g), cut into small florets

1 lb (450 g) farfalle

Freshly grated Parmesan cheese, for serving

TIP Mix up the combination of herbs in this pesto. Basil can be used in place of thyme, and you can throw in some mint or oregano, too. Broccoli makes a fun, fresh replacement for the cauliflower.

Bring a large pot of water to a boil. Generously salt.

Meanwhile, make the pesto: In a food processor, combine thyme, marjoram, parsley, Pecorino Romano, hazelnuts, olive oil and nutmeg. Process until smooth. Season with salt and pepper. Transfer pesto to a large bowl.

Add cauliflower to boiling water. Blanch cauliflower until tender, 3 to 4 minutes. Remove cauliflower with a spider or slotted spoon and set aside. Add pasta to boiling water and cook until al dente.

Drain pasta, reserving 3 tbsp (45 mL) of the pasta water. Add 2 to 3 tbsp (30 to 45 mL) pasta water to the pesto to loosen. Add pasta and cauliflower. Toss to combine. Serve topped with freshly grated Parmesan.

Asparagus and Shrimp Linguine

This is the perfect pasta to make on a first date, trust me. Not only is it ready in no time (which gives you more time to spend with your other half), but it looks really fancy. Serve it with a chilled white wine and you're on your way to having a great night! MAKES 4 TO 6 SERVINGS

1 lb (450 g) asparagus

1 lb (450 g) linguine

2 tbsp (30 mL) extra-virgin olive oil

2 tbsp (30 mL) butter

2 French shallots, finely chopped

1 lb (450 g) large or extra-large shrimp, peeled and deveined

3 tbsp (45 mL) brandy

1 cup (250 mL) whipping cream (35%)

Leaves from 1 to 2 sprigs tarragon, chopped

Salt and freshly ground pepper

Freshly grated Parmesan cheese, for serving

Snap ends off asparagus. Peel asparagus if too woody. Cut into 2-inch (5 cm) pieces and steam until tender-crisp, 7 to 10 minutes. Set aside.

Bring a large pot of water to a boil. Generously salt. Add pasta and cook until al dente.

Meanwhile, heat a large skillet over medium-high heat. Add olive oil and butter. When butter has melted, add shallots. Cook, stirring frequently, until soft. Add shrimp and asparagus; cook, stirring, for 2 to 3 minutes. Remove skillet from heat. Add brandy. Return skillet to heat and let brandy warm. Ignite with a long match. The alcohol should burn off in a few seconds and the flame will die out. (If the flame gets out of hand, immediately cover the pan with a tight-fitting lid to extinguish flame. Remove from heat.)

Stir in cream and cook sauce until reduced and starting to thicken, about 5 minutes. Add tarragon and season with salt and pepper.

Drain pasta, reserving some of the pasta water. Add pasta to pan and toss to coat with sauce. If needed, add a little pasta water to loosen sauce. Serve topped with freshly grated Parmesan.

Stefano's Mac and Cheese

You can make mac and cheese from a box, but once you see how easy it is to make my recipe for this childhood favourite, you'll never go back to the packaged version. Rich and creamy with three kinds of cheese and a crispy bread crumb topping, this mac and cheese is definitely a classic. MAKES 4 TO 6 SERVINGS

4 tbsp (60 mL) butter

1 lb (450 g) macaroni

1 small onion, chopped

1 garlic clove, minced

1 celery stalk, diced

Salt and freshly ground pepper

2 tbsp (30 mL) all-purpose flour

2 ½ cups (625 mL) milk

½ cup (125 mL) whipping cream (35%)

2 cups (500 mL) grated aged Cheddar

1 cup (250 mL) shredded
mozzarella cheese

½ cup (125 mL) grated Pecorino
Romano cheese

¼ cup (60 mL) fresh or dry bread crumbs

1 tbsp (15 mL) chopped fresh Italian parsley

2 tbsp (30 mL) olive oil

Grated zest of 1 lemon

Preheat oven to 400°F (200°C). Grease a large baking dish with 1 tbsp (15 mL) butter.

Bring a large pot of water to a boil. Generously salt. Add macaroni and cook until al dente.

Meanwhile, melt 1 tbsp (15 mL) butter in a large skillet over medium heat. Add onions, garlic, celery, and salt and pepper to taste. Cook veggies, stirring frequently, until they begin to soften, 3 to 5 minutes. Set aside.

To make the béchamel sauce: Melt the remaining 2 tbsp (30 mL) butter in a large saucepan over medium heat. Add flour and stir to combine to make a roux. Cook, stirring constantly, for 2 or 3 minutes, without browning flour. Gradually whisk in milk, smoothly blending the roux into the milk. Add cream. Bring to a boil, whisking constantly. Reduce heat and simmer, whisking frequently, until sauce thickens, about 5 minutes.

Season béchamel with salt and pepper. Remove from heat and stir in 1 cup (250 mL) Cheddar, ½ cup (125 mL) mozzarella and ¼ cup (60 mL) Pecorino Romano, stirring until cheese is melted. Add veggies and drained pasta. Stir to combine. Transfer to baking dish. Sprinkle with remaining 1 cup (250 mL) Cheddar, ½ cup (125 mL) mozzarella and ¼ cup (60 mL) Pecorino Romano.

Combine bread crumbs, parsley, olive oil and lemon zest in a small bowl. Sprinkle mixture over cheese.

Bake mac and cheese until bubbling and golden brown, about 20 minutes.

Pasta with Mushroom and Bacon Cream Sauce

This was one of the first dishes we made on *In the Kitchen*, and when most of the crew asked me for the recipe, I knew it was a winner. The super-simple but oh-so-delicious combination of smoky bacon and thyme in a creamy sauce will make everyone happy. **MAKES 4 TO 6 SERVINGS**

1 lb (450 g) rigatoni or other short pasta

1 tbsp (15 mL) unsalted butter

2 tbsp (30 mL) extra-virgin olive oil

1 small onion, diced

5 oz (140 g) thick-cut bacon, chopped

5 oz (140 g) shiitake mushrooms, stems removed, sliced or chopped

5 oz (140 g) button or brown mushrooms

Leaves from 3 or 4 sprigs thyme

Salt and freshly ground pepper

½ cup (125 mL) white wine

1 cup (250 mL) whipping cream (35%)

Freshly grated Parmesan cheese, for serving

Bring a large of pot of water to a boil. Generously salt. Start making the sauce, then add pasta to boiling water just before you add the wine to the sauce. Cook pasta until al dente.

In a large sauté pan, melt butter with olive oil over medium-high heat. Add onions and bacon and cook, stirring frequently, until onions begin to soften and bacon begins to crisp, 3 to 5 minutes. Add mushrooms and thyme. Cook until mushrooms are golden brown, 5 to 7 minutes. Season with salt and pepper. (Start cooking your pasta now.) Deglaze pan with white wine and cook until most of the liquid has evaporated, 4 to 5 minutes more. Add cream and bring to a boil. Reduce heat and simmer for another 4 to 5 minutes. Taste and adjust seasoning.

Drain pasta, reserving about ¼ cup (60 mL) of the pasta water. Add pasta to sauce, adding a little of the pasta water, if needed, to loosen the sauce. Toss to combine. Serve topped with freshly grated Parmesan and freshly ground pepper.

TIP Use whichever mix of mushrooms you like in this recipe, but only include one mushroom that has big, intense flavour. The other mushrooms should play a more supporting role.

Butternut Squash Cannelloni with Sage Cream Sauce

The flavour combination of roasted butternut squash and sage is amazing and a nice change from tomato-based pastas. Keep this beautiful, hearty pasta dish in your back pocket to serve at your next dinner party. **MAKES 4 TO 6 SERVINGS**

BUTTERNUT SQUASH CANNELLONI

1 medium butternut squash

2 tbsp (30 mL) olive oil

Salt and freshly ground pepper

1 large egg

1 lb (450 g) ricotta cheese

1 to 1 ½ cups (250 to 375 mL) grated Parmesan cheese

Pinch of freshly grated nutmeg

1 package (13 oz/340 g) fresh lasagna sheets (page 108 or store-bought)

SAGE CREAM SAUCE

3 tbsp (45 mL) unsalted butter

1 shallot, finely chopped

Handful of fresh sage leaves, chopped

¼ cup (60 mL) all-purpose flour

¼ cup (60 mL) dry white wine

2 cups (500 mL) chicken stock

2 cups (500 mL) whipping cream (35%)

TO ASSEMBLE

Grated Parmesan or pecorino cheese, to taste

Handful of chopped toasted walnuts, for garnish

1 tsp (5 mL) chopped fresh sage, for garnish

Preheat oven to 400°F (200°C). Butter a large baking dish.

To make the butternut squash cannelloni: Cut butternut squash in half and scrape out seeds with a spoon. Place squash halves cut side up on a baking sheet. Drizzle with olive oil and season with salt and pepper. Roast squash until tender, 45 to 60 minutes. Let cool completely.

Spoon butternut squash flesh into a food processor. Add egg, ricotta, 1 cup (250 mL) Parmesan, nutmeg, and salt and pepper to taste. Pulse until smooth. If mixture feels loose, mix in ½ cup (125 mL) more Parmesan. Set aside.

To make the sage cream sauce: Melt butter in a medium saucepan over medium heat. Add shallot and sage. Cook, stirring frequently, until shallot starts to soften, 2 to 3 minutes. Add flour and stir to combine to make a roux. Cook, stirring constantly, for 2 or 3 minutes, without browning flour. Gradually whisk in wine, chicken stock and cream. Bring to a boil, whisking frequently. Reduce heat and simmer, whisking often, until sauce thickens, about 5 minutes. Season with salt and pepper. Spread sauce in prepared baking dish. Set aside.

Preheat oven to 350°F (180°C).

Bring a large pot of water to a boil. Generously salt. Cut pasta sheets into 6- × 5 ½-inch (15 × 13 cm) rectangles. (You'll need 12 to 16 rectangles.) Blanch pasta in boiling water until al dente. Drain on clean kitchen towels.

Divide filling among cooked pasta rectangles and roll up. Arrange cannelloni seam side down in baking dish with sauce. Cover with grated Parmesan.

Bake until sauce bubbles, filling is hot and cheese is golden brown, about 20 minutes. Serve cannelloni garnished with toasted walnuts and chopped sage, if desired.

TIP Instead of squash, you can easily use sweet potato. If fresh lasagna sheets are not available, dried store-bought cannelloni tubes will work well, too.

Homemade Gnocchi with Butter and Sage

It takes a little bit of technique to make gnocchi, but don't be intimidated. This recipe is foolproof. Just be organized, follow my recipe and enjoy all the compliments you'll get when you bring it to the table! MAKES 4 TO 6 SERVINGS

2 ¼ lb (1 kg) russet potatoes

2 large egg yolks

1 ¾ cups (425 mL) semolina

4 tbsp (60 mL) unsalted butter

1 tbsp (15 mL) chopped fresh sage

Freshly grated Parmesan cheese, for serving

TIP When making gnocchi, try not to add too much flour—if you do, you could lose that fluffy texture. Once your dough stops sticking to your wooden board, it is ready.

Preheat oven to 350°F (180°C).

Pierce potatoes with a fork. Bake on oven rack until tender, about 1 hour depending on their size. (Alternatively, boil potatoes, unpeeled, until tender.)

Cut warm potatoes in half lengthwise and scoop out flesh with a spoon. Pass through a potato ricer (or use a potato masher). Shape puréed potatoes into a mound on work surface and make a well in the centre. Add egg yolks and semolina to the well and beat with a fork until combined. As you beat, begin to incorporate potato from the sides of the well. When potato is fully incorporated, knead dough just until it comes together and is smooth.

Divide dough into 6 equal pieces. Roll each piece into a rope 1 inch (2.5 cm) thick. Cut each log into ½-inch (1 cm) pieces. Roll each piece on a gnocchi board or the tines of a fork.

Bring a large pot of water to a boil. Generously salt. Add gnocchi and cook until they float to the surface, about 2 minutes. Gently drain or remove with a slotted spoon.

Meanwhile, melt butter in a large skillet over medium heat. Add sage. When butter begins to foam, add cooked gnocchi and cook, turning to coat in butter, about 2 minutes. Serve topped with grated Parmesan.

Orecchiette with Sausage and Rapini

These "little ears" of pasta are crazy good. The sweet Italian sausage and slightly bitter rapini are perfectly balanced flavours. Top it with some freshly grated Parmesan cheese and you've got magic! **MAKES 4 TO 6 SERVINGS**

1 lb (450 g) orecchiette

3 tbsp (45 mL) olive oil

2 shallots, sliced

4 Italian sausages (mild or hot), casings removed

1 bunch rapini, coarsely chopped and blanched

Salt and freshly ground pepper

Freshly grated or shaved Parmesan cheese, to taste

Bring a large pot of water to a boil. Generously salt. Add pasta and cook until al dente.

Meanwhile, heat olive oil in a large skillet over medium heat. Add shallots and cook, stirring frequently, until they start to soften, 2 to 3 minutes. Add sausage meat and fry until meat is golden brown, 8 to 10 minutes. Add blanched rapini. Sauté until meat is cooked through and rapini is tender, 3 to 5 minutes.

Drain pasta, reserving some of the cooking water. Add pasta to sauce and toss to combine. If needed, add a little of the pasta water to loosen the mixture. Season with salt and pepper. Serve topped with grated or shaved Parmesan.

Fettuccine with Clams and Tomatoes

My daughter Emilia has been in love with this recipe since she was three years old. Kids liking clams, who knew! Everything is cooked in one pan and it takes no time to prepare. If my fussy eater loves it, I'm sure you will too! **MAKES 4 TO 6 SERVINGS**

3 ½ lb (1.5 kg) fresh clams, such as littleneck or Manila

¼ cup (60 mL) extra-virgin olive oil

½ cured chorizo sausage, chopped

2 garlic cloves, chopped

½ onion, chopped

1 tbsp (15 mL) hot pepper flakes, or to taste

1 pint (500 mL) cherry tomatoes, halved

¼ cup (60 mL) clam juice

Splash of white wine

1 lb (450 g) fettuccine or other long pasta

Large handful of arugula

Salt and freshly ground pepper

Bring a large pot of water to a boil. Generously salt.

Meanwhile, begin the sauce: Discard any clams with cracked shells or that do not close when tapped.

In a large saucepan over medium-high heat, heat olive oil. Add chorizo, garlic, onions and hot pepper flakes. Cook, stirring frequently, until onions start to soften. Add cherry tomatoes and cook until their skins start to wrinkle. Add clams, clam juice and white wine. Cover and cook until clams start to open, 3 to 6 minutes. Discard any clams that remain closed.

Meanwhile, add pasta to boiling water and cook until al dente. Drain pasta and add to clams. Toss to combine. Add arugula and toss to mix. Season with salt and pepper. Serve immediately.

TIP A spicy Italian sausage can replace the chorizo sausage in this dish. If you like, use mussels instead of clams . . . or hey, use both!

Pasta Timballo

When you need a show-stopping recipe for a special dinner, this is the one to choose. It takes a little bit of time to make the components, but when you bring them all together and see the impressive results, you'll look for an occasion to make it again! **MAKES 6 SERVINGS**

TIMBALLO FILLING

2 tbsp (30 mL) olive oil

1 onion, chopped

1 carrot, diced

1 roasted red pepper, diced

1 can (14 oz/398 mL) diced tomatoes

1 tsp (5 mL) dried oregano

Salt and freshly ground pepper

1 to 2 Italian sausages (hot or mild)

11 oz (310 g) rigatoni (about three-quarters of a 1-lb/450 g package)

1 ball (12 oz/340 g) smoked mozzarella cheese, diced

5 basil leaves, chopped

Handful of Italian parsley, chopped

2 hard-boiled eggs, chopped

¼ cup (60 mL) grated Parmesan cheese

1 tbsp (15 mL) chopped hot peppers packed in oil, or to taste (optional)

TO ASSEMBLE

4 medium eggplants

About 1 cup (250 mL) olive oil, plus more for finishing

Freshly grated Parmesan cheese, for finishing

To make the timballo filling: In a large saucepan over medium heat, heat olive oil. Add onions and carrots and cook, stirring frequently, until softened, 3 to 4 minutes. Add roasted red peppers, tomatoes, oregano, and salt and pepper to taste. Bring to a boil. Reduce heat, cover and simmer for about 15 minutes.

Meanwhile, remove sausage meat from casing. Roll meat into ½-inch (1 cm) mini meatballs. Add meatballs to simmering sauce. Cover and simmer until meatballs are just cooked through, 10 to 15 minutes. Set aside.

Bring a large pot of water to a boil. Generously salt. Add pasta and cook until al dente. Drain and let cool.

In a large bowl, combine pasta, meatballs and sauce, mozzarella, basil, parsley, eggs, Parmesan and hot peppers, if desired. Mix well. Set aside.

To assemble the timballo, cut the eggplants lengthwise into ½-inch (1 cm) slices.

Pour enough olive oil into a large skillet to come ½ inch (1 cm) up the sides of the pan. Heat over medium heat. When oil is hot, fry eggplant slices in batches until golden brown on both sides, 2 to 4 minutes per side. Drain on paper towels and pat with more paper towels to remove any excess oil. Let cool.

Preheat oven to 375°F (190°C). Generously butter or oil a 9-inch (2.5 L) spring-form pan.

Line bottom and sides of pan with eggplant slices, overlapping slightly and allowing ends to hang over sides. Add filling. Cover with the remaining eggplant slices, then fold overlapping ends over to completely enclose filling. Press down to make sure filling is compact.

Bake timballo until filling is heated through, 30 to 35 minutes. Let rest for 20 minutes before serving. If you serve the timballo warm, it will be loose in structure. If you cool it completely, the timballo will be firmer. Remove sides of springform pan and transfer timballo to a serving plate. Drizzle with olive oil and garnish with freshly grated Parmesan. Cut into wedges and serve.

TIP When making this dish, there are two very important things to keep in mind: always use a short pasta that is hollow, and ensure you grease your baking dish well so the timballo remains intact when it's unmoulded.

SALADS & SIDES

Green Salad with Fresh Herbs

This simple salad is the perfect side for almost any main. The lettuces, a combination of peppery watercress and buttery mâche, are a light, delicate base and the fresh herbs—tarragon, chive and basil—take this salad to a whole new level of "fresh." **MAKES 6 TO 8 SERVINGS**

8 cups (2 L) mâche lettuce (a 5-oz/ 140 g package)

1 small bunch watercress, woody stems removed

1 tbsp (15 mL) chopped fresh chives

1 tbsp (15 mL) chopped fresh tarragon

Handful of basil leaves, torn

Grated zest of ½ lemon

⅓ cup (75 mL) extra-virgin olive oil

3 tbsp (45 mL) white balsamic vinegar

Salt and freshly ground pepper

TIP Get creative with your greens and try different kinds of lettuces, such as baby arugula or baby spinach, in your salads.

Combine mâche lettuce, watercress, chives, tarragon, basil and lemon zest in a large bowl. Drizzle with olive oil and vinegar. Season with salt and pepper. Toss to combine. Taste and adjust seasoning.

Frisée, Fennel and Apple Salad

Three of my favourite ingredients in one tasty salad! Here, a perfect balance of flavours—bitter frisée, sweet fennel and tart apple—marry to create a flavour explosion in every bite. This salad is easy enough to serve on a weeknight, but special enough for entertaining. **MAKES 8 TO 10 SERVINGS**

1 large head or 2 small heads frisée, leaves torn into smaller pieces

2 Belgian endives, sliced

3 radishes, thinly sliced

1 tart apple, thinly sliced

½ fennel bulb, cored and thinly sliced crosswise

Handful of pomegranate seeds, for garnish

Handful of toasted hazelnuts, for garnish

DRESSING

⅓ cup (75 mL) champagne vinegar

2 tsp (10 mL) minced shallot

2 tsp (10 mL) Dijon mustard

½ cup (125 mL) extra-virgin olive oil

Salt and freshly ground pepper

Combine frisée, endives, radishes, apple and fennel in a large bowl.

To make the dressing: Combine vinegar, shallot and mustard in a small bowl; whisk to combine. Gradually whisk in olive oil until emulsified. Season with salt and pepper. Taste and adjust seasoning.

Right before serving, toss salad with dressing. Garnish with pomegranate seeds and hazelnuts.

TIP The apple can be replaced with sweet peach slices or juicy orange segments.

Arugula, Fig and Walnut Salad

It may look like something fancy you would find in a restaurant, but this salad couldn't be easier to make. Just place tender, sweet figs, crunchy walnuts and creamy crumbled goat cheese over a bed of fresh arugula and drizzle with the super-simple dressing. It's a great recipe to keep in mind when entertaining. **MAKES 4 SERVINGS**

6 large handfuls of baby arugula

Salt and freshly ground pepper

⅓ cup (75 mL) extra-virgin olive oil

3 tbsp (45 mL) white balsamic vinegar

6 fresh figs, cut in quarters

¼ cup (60 mL) chopped walnuts

4 to 6 oz (115 to 170 g) soft goat cheese, crumbled

TIP Hazelnuts or pine nuts can be substituted for the walnuts in this dish. In place of nuts altogether, you can finish with a drizzle of a nut oil, like walnut or hazelnut. This recipe is also delicious with a crumble of blue cheese over the top.

Place arugula in a large bowl. Season with salt and pepper and sprinkle with olive oil and vinegar. Toss to combine. Taste and adjust seasoning. Transfer dressed greens to a platter or plates and garnish with figs, walnuts and goat cheese.

Classic Tabbouleh

Here's a hearty, healthy Middle Eastern favourite that almost needs no introduction. I know you'll love this recipe. It's got the goodness of fresh mint, parsley and bulgur wheat in a full-flavoured side dish. Serve it with my falafel balls (page 176) and some grilled pita and you've got one delicious dinner! MAKES 4 TO 6 SERVINGS

1 cup (250 mL) water

½ cup (125 mL) finely ground bulgur

1 tomato, finely diced

1 garlic clove, minced

Leaves from 1 small bunch parsley, chopped

Leaves from 1 small bunch mint, chopped

½ cup (125 mL) extra-virgin olive oil

¼ cup (60 mL) fresh lemon juice (from about 1 lemon)

Salt and freshly ground pepper

In a medium saucepan, bring salted water to a boil. Add bulgur. Turn off the heat, cover and let bulgur sit for 5 minutes. Transfer bulgur to a baking sheet and spread out. Let cool completely.

In a large bowl, combine bulgur, tomato, garlic, parsley, mint, olive oil, lemon juice, and salt and pepper to taste. Toss to combine. Taste and adjust seasoning.

Carrot Salad with Citrus Dressing

Few salads are delicious both hot and cold, but this one sure is! Serve this carrot salad warm as a veggie side with beef or poultry or serve it as a refreshing summer salad with fish or as part of a cold buffet. **MAKES 4 SERVINGS**

4 carrots, sliced

1 garlic clove, minced

Pinch of cumin

Juice of ½ orange

Juice of ½ lemon

2 tbsp (30 mL) extra-virgin olive oil

1 tbsp (15 mL) chopped fresh cilantro

Salt and freshly ground pepper

TIP Omit the cumin, if you like. Cilantro can be replaced with some fresh Italian parsley.

Blanch carrots in boiling salted water until tender-crisp. Drain and transfer to a medium bowl. Add garlic, cumin, orange juice, lemon juice, olive oil and cilantro. Toss to combine. Season with salt and pepper. Taste and adjust seasoning. Serve warm or cold.

Orange and Brussels Sprout Salad

These aren't your grandma's Brussels sprouts! This colourful side dish, with pecans, cranberries and zesty orange segments, is a great way to shake up your holiday menu and a gourmet addition to any dinner table. Just toss and serve!

MAKES 6 TO 8 SERVINGS.

1 to 1 ¼ lb (450 to 565 g) Brussels sprouts, trimmed and halved

2 mandarins or clementines

1 tbsp (15 mL) grated orange zest

¼ cup (60 mL) fresh orange juice

3 tbsp (45 mL) sherry vinegar

2 tsp (10 mL) grainy Dijon mustard

2 tsp (10 mL) liquid honey

2 tsp (10 mL) chopped fresh ginger

Tiny pinch each of allspice, cinnamon, ground cloves and nutmeg

Pinch of cayenne pepper, or to taste

Salt and freshly ground pepper

⅓ cup (75 mL) extra-virgin olive oil

⅓ cup (75 mL) chopped pecans, toasted

⅓ cup (75 mL) dried cranberries

Add Brussels sprouts to a pot of boiling salted water and cook until just tender-crisp, 3 to 4 minutes. Drain and transfer to an ice bath to stop the cooking process. When cooled, drain well and pat dry. Transfer to a large bowl.

Peel oranges with a knife, cutting away white pith. Working over a bowl, cut between fruit and membranes to release segments. Set aside.

To make the vinaigrette: In a small bowl, combine orange zest, orange juice, vinegar, mustard, honey, ginger, allspice, cinnamon, cloves, nutmeg, cayenne, and salt and pepper to taste. Whisk to combine. Gradually whisk in olive oil until emulsified. Taste and adjust seasoning. Add more sherry vinegar if you prefer a tarter vinaigrette, or add more honey if you prefer a sweeter vinaigrette.

Toss Brussels sprouts with vinaigrette. Add mandarin segments, pecans and cranberries. Toss to combine.

TIP You can make this salad with maple syrup instead of honey. The salad is also tasty if you replace the cranberries with raisins.

Asparagus, Mint and Feta Salad

Here's a fun new way to enjoy asparagus with a Mediterranean twist. Asparagus spears are shaved into long, thin ribbons, then mixed with fresh mint, salty feta cheese and a handful of crunchy pistachios. It's the perfect side to pair with any grilled meat, especially lamb. **MAKES 4 TO 6 SERVINGS**

1 large bunch asparagus, trimmed

½ small red onion, sliced

½ cup (125 mL) extra-virgin olive oil

¼ cup (60 mL) red wine vinegar

2 tbsp (30 mL) chopped fresh mint

Grated lemon zest, to taste

Salt and freshly ground pepper

¼ cup (60 mL) chopped raw pistachio nuts

⅓ cup (75 mL) feta cheese, crumbled

TIP You can replace the mint with fresh basil. Sherry vinegar or a young balsamic vinegar can be a flavourful twist on the red wine vinegar.

Using a vegetable peeler, peel each asparagus spear into long, thin strips. Place in a large bowl. Add red onion, olive oil, vinegar, mint, lemon zest, and salt and pepper to taste. Toss to combine. Taste and adjust seasoning. Serve garnished with chopped pistachios and crumbled feta.

Broccoli Caesar Salad

Be careful, this just may become your new go-to potluck dish. If you enjoy the flavours of a Caesar salad, this warm broccoli-filled twist on the original will make you fall in love all over again. **MAKES 4 SERVINGS**

1 large bunch broccoli, cut into florets

Juice of 1 lemon

2 garlic cloves, minced

¼ cup (60 mL) grated Parmesan cheese

3 tbsp (45 mL) mayonnaise

3 tbsp (45 mL) olive oil

1 tbsp (15 mL) Dijon mustard

1 tsp (5 mL) Worcestershire sauce

Salt and freshly ground pepper

2 slices pancetta or bacon, cooked and chopped

Freshly grated or shaved Parmesan cheese, for garnish

Blanch or steam broccoli florets until tender-crisp. Drain well and let cool.

In a large bowl, combine lemon juice, garlic, ¼ cup (60 mL) Parmesan, mayonnaise, olive oil, mustard, Worcestershire sauce, and salt and pepper to taste. Whisk to combine. Add broccoli and toss to combine. Serve topped with pancetta and freshly grated or shaved Parmesan.

Classic Greek Salad

With its big chunks of vegetables and simple oil-and-vinegar dressing, this dish is based on the Greek "village salad." I make this for my family at least once a week—there's something about the combination of cucumber, tomatoes, feta and olives that we just can't get enough of. Pair it with meat or fish if you like, but be sure to make it a regular at your house as well! MAKES 4 SERVINGS

½ pint (250 mL) cherry tomatoes, halved (or 2 large tomatoes, cut in wedges)

½ red onion, sliced

1 medium cucumber, chopped

1 sweet green pepper, chopped

Handful of Italian parsley, chopped

¼ cup (60 mL) extra-virgin olive oil

4 tsp (20 mL) red wine vinegar

Salt and freshly ground pepper

2 handfuls pitted kalamata olives

8 oz (225 g) feta cheese, crumbled or cubed

Combine tomatoes, onion, cucumber, green pepper and parsley in a large bowl.

Drizzle salad with olive oil and red wine vinegar. Season with salt and pepper. Toss to combine. Taste and adjust seasoning. Serve garnished with black olives and feta.

Apple and Carrot Coleslaw with Cumin

Carrots, cranberries and cumin are added to tangy apple in this fun, fresh spin on ordinary coleslaw. If you've never tried cumin before, this salad is the perfect way to introduce it to your family—everyone will love the warm, earthy flavour that it adds to the dish. **MAKES 4 SERVINGS**

4 medium carrots, grated

1 apple, diced

½ cup (125 mL) dried cranberries, coarsely chopped

1 ½ tsp (7 mL) cumin seeds, toasted and ground

¼ cup (60 mL) extra-virgin olive oil

Juice of ½ lemon

Salt and freshly ground pepper

In a large bowl, combine carrots, apple, cranberries, cumin, olive oil, lemon juice, and salt and pepper to taste. Mix well. Let salad sit in fridge for 10 to 15 minutes to allow flavours to marry. Taste and adjust seasoning, adding a little more olive oil or lemon juice, as needed.

Mango Cabbage Slaw

Take cabbage slaw to a whole new level with the addition of sweet mango chunks and crunchy cashews. No matter whether you're a fan of a creamy or tangy dressing in your slaw, this one is a perfect cross between the two. Serve it up at any barbecue as a great side for grilled chicken or ribs. MAKES 4 TO 6 SERVINGS

2 mangoes, peeled and diced

1 small green cabbage, shredded (about 8 cups/2 L)

2 carrots, shredded

½ red onion, sliced

2 tbsp (30 mL) chopped fresh cilantro

Handful of raw cashews

DRESSING

6 tbsp (90 mL) mayonnaise

6 tbsp (90 mL) apple cider vinegar

2 tbsp (30 mL) vegetable oil

1 tbsp (15 mL) honey

2 tsp (10 mL) Jerk Marinade (page 261) or hot pepper sauce

Salt and freshly ground pepper

TIP Red cabbage can be used to inject a hit of colour in this slaw. Feel free to use parsley if cilantro is not available.

Combine mangoes, cabbage, carrots, onion and cilantro in a large bowl.

To make the dressing: In a small bowl, combine mayonnaise, cider vinegar, vegetable oil, honey, Jerk Marinade, and salt and pepper to taste. Whisk to combine.

Toss salad with dressing. Garnish with cashews.

Rosemary Fougasse

This rustic French flatbread will be a stunning addition to your next dinner party. Making fresh bread is impressive in itself, but when it's such a pretty design, your guests will be wowed by the results. Simply follow the step-by-step instructions and you'll be a bread maker in no time! **MAKES 8 TO 10 SERVINGS**

2 ¾ to 3 cups (675 to 750 mL)
   all-purpose flour
1 tbsp (15 mL) salt
3 to 4 tsp (15 to 20 mL) finely
   chopped fresh rosemary
1 cup (250 mL) warm water

1 tbsp (15 mL) sugar
2 tsp (10 mL) active dry yeast
2 tbsp (30 mL) extra-virgin olive oil,
   plus more for brushing
Coarse sea salt, for sprinkling

In a large bowl, stir together 2 ¾ cups (675 mL) flour, salt and rosemary. Set aside.

In a small bowl, stir together warm water, sugar and yeast. Let stand until foamy, 5 to 10 minutes.

Add yeast mixture and 2 tbsp (30 mL) olive oil to flour mixture. Stir to combine and form dough into a ball. On a lightly floured work surface, knead dough until smooth and elastic, 7 to 8 minutes, adding more flour if dough is too sticky.

Put the ball of dough in an oiled bowl and cover with plastic wrap. Let rise in a warm place until it doubles in volume, 45 to 60 minutes.

Preheat oven to 425°F (220°C). Lightly oil a baking sheet.

Sprinkle work surface with flour. Punch down dough. Roll out dough into an oval ¾ to 1 inch (2 to 2.5 cm) thick.

To create a leaf pattern in the bread, use a sharp paring knife or pastry scraper and cut a slit down the middle of the bread, cutting all the way through and leaving a 1-inch (2.5 cm) border at each end of the cut. Cut 5 diagonal slits on each side of it, leaving a 1-inch (2.5 cm) border at each end of the cuts. Delicately open up the slits with your fingers to create a more prominent design.

Transfer dough to baking sheet. Brush with olive oil and sprinkle with coarse sea salt. Bake until golden brown, 18 to 20 minutes. Let cool on a rack.

(photo on next page)

TIP You can make the dough 1 day ahead. Instead of letting the dough rise in a warm place, cover and put in fridge overnight. The next day, bring dough to room temperature, then punch dough and proceed as above.

Party-Style Focaccia

Can't decide which flatbread to make? You don't have to pick just one! Dress up pizza dough with four of your favourite flatbread toppings—veggies, olives, cheeses or herbs—and mix and match as you please. Bakes up fast, and tastes so delicious! **MAKES 10 TO 12 SERVINGS**

2 lb (900 g) pizza dough,
    at room temperature

Extra-virgin olive oil, for drizzling

Handful of pitted black olives, chopped

Handful of pitted green olives, chopped

2 tbsp (30 mL) finely chopped
    fresh rosemary

Handful of roasted red peppers,
    chopped

Coarse sea salt or kosher salt

Preheat oven to 375°F (190°C). Brush a large baking sheet with olive oil.

Dust work surface with flour. Roll out pizza dough to fit baking sheet, about ¾ inch (2 cm) thick. Transfer dough to baking sheet, gently stretching it to fit, as needed. Let dough rise in a warm, draft-free spot until puffed, about 15 minutes.

With your fingertips, dimple the dough all over. Generously drizzle with olive oil.

Top each quarter of the dough with a different topping (black olives, green olives, rosemary, roasted red peppers). Sprinkle with salt to taste.

Bake focaccia until golden brown and cooked through, 20 to 25 minutes.

TIP If you're stuck for the perfect four-flavour combination on this focaccia, just think of your four favourite pizza toppings and fill 'er up!

Buttermilk Biscuits

Everyone needs a perfect biscuit recipe, and this is the one I always reach for. Make a bunch of these light, flaky gems when you need a little something to soak up your gravy. They're at their best hot and fresh, straight out of the oven—and don't forget the butter! **MAKES 8 BISCUITS**

2 cups (500 mL) all-purpose flour

4 tsp (20 mL) baking powder

½ tsp (2 mL) baking soda

½ tsp (2 mL) salt

3 tbsp (45 mL) shortening

2 tbsp (30 mL) cold unsalted butter, cut in cubes

1 cup (250 mL) buttermilk

1 egg beaten with 1 tbsp (15 mL) water, for egg wash

TIP Make a double batch of this recipe and freeze biscuits, without egg wash, in an air-tight container. Brush frozen biscuits with egg wash and bake at 425°F (220°C) for 25 to 30 minutes.

Preheat oven to 425°F (220°C). Line a small baking sheet with parchment paper.

Combine flour, baking powder, baking soda and salt in a large bowl. Stir with a whisk to thoroughly combine.

Cut shortening and butter into flour mixture, rubbing fat into flour with your fingertips until the mixture resembles coarse crumbs. (Some bigger clumps are okay.)

Stir in milk with a wooden spoon just until dough starts to come together. Do not over-mix.

Lightly flour work surface. Turn out dough and knead a few times, just until dough comes together. Don't overwork the dough or the biscuits will be tough.

Shape dough into a round and flatten to 1-inch (2.5 cm) thickness. Lightly dust with flour if dough is too sticky. Cut dough into 6 rounds with 3-inch (8 cm) cookie cutter. Gently bring scraps of dough together and shape 2 more biscuits. Transfer to baking sheet. Lightly brush tops with egg wash.

Bake biscuits until golden brown on top and bottom, 15 to 20 minutes.

Four-Cheese Garlic Bread

A big plate of spaghetti just isn't the same without a wedge of garlic bread. This combination of Cheddar, mozzarella, Parmesan and jalapeño Havarti cheeses is over the top, and the garlicky, buttery spread takes this recipe to another level of flavour. Serve a slice of this classic cheesy bread with soup or a bowl of chili. **MAKES 6 TO 8 SERVINGS**

⅓ cup (75 mL) butter, at room temperature

2 to 3 garlic cloves, chopped

¼ cup (60 mL) chopped fresh Italian parsley

1 tsp (5 mL) chopped fresh or dried thyme

1 tsp (5 mL) paprika

Salt and freshly ground pepper

1 baguette (can be day-old), cut in half horizontally

¾ cup (175 mL) shredded Cheddar cheese

¾ cup (175 mL) shredded mozzarella cheese

¾ cup (175 mL) shredded jalapeño Havarti cheese

¼ cup (60 mL) grated Parmesan cheese

Preheat oven to 400°F (200°C). Line a baking sheet with parchment paper.

To make the garlic butter: Stir together butter, garlic, parsley, thyme, paprika, and salt and pepper to taste.

Spread garlic butter on both halves of bread. Cover with cheeses. Transfer to prepared baking sheet.

Bake until cheese is melted and bread is toasted, 10 to 15 minutes. To speed up the process, finish under the broiler, if desired.

TIP Change up the selection of cheeses in this recipe—just make sure the cheeses you pick are good melters.

Easy Skillet Corn Bread

This couldn't-be-easier batter is baked up in a skillet—it's the perfect quick bread to make on a weeknight. The kids will love the slight sweetness of the dense and tasty bread, and when you slather it with my honey butter, you may not need to serve anything else for dinner! **MAKES 8 SERVINGS**

SKILLET CORN BREAD

1 ¼ cups (300 mL) all-purpose flour

¾ cup (175 mL) cornmeal

¼ cup (60 mL) sugar

2 tsp (10 mL) baking powder

1 tsp (5 mL) salt

1 large egg

1 cup (250 mL) milk

½ cup (125 mL) vegetable oil

HONEY BUTTER

1 cup (250 mL) unsalted butter, softened

¼ cup (60 mL) honey

Hot pepper sauce, to taste

Salt

1 tsp (5 mL) chopped fresh chives (optional)

To make the corn bread: Preheat oven to 375°F (190°C). Brush an 8-inch (20 cm) cast-iron skillet with oil. Heat skillet over medium-low heat for 10 minutes so pan is hot when corn bread batter is added.

In a medium bowl, stir together flour, cornmeal, sugar, baking powder and salt.

In a small bowl, beat egg. Add milk and oil. Whisk to combine. Add wet ingredients to dry ingredients and stir just to combine. Don't over-mix.

Pour batter into preheated skillet and bake until a toothpick inserted in centre of corn bread comes out clean, 35 to 40 minutes.

While corn bread is baking, make the honey butter: Combine butter, honey, hot sauce and salt to taste in a medium bowl. Beat with an electric mixer or stir vigorously until well combined. Transfer to a serving dish and garnish with chopped chives, if desired.

Serve corn bread warm with honey butter.

Broccolini with Lemon and Capers

Serve this super-healthy side with almost anything—pastas, roasts or grilled fish. If you can't find broccolini at the grocery store, just replace it with rapini, broccoli florets or Swiss chard. There couldn't be a more delicious way to eat your greens! **MAKES 6 SERVINGS**

2 bunches broccolini

3 tbsp (45 mL) olive oil

2 garlic cloves, chopped

1 tbsp (15 mL) capers

Chopped hot peppers packed in oil,
    to taste (optional)

2 tsp (10 mL) grated lemon zest

Salt and freshly ground pepper

Juice of ½ lemon

TIP Give this dish a whole new flavour dimension by using an orange instead of a lemon.

Add broccolini to a pot of boiling salted water. Cook until tender-crisp, about 3 minutes. Drain.

Meanwhile, heat olive oil in a large skillet over medium heat. Add garlic, capers and hot peppers, if desired. Cook, stirring, for 1 minute. Add broccolini, lemon zest, and salt and pepper to taste. Cook, stirring frequently, until broccolini is tender and heated through, 3 to 5 minutes. Sprinkle with a little lemon juice and serve immediately.

Peas with Prosciutto

Peas with prosciutto is the quintessential Italian summer side dish, especially when peas are in season. If you don't have fresh peas from the garden, you can still make this versatile side dish all year long—just use good-quality frozen peas. It's super-tasty as a side for lamb or roast beef. **MAKES 4 SERVINGS**

1 tbsp (15 mL) butter

1 tbsp (15 mL) olive oil

3 to 4 thin or thick slices prosciutto, diced

2 green onions, chopped

2 cups (500 mL) fresh or thawed frozen peas (12-oz/340 g bag frozen)

Pinch of hot pepper flakes (optional)

Salt and freshly ground pepper

Melt butter with olive oil in a large skillet over medium heat. When butter has melted, add prosciutto and green onions. Fry until prosciutto is lightly golden, about 2 minutes.

Add peas and toss to combine. Season with salt and pepper and hot pepper flakes, if desired. Cook until peas are heated through, 3 to 4 minutes.

TIP You can replace the prosciutto with regular ham or pancetta.

Roasted Carrots and Brussels Sprouts in Miso Honey

This sweet roasted veggie dish was one of the big hits on *In the Kitchen*. Folks in the audience couldn't wait for a taste of these amazing miso-and-honey-coated veggies. Keep a small container of miso paste in your pantry—it adds a distinctively delicious flavour to so many dishes. **MAKES 4 SERVINGS**

1 bunch small carrots (about 1 lb /450 g), peeled and cut in half crosswise

3 cups Brussels sprouts, trimmed and cut in half

2 tbsp (30 mL) olive oil

2 tbsp (30 mL) liquid honey

1 tbsp (15 mL) water

1 tbsp (15 mL) miso paste, preferably white

2 tsp (10 mL) chopped fresh ginger

Salt and freshly ground pepper

White and black sesame seeds, for garnish

Handful of cilantro leaves, for garnish

Preheat oven to 425°F (220°C).

In a large bowl, combine carrots, Brussels sprouts, olive oil, honey, water, miso, ginger, and salt and pepper to taste. Toss to combine well.

Transfer to a baking sheet. Roast, turning vegetables occasionally, until tender and golden brown, 15 to 20 minutes. Serve garnished with sesame seeds and cilantro.

Easy Potato and Zucchini Pancakes

These delicious little savoury pancakes are a side dish treat any night of the week and a creative way to bring veggies to the table. Serve them with a bowl of my creamy Dill Yogurt Dip and you have a match made in heaven. They'll also be a popular addition to a brunch buffet table—no one can resist these little guys!

MAKES 4 SERVINGS

DILL YOGURT DIP
¾ cup (175 mL) sour cream
¾ cup (175 mL) plain yogurt
1 tbsp (15 mL) olive oil (optional)
3 tbsp (45 mL) chopped fresh dill
Salt and freshly ground pepper

EASY POTATO AND ZUCCHINI PANCAKES
2 medium russet potatoes, peeled and grated
1 small zucchini, grated
½ onion, grated
2 garlic cloves, chopped
2 tbsp (30 mL) chopped fresh chives
Salt and freshly ground pepper
¼ cup (60 mL) olive or vegetable oil

To make the dill yogurt dip: In a small bowl, stir together sour cream, yogurt, olive oil (if desired), dill, and salt and pepper to taste. Stir to combine. Set aside.

To make the potato and zucchini pancakes: In a medium bowl, combine potato, zucchini, onion, garlic and chives. Season with salt and pepper. Toss to mix well.

Heat oil in a large nonstick skillet over medium-high heat. When oil is hot, add heaping tablespoonfuls of potato mixture, working in batches to avoid crowding the pan. Press gently with a spatula to flatten. Cook until crispy, browned and tender, 4 to 5 minutes per side, adding more oil to the pan as needed. Drain on paper towels.

Serve 3 to 4 pancakes per serving for a side dish. Serve with Dill Yogurt Dip.

(photo on next page)

Cauliflower "Couscous"

Cauliflower may not get a lot of play on your table, but give it a try—it's filled with fibre and nutrients. Beyond being good for you, when the florets are whizzed in the food processor, they turn into tiny pieces that look remarkably like grains of couscous. The kids will love watching the magic transformation! **MAKES 4 SERVINGS**

1 fresh red finger chili

1 head cauliflower, cut into florets

1 small garlic clove, minced

⅓ cup (75 mL) olive oil

2 to 3 tbsp (30 to 45 mL) apple cider vinegar

1 tsp (5 mL) curry powder, or to taste

Salt and freshly ground pepper

1 Granny Smith apple, diced

2 green onions, sliced

¼ cup (60 mL) toasted slivered almonds

¼ cup (60 mL) raisins

⅓ cup (75 mL) chopped fresh mint

Finely chop half the finger chili; set aside. Thinly slice remaining half; set aside for garnish.

Place cauliflower florets in a food processor and pulse until the size of grains of couscous.

In a large bowl, combine garlic, olive oil, vinegar, curry powder, reserved chopped chili, and salt and pepper to taste. Stir well. Add cauliflower "couscous" and toss to coat. Add apple, green onions, almonds, raisins and mint. Toss to combine. Serve garnished with sliced chili, if desired.

Couscous with Pistachios, Almonds and Apricots

One of my best friends is from Morocco and, when we were young, he introduced me to couscous. It's like a blank canvas for flavour and lends itself to so many versatile flavour combinations. Playing around with a mix of pistachios, almonds and apricots has definitely resulted in my favourite couscous combo—you can feel free to experiment with the recipe, too! **MAKES 4 TO 6 SERVINGS**

1 ¼ cups (300 mL) boiling water

1 ¼ cups (300 mL) instant couscous

2 tbsp (30 mL) butter or olive oil

Pinch of ground cardamom (optional)

Salt and freshly ground pepper

1 tbsp (15 mL) chopped toasted raw pistachio nuts

1 tbsp (15 mL) chopped toasted blanched almonds

2 tbsp (30 mL) chopped dried apricots

2 green onions, chopped

TIP Replace the couscous with bulgur or quinoa. It's also delicious with dried cranberries or raisins in place of the apricots.

Bring water to a boil in a medium saucepan. Stir in couscous, butter, cardamom (if desired), and salt and pepper to taste. Remove from heat, cover and let sit for 5 minutes. Fluff with a fork and stir in nuts, apricots and green onions.

Italian Grilled Vegetables

I grill meals on the barbecue winter, spring, summer and fall, and one of my go-to side dishes is definitely these Italian grilled vegetables. Just barbecue a slew of zucchini, sweet peppers, onion, eggplant and portobellos, and you have a platter that's a real crowd-pleaser. Enjoy the special smoky flavour of this dish any time of year. **MAKES ABOUT 8 SERVINGS**

2 small eggplants, sliced crosswise

3 medium zucchinis, sliced crosswise on the diagonal

4 sweet peppers (different colours), quartered

1 large red onion, sliced

3 or 4 small portobello mushrooms, stemmed

Extra-virgin olive oil

Salt and freshly ground pepper

Balsamic vinegar, as needed

Handful of fresh herbs, such as basil, parsley and oregano, for finishing

Preheat grill to medium-high. Clean and oil grill.

In a large bowl, combine eggplants, zucchinis, peppers, onions and mushrooms. Drizzle with enough olive oil to coat. Season with salt and pepper.

Add vegetables to grill, cooking in batches and turning as needed, until grill-marked and tender, 5 to 10 minutes.

Transfer grilled vegetables to a platter or salad bowl. Drizzle with balsamic vinegar and more olive oil. Season with salt and pepper. Serve topped with chopped herbs.

Cheesy Stuffed Tomatoes

These veggie-stuffed tomatoes are a classic steakhouse side. Made with fresh thyme and covered in lots of mozzarella and Parmesan, they add a nice hit of colour to your plate. But they don't have to stay on the side of your plate—move them to the middle as the main act! Serve two tomatoes as a hearty meat-free dinner. **MAKES 4 SERVINGS**

3 tbsp (45 mL) olive oil

1 small onion, finely chopped

2 small eggplants, diced

1 yellow zucchini, diced

1 green zucchini, diced

1 garlic clove, minced

Leaves from 2 sprigs thyme, finely chopped

Salt and freshly ground pepper

4 medium vine-ripened tomatoes

3 to 4 tbsp (45 to 60 mL) shredded mozzarella cheese

2 tbsp (30 mL) grated Parmesan cheese

TIP Add some fresh basil and parsley to the stuffing for an extra hit of freshness. Whatever cheese you have on hand is fine to use—it just needs to be a good melting cheese.

Preheat oven to 350°F (180°C).

Heat olive oil in a large sauté pan over medium to medium-high heat. When oil is hot, add onions, eggplants, zucchini, garlic and thyme. Season with salt and pepper. Sauté until vegetables are tender, 7 to 10 minutes.

Meanwhile, cut tops off each tomato and scoop out seeds and pulp with a melon baller or spoon. Stuff tomatoes with the vegetable mixture. Transfer to a small baking dish, and bake until tomatoes start to soften and skins begin to wrinkle, 20 to 25 minutes.

Remove tomatoes from oven and preheat broiler. Top each tomato evenly with mozzarella and Parmesan. Broil tomatoes until the cheese is melted and lightly golden brown. Serve hot.

Mashed Sweet Potatoes

Mashed potatoes is one of the most classic sides of all time, but it's fun to shake up your mash every now and then. Add the vibrant colour, vitamins and nutrients of sweet potatoes to the mix the next time you're boiling up a pot. This rich and creamy dish goes with almost anything. **MAKES 4 TO 6 SERVINGS**

4 sweet potatoes, peeled and cubed

¼ cup (60 mL) extra-virgin olive oil

¼ to ⅓ cup (60 to 75 mL) whipping cream (35%)

Salt and freshly ground pepper

In a saucepan, cook potatoes in boiling salted water until tender. Drain well, return to pot and set over hot element to remove excess moisture. Remove from heat.

Add olive oil, ¼ cup (60 mL) cream, and salt and pepper to taste. Mash until smooth, adding more cream if needed.

Parsnip Purée

This rich and creamy purée, scented with just a hint of nutmeg, is a nice change from mashed potatoes. It's an easy, flavourful side that's perfect with roasted meats and super-saucy stews. MAKES 4 SERVINGS

6 large parsnips, peeled and cut in large pieces

1 medium Yukon Gold potato, peeled and cut in large pieces

⅓ to ½ cup (75 to 125 mL) whipping cream (35%), heated until warm to the touch

3 tbsp (45 mL) butter, at room temperature

Pinch of freshly grated nutmeg

Salt and freshly ground pepper

1 tbsp (15 mL) chopped fresh parsley, for garnish

Olive oil, for finishing (optional)

In a pot of salted water, bring parsnips and potato to a boil. Cook until tender, 15 to 20 minutes. Drain well.

Transfer parsnips and potato to a food processor. Add ⅓ cup (75 mL) cream, butter, nutmeg, and salt and pepper to taste. Pulse until smooth, adding more cream, if desired, for a creamier purée. Taste and adjust seasoning. Serve garnished with chopped parsley and a drizzle of olive oil, if desired.

Mashed Potatoes with Sour Cream and Chives

Mashed potatoes are a staple of weekend eating, holiday meals and any dinner that calls for a big, hearty spread. If you don't serve mashed potatoes, you just might have a protest on your hands! Make this classic creamy mash anytime—it's sensational topped with heaps of sour cream and chives. **MAKES 6 SERVINGS**

6 medium Yukon Gold potatoes (unpeeled), washed

2 garlic cloves

2 heaping tbsp (35 mL) butter

⅓ to ½ cup (75 to 125 mL) sour cream

¼ cup (60 mL) grated Parmesan cheese

2 tbsp (30 mL) chopped fresh chives

Pinch of freshly grated nutmeg

Pinch of cayenne pepper, or to taste

Salt and freshly ground pepper

In a pot of salted water, bring potatoes to a boil. Add garlic cloves. Reduce heat and simmer, covered, until potatoes are fork-tender, 20 to 25 minutes. Drain.

Peel potatoes. Return potatoes and garlic to pot or transfer to a large bowl. Add butter and ⅓ cup (75 mL) sour cream. Mash until smooth, adding more sour cream, if desired. Stir in Parmesan and chives. Season with nutmeg, cayenne, and salt and pepper to taste.

Prosciutto-Wrapped Potato Bites

These mini potato bites are a real hit at my house. Customize them to your family's liking by substituting your favourite cheese, or rolling them in the cured meat of your choice—make them your perfect potato bite. They're great served as a side at dinnertime or a pass-around at a cocktail party. **MAKES 4 SERVINGS**

1 lb (450 g) new potatoes or
    baby red potatoes (unpeeled)

5 oz (140 g) thinly sliced prosciutto

7 oz (200 g) provolone cheese,
    cut in small cubes

Salt and freshly ground pepper

1 tbsp (15 mL) butter

1 tbsp (15 mL) extra-virgin olive oil

1 sprig rosemary

1 garlic clove, smashed

In a pot of salted water, bring potatoes to a boil. Cook until they are almost fork-tender, 15 to 20 minutes, depending on size of potatoes.

Cut prosciutto slices in half lengthwise.

Slice the cooked potatoes in half. Sandwich a cube of provolone between the potato halves. Wrap prosciutto around each potato sandwich and secure with a toothpick. Lightly season with salt and pepper.

Melt butter with olive oil in a large skillet over medium heat. Add rosemary and garlic and let infuse the oil and butter for 1 minute. Remove rosemary and garlic. Add potato sandwiches to pan and cook, turning frequently, until the prosciutto is crispy and the cheese is melted. If the cheese is not melted, transfer to a 350°F (180°C) oven and bake until the cheese is fully melted.

TIP Don't have any prosciutto? No problem—just use pancetta or regular bacon in this recipe.

Baked Fries

I challenged myself to come up with a recipe for baked fries that was as good as the deep-fried version. All you need is potatoes, olive oil and a little S&P, and they bake up golden and crispy. If you're looking to eat healthier, treat your family to these great fries—they won't miss the deep-fryer, I promise!

MAKES 4 TO 6 SERVINGS

4 russet potatoes (unpeeled)
About ¼ cup (60 mL) extra-virgin olive oil
Sea salt and freshly ground black pepper

TIP Swap sweet potatoes for regular potatoes for these fries. The cooking time will be the same.

Preheat oven to 425°F (220°C).

Cut each potato into 6 to 8 wedges. Transfer to a large bowl, coat generously with olive oil and season with salt and pepper. Toss to combine.

Spread wedges in a single layer on a large nonstick baking sheet. (Use 2 baking sheets if fries are overlapping.) Bake fries, turning occasionally, until golden brown and fork-tender, 30 to 35 minutes.

Crispy Vegetable Fries

I made these cool Crispy Vegetable Fries on *In the Kitchen* as part of a healthier fish and chips dinner. Substituting nutrient-packed root veggies, such as carrots, parsnips and sweet potatoes, is a tasty alternative to straight-up potato fries. The egg white coating helps the strips get crispy in the oven, and you'll love the slight hit of spice from the chili powder. **MAKES 4 SERVINGS**

1 large russet potato, peeled

1 large sweet potato, peeled

2 parsnips, peeled

2 carrots, peeled

1 small red onion

2 large egg whites

2 tbsp (30 mL) olive oil

1 tsp (5 mL) chili powder

Salt and freshly ground pepper

Place racks in top and bottom thirds of oven and preheat oven to 425°F (220°C). Line 2 baking sheets with parchment paper.

Cut all the vegetables into ½-inch (1 cm) thick fries.

In a large bowl, whip egg whites until light and frothy. Whisk in olive oil. Toss vegetables in egg white mixture to coat well. Season with chili powder and salt and pepper to taste.

Divide vegetable fries between baking sheets, making sure they don't touch. Bake, rotating and switching baking sheets halfway, until crispy on the outside and tender on the inside, 20 to 25 minutes.

Crispy Smashed Paprika Potatoes

These addictive smashed potatoes are crispy and golden brown on the outside and tender and creamy on the inside. In my house we like to smash our potatoes with a bit of smoked paprika, but feel free to add whichever spice or herb your family likes. Maybe try a little chopped rosemary with your spuds . . . just like nonna used to make! MAKES 4 TO 6 SERVINGS

12 small Yukon Gold potatoes

¼ cup (60 mL) olive oil

Salt and freshly ground pepper

1 tsp (5 mL) smoked paprika

1 tbsp (15 mL) chopped fresh chives, for garnish

In a pot of salted water, bring potatoes to a boil. Reduce heat, cover and simmer until potatoes are just cooked through, 15 to 20 minutes. Drain.

Preheat oven to 425°F (220°C). Drizzle a baking sheet with some of the oil.

Using a meat mallet, a rolling pin or your hand, gently crush each potato into a thick pancake. With a spatula, transfer to baking sheet and brush generously with oil. Season with salt and pepper.

Bake until potatoes are golden brown and very crispy, 25 to 30 minutes.

Sprinkle potatoes with smoked paprika and garnish with chives.

Lemony Greek Roasted Potatoes

There is a small Greek restaurant in our neighbourhood and I just love their lemon-infused roasted potatoes. I love them so much, I had to figure out how to make them myself, anytime I wanted. It took some time to experiment with the ingredients, but I eventually arrived at takeout-worthy potatoes. Now you can enjoy the lemony goodness of this flavourful side dish anytime you like, too!

MAKES 4 SERVINGS

4 medium Yukon Gold or russet potatoes, peeled and cut in quarters

Juice of 1 lemon

¼ cup (60 mL) olive oil

2 tbsp (30 mL) chicken stock or water

Pinch of dried oregano

1 garlic clove, chopped

Coarse salt and freshly cracked black pepper

Preheat oven to 350°F (180°C).

In a large bowl, combine potatoes, lemon juice, olive oil, chicken stock, oregano, garlic, and salt and pepper to taste. Toss to coat potatoes.

Transfer potatoes and any liquid in bowl to a small roasting pan. Cover with foil and roast potatoes, turning occasionally, until tender, 30 to 40 minutes. Remove foil and roast until golden brown, 10 to 15 minutes more.

TIP To change up the flavours of these roasted potatoes, experiment with other fresh herbs, such as rosemary or thyme.

Beer-Battered Onion Rings

You may think onion rings are reserved for visits to the local burger joint, but they're actually fun and easy to make at home. Serve them stacked high on a plate, all hot and crispy, with spicy mayo dip—your friends and family will be amazed. MAKES 4 SERVINGS

BEER BATTER
1 ½ cups (375 mL) all-purpose flour
1 tsp (5 mL) salt
1 tsp (5 mL) baking powder
1 bottle (12 oz/355 mL) lager

TO ASSEMBLE
Vegetable oil, for deep-frying
2 Vidalia or Spanish onions, sliced into rings
Flour, for dredging
Salt
Spicy Mayo Dip (page 56)

To make the beer batter: In a large bowl, stir together flour, salt and baking powder. Whisk in beer until smooth. Let batter rest for 15 to 30 minutes.

Meanwhile, add oil to a deep-fryer or pour enough oil into a deep saucepan to come 2 to 3 inches (5 to 8 cm) up sides of pan. Heat oil over medium heat to 375°F (190°C).

Working in batches, dredge onion rings in flour, shaking off excess. Then dip into batter to evenly coat. Carefully add them to the hot oil. Fry, turning once, until tender and golden brown, about 3 minutes. Drain on paper towels. Sprinkle with salt. Serve with Spicy Mayo Dip, if desired.

TIP Use the same batter to coat a selection of other vegetables—it's a fun way to serve them up!

Mixed Mushroom Polenta

I ate a lot of polenta growing up—it was a total staple in our Italian family. Some people are a bit intimidated at the thought of making this creamy dish from scratch, but I'm here to tell you it couldn't be easier. Polenta has a neutral flavour that just begs you to add whatever flavour you like. I suggest starting with this incredibly delicious mixed mushroom recipe—you'll be a pro in no time!

MAKES 6 SERVINGS

1 oz (28 g) dried porcini mushrooms

5 cups (1.25 L) water

1 tsp (5 mL) salt

1 ½ cups (375 mL) finely ground cornmeal

¼ cup (60 mL) + 3 tbsp (45 mL) butter

4 cups (1 L) sliced cremini mushrooms

Leaves from 1 sprig thyme, chopped

Salt and freshly ground pepper

¾ cup (175 mL) grated Parmesan cheese

4 oz (115 g) fontina cheese, shredded

½ cup (125 mL) whipping cream (35%), warmed

Chopped fresh chives, for garnish

Freshly grated Parmesan cheese, for finishing (optional)

TIP Replace the thyme with some finely chopped rosemary. For a really different flavour, use Cheddar instead of fontina.

Soak dried porcini mushrooms in hot water for 20 minutes. Drain, reserving soaking liquid. Chop mushrooms and set aside.

Bring water and salt to a boil in a large saucepan. While whisking, add the cornmeal a little at a time. (Whisking will help prevent lumps.) Reduce heat to medium-low and cook polenta, stirring constantly, until thick enough to mound on a spoon, 20 to 25 minutes. Cover and keep warm.

Heat a large skillet over medium-high heat. Add 3 tbsp (45 mL) butter. When butter melts, add cremini mushrooms, porcini mushrooms and thyme. Season with salt and pepper. Sauté until golden brown, 5 to 7 minutes. Remove from heat.

If polenta has become too thick, thin with a little hot water to preferred consistency. Add mushroom soaking liquid, ¼ cup (60 mL) butter, ¾ cup (175 mL) Parmesan, fontina and cream. Stir until cheeses are melted. Transfer to a serving dish. Top with mushroom mixture. Garnish with chives. Finish with freshly grated Parmesan, if desired.

Risotto Milanese

To me, risotto is the ultimate comfort food. This risotto, probably the simplest version ever, is a true classic from northern Italy. Made with saffron and white wine, it has a lovely subtle flavour that makes it perfect to pair with a hearty piece of meat. Practise your risotto-making skills with this easy recipe.

MAKES 4 TO 6 SERVINGS

4 cups (1 L) chicken stock

Pinch of saffron

4 tbsp (60 mL) butter

1 tbsp (15 mL) extra-virgin olive oil

1 large onion, finely chopped

2 cups (500 mL) arborio, carnaroli or vialone nano rice

Salt and freshly ground pepper

1 ¼ cups (300 mL) dry white wine

Splash of whipping cream (35%)

Freshly grated Parmesan cheese, to finish

TIP Remember that the best stock makes the best risotto—use as good a quality stock as you can. For some added texture, stir in some shredded fontina cheese—your guests will love it.

In a saucepan, bring chicken stock to a boil, then reduce heat to a simmer. Add saffron.

In a braising pot or deep skillet, melt 2 tbsp (30 mL) butter with oil over medium to medium-high heat. Add onions and sauté until softened, 3 to 5 minutes. Add rice and season with salt and pepper. Cook rice for 1 to 2 minutes, stirring occasionally so rice is thoroughly coated with oil and butter.

Add wine. Let wine reduce until most of the liquid is evaporated and pan is dry. Add 1 ladleful of simmering stock. Cook, stirring frequently, until stock is completely absorbed into the rice and the pan is dry. Continue to add stock 1 ladleful at a time, stirring until stock is absorbed and the pan is dry before adding more. Cook until rice is tender yet still firm, about 20 minutes.

Remove risotto from heat. Add cream, remaining 2 tbsp (30 mL) butter and Parmesan to taste. Serve sprinkled with additional Parmesan.

Island Rice and Peas

Pure Caribbean comfort food, this easy version of rice and peas is flavoured with coconut milk, ginger and fresh thyme. **MAKES 4 TO 6 SERVINGS**

2 tbsp (30 mL) vegetable oil

1 small onion, finely chopped

1 garlic clove, minced

2 tsp (10 mL) chopped fresh ginger

1 ½ cups (375 mL) parboiled/converted rice

Salt and freshly ground pepper

2 sprigs thyme

1 ¾ cups (425 mL) coconut milk

1 ¼ cups (300 mL) water

1 can (14 oz/398 mL) pigeon peas or red kidney beans, drained and rinsed

In a medium saucepan, heat oil over medium-high heat. When oil is hot, add onion, garlic and ginger. Sauté for 2 to 3 minutes. Add rice and toss for 2 minutes, until rice is completely coated in oil. Season with salt and pepper.

Add thyme, coconut milk and water. Bring to a boil, then reduce heat to low. Stir in pigeon peas. Cover and simmer for 20 minutes. Remove from heat and let stand, covered, for 8 to 10 minutes. Fluff with a fork. Serve.

EVERYDAY MAINS

Falafel Sandwiches

These hearty Middle Eastern sandwiches are always popular, and once you try them, you'll know why! Rolled in pita bread, they're a satisfying meatless main made with spiced chickpea fritters and lots of fresh fixings. Don't forget to drizzle lots of tahini sauce on your falafels for a tangy, creamy hit of goodness.

MAKES 6 SERVINGS

FALAFELS

1 ½ cups (375 mL) dried chickpeas

1 to 2 tbsp (15 to 30 mL) water

½ onion, coarsely chopped

2 garlic cloves, coarsely chopped

1 cup (250 mL) chopped fresh parsley or cilantro

1 tsp (5 mL) baking powder

1 tsp (5 mL) ground cumin

Pinch of dried oregano

Salt and freshly ground pepper

TO ASSEMBLE

Vegetable oil, for deep-frying

6 medium to large pitas, top third cut off

Lettuce leaves

Tomato slices

Onion slices

Pickled turnips

Tahini sauce

To make the falafels: Soak chickpeas in water to cover by 2 to 3 inches (5 to 8 cm). Refrigerate for 24 hours. The chickpeas should triple in volume.

Drain and rinse chickpeas. Place chickpeas in a food processor. Pulse until mixture has a coarse meal texture, adding 1 to 2 tbsp (15 to 30 mL) water, if needed. Add onions, garlic, parsley, baking powder, cumin, oregano, and salt and pepper to taste. Pulse until mixture is finely ground.

Measure heaping tablespoons (18 mL) of the mixture and roll into 1 ½-inch (4 cm) balls or discs.

Add oil to a deep-fryer or pour enough oil into a deep skillet to come 2 to 3 inches (5 to 8 cm) up sides of pan. Heat oil over medium heat to 350°F (180°C). Working in batches if necessary, fry falafels, turning occasionally, until golden brown, 3 to 5 minutes. Drain on paper towels.

Divide falafels among pita pockets. Tuck in lettuce, tomato, onions and pickled turnip. Drizzle in tahini sauce. Roll up sandwich and serve.

Layered Cheese and Vegetable Pie

This rustic and hearty vegetable pie will impress any vegetarian sitting at your table. Layered with roasted red peppers, eggplant, zucchini and Emmental cheese, it's packed with flavour and perfect for brunch, lunch and dinner . . . you choose! **MAKES 6 TO 8 SERVINGS**

PASTRY

2 ⅓ cups (575 mL) all-purpose flour

2 tbsp (30 mL) grated Parmesan cheese

Pinch of salt

⅔ cup (150 mL) water

⅓ cup (75 mL) olive oil

CHEESE AND VEGETABLE FILLING

3 medium potatoes, peeled and sliced lengthwise

2 medium zucchinis, sliced lengthwise

3 tbsp (45 mL) olive oil

3 small eggplants, sliced lengthwise

2 roasted red peppers, sliced

About 2 cups (500 mL) baby spinach

7 oz (200 g) Emmental cheese, sliced

Leaves from 5 sprigs fresh thyme, finely chopped

6 to 8 basil leaves, finely chopped

1 egg white, beaten, for egg wash

To make the pastry: In a large bowl, stir together flour, Parmesan and salt. Add water and olive oil. Stir until dough comes together, adding more flour if too sticky or more water if dry. Remove dough from bowl and gently knead a few times until smooth. The dough should feel a little like pizza dough. Wrap dough in plastic wrap and let it rest for 20 to 30 minutes.

Meanwhile, make the filling: Bring a large skillet of water to a boil. Add potatoes and zucchinis, and cook just until they are tender but still firm enough to hold their shape. Drain and set aside.

Heat 3 tbsp (45 mL) olive oil in same skillet over medium-high heat. When oil is hot, add a few slices of eggplant—don't crowd the pan. Fry eggplant in batches, adding more oil if pan is dry, until tender and golden on both sides. Drain on paper towels. Set aside.

Preheat oven at 375°F (190°C).

To assemble the pie: Lightly flour work surface and rolling pin. Roll out two-thirds of pastry to ¼-inch (5 mm) thickness. Fit pastry into 9-inch (20 cm) springform pan so pastry hangs over the sides of the pan by about 1 inch (2.5 cm). Layer in half of the vegetables (potato, eggplant, zucchini, red peppers and spinach), followed by half the Emmental cheese and half the thyme and basil. Repeat with remaining vegetables, cheese and herbs.

Roll out remaining pastry to ¼-inch (5 mm) thickness and place over pie. Press top and bottom pastry edges together and fold inward to seal pie. Brush top evenly with beaten egg white. Poke a few holes in top of pie to allow steam to escape while baking.

Bake pie until pastry is golden brown and vegetables are tender, about 50 minutes. Remove sides of pan, cut pie in wedges and serve warm.

TIP Make it easy on yourself and use store-bought pastry for this recipe. Feel free to replace the Emmental with a tangy goat cheese or a nice strong Cheddar.

Mixed Mushroom Pot Pie

This tasty dish is a meatless version of the classic beef and chicken pot pies. It's full of rich, earthy flavours, and the mushrooms and lentils lend a surprising hearty texture. Your carnivore friends won't miss the meat in this one! **MAKES 4 SERVINGS**

1 oz (28 g) mixed dried mushrooms, such as porcini, chanterelles and black trumpets

2 tbsp (30 mL) butter

1 tbsp (15 mL) olive oil

1 small onion, chopped

1 leek (white and pale green part only), chopped

2 celery stalks, chopped

1 garlic clove, chopped

Salt and freshly ground pepper

1 lb (450 g) mixed fresh mushrooms, such as portobello, cremini, shiitake and oyster, thickly sliced or diced

1 tbsp (15 mL) chopped fresh rosemary

1 tbsp (15 mL) chopped fresh thyme

2 tbsp (30 mL) all-purpose flour

1 tbsp (15 mL) tomato paste

½ cup (125 mL) red wine

2 cups (500 mL) vegetable stock

1 tsp (5 mL) soy sauce or tamari

1 can (14 oz/398 mL) brown lentils, drained and rinsed

2 carrots, diced

1 parsnip, diced

1 large potato, peeled and diced

2 cups (500 mL) Brussels sprouts, trimmed, cut in half and blanched

1 cup (250 mL) frozen or fresh peas

2 sheets rolled puff pastry, preferably all-butter (1-lb/450 g package), thawed if frozen

1 egg beaten with 1 tbsp (15 mL) water, for egg wash

1 tbsp (15 mL) chopped fresh parsley, for garnish

Soak dried mushrooms in hot water until rehydrated, 15 to 20 minutes. Drain, reserving soaking liquid. Chop mushrooms and set aside.

Melt butter with oil in a large skillet over medium heat. Add onions, leek, celery and garlic. Cook, stirring occasionally, until vegetables start to soften, about 3 minutes. Season with salt and pepper.

Increase heat to medium-high. Add fresh mushrooms, rosemary, thyme, and salt and pepper to taste. Sauté until mushrooms are golden, 8 to 10 minutes. Stir in soaked mushrooms. Cook for 2 to 3 minutes more.

Sprinkle with flour and stir. Cook for 1 to 2 minutes. Stir in tomato paste and cook for 1 minute. Gradually stir in wine and stock. Add mushroom soaking liquid, soy sauce, lentils, carrots, parsnips and potatoes. Bring to a boil. Reduce heat and simmer, stirring occasionally, until vegetables are tender, 15 to 20 minutes. Stir in blanched Brussels sprouts and peas. Remove from heat.

Preheat oven to 425°F (220°C). Butter 4 large ovenproof bowls or large French onion soup crocks.

Lightly dust work surface with flour. Unfold puff pastry on work surface. Using one of the bowls as a guide, cut pastry circles about ½ inch (1 cm) bigger than the bowl.

Divide mushroom mixture among bowls. Top with pastry circles and press gently so pastry adheres to bowls. Brush with egg wash and a cut a few steam vents. Transfer to a baking sheet.

Bake pot pies until filling is bubbling and pastry is golden brown, about 15 minutes. Serve hot, garnished with chopped parsley, if desired.

Italian Shepherd's Pie

Where I come from, shepherd's pie is huge. I love this recipe, which puts an Italian flavour twist on the traditional mix of lamb, potato and corn, this time using a combo of sausage, mushrooms and roasted peppers. Make it in advance and keep it in the freezer for your next casual get-together—a delicious, hearty casserole, ready to go. MAKES 6 SERVINGS

2 oz (55 g) dried porcini mushrooms

4 tbsp (60 mL) butter

12 oz (340 g) Italian sausage, casings removed

12 oz (340 g) cremini or button mushrooms, sliced

3 tbsp (45 mL) chopped fresh Italian parsley

Salt and freshly ground pepper

2 ¼ lb (1 kg) Yukon Gold potatoes (unpeeled)

½ cup (125 mL) milk

Pinch of freshly grated nutmeg

¾ cup (175 mL) grated Parmesan cheese

3 large eggs

2 tbsp (30 mL) fresh bread crumbs

3 to 4 roasted red peppers

1 egg yolk, beaten

To make the meat filling: Soak dried porcini mushrooms in hot water for about 15 minutes. Drain, reserving mushroom liquid. Chop mushrooms and set aside.

In a large skillet over medium to medium-high heat, melt 2 tbsp (30 mL) butter. Add sausage meat and cremini mushrooms. Sauté for 2 minutes, breaking up sausage meat with a wooden spoon. Add porcini mushrooms. Cook until mushrooms are golden brown and sausage meat is cooked through, 10 to 12 minutes. Add mushroom soaking liquid and let reduce until most of the liquid has evaporated. Stir in parsley and season with salt and pepper. Remove from heat.

To make the potato topping: Cook potatoes in boiling salted water until tender. Peel potatoes while still hot. Pass through a potato ricer into the pot they were cooked in (or use a potato masher). Place pot over low heat. Add 2 tbsp (30 mL) butter, milk, nutmeg, and salt and pepper to taste. Stir until smooth. Remove from heat. Stir in Parmesan. Add eggs, one at a time, stirring vigorously after each addition to prevent the eggs from coagulating.

To assemble the shepherd's pie: Preheat oven to 350°F (180°C). Butter a 9-inch (2.5 L) square baking dish and dust bottom and sides with bread crumbs. Spoon meat mixture into prepared dish. Evenly top with roasted red peppers, then top with mashed potato mixture. Brush with egg yolk.

Bake until top is golden brown and filling is piping hot, 15 to 20 minutes.

TIP You can make a more traditional version of shepherd's pie by using ground beef, lamb or pork instead of the sausage meat.

To freeze shepherd's pie: Use a pan that is freezer-to-oven safe. Assemble pie but do not brush the top with the egg yolk. Cool completely. Wrap airtight and freeze for up to 2 weeks for best results or up to 1 month. Bake, covered, at 375°F (190°C) until steaming hot, 1 hour to 1 hour 15 minutes. Uncover and broil until top is golden brown.

Mini Chicken Pot Pies

When you have leftover chicken in the fridge, this is the perfect recipe to put it to good use. Size doesn't matter here—these pies are small but mighty good. Lay them out as part of a buffet or serve two per person as a dinner main. I promise, the kids will love them! **MAKES 12 SERVINGS**

PASTRY

2 cups (500 mL) all-purpose flour

Pinch of salt

1 cup (250 mL) cold unsalted butter, cut in cubes

⅓ cup (75 mL) ice water

CHICKEN FILLING

1 tbsp (15 mL) butter

1 tbsp (15 mL) olive oil

1 carrot, diced

1 celery stalk, diced

1 onion, finely chopped

1 cup (250 mL) diced fennel

Leaves from 1 sprig thyme

Salt and freshly ground pepper

1 tbsp (15 mL) all-purpose flour

¼ cup (60 mL) white wine

1 ½ cups (375 mL) chicken stock

2 cups (500 mL) cooked chicken cut in ¾-inch (2 cm) cubes

1 cup (250 mL) fresh or frozen peas

1 egg beaten with 2 tbsp (30 mL) milk, for egg wash

To make the pastry: Combine flour and salt in a food processor. Pulse to mix. Add butter. Pulse a few times to cut butter into flour. You want the consistency of coarse meal. Do not over-mix or the butter will start to melt. Add water and pulse just until dough starts to come together. Remove from bowl and shape dough into a disc. Wrap in plastic wrap. Let dough rest in the fridge for 1 hour.

Meanwhile, make the filling: Melt butter with olive oil in a large saucepan over medium heat. When butter has melted, add carrots, celery, onions, fennel and thyme. Season with salt and pepper. Cook, stirring occasionally, until vegetables start to soften, about 5 minutes.

Stir in flour and cook for 1 to 2 minutes. Slowly stir in wine. Let wine reduce until almost all the liquid has evaporated. Add chicken stock and chicken. Bring to a boil, then reduce heat to a simmer. If using fresh peas, add now. Cook, stirring occasionally, until sauce has thickened slightly, 5 to 10 minutes. If using frozen peas, add now. Taste filling and adjust seasoning. Let cool before filling pies.

Preheat oven to 400°F (200°C). Cut 12 parchment-paper strips about 7 inches × 1 inch (18 × 2.5 cm). Line sides of 12 muffin cups with parchment strips.

Lightly flour work surface. Roll out pastry to about ¼-inch (5 mm) thickness. Cut out 12 circles 5 ½ inches (13 cm) wide and another 12 circles 3 inches (8 cm) wide. Fit larger pastry circles into muffin cups. Divide filling among pies. Cover with pastry tops. Crimp edges to seal. Brush tops with egg wash. Cut 2 or 3 slits in tops to allow steam to escape.

Bake pies at 400°F (200°C) for 15 minutes to set the pastry. Reduce heat to 350°F (180°C) and continue to bake until pastry is golden brown and filling is bubbling, 25 to 30 minutes more. Let pies rest for 10 minutes before serving.

TIP We made these in individual servings on the show, but you can make one big pie, if you prefer. For convenience, use whichever vegetables you have in the fridge.

Frittata with Potatoes and Spinach

When I was growing up, my mom must have made frittata at least once a week. She would change up the flavour combinations, always using different meats, veggies and herbs—whatever she had in the kitchen. Best of all, she would use the leftovers to make me a frittata sandwich to take to school the next day. Love you, Mom... thanks! **MAKES 4 SERVINGS**

6 large eggs

Handful of chopped fresh parsley

Salt and freshly ground pepper

⅔ cup (150 mL) shredded Cheddar cheese

⅓ cup (75 mL) olive oil

1 small onion, finely chopped

½ sweet red pepper, diced

1 Yukon Gold potato, peeled, blanched and cut in small cubes

2 cups (500 mL) baby spinach

In a large bowl, whisk together eggs, parsley, and salt and pepper to taste. Stir in cheese. Set aside.

In a 10-inch (25 cm) nonstick skillet over medium-high heat, heat olive oil. When oil is hot, sauté onions and red pepper until they begin to soften, about 2 minutes. Add the potatoes and sauté for 2 to 3 minutes more. Add spinach to pan and sauté until spinach just starts to wilt, about 1 minute. Season with salt and pepper.

Reduce heat to medium and add the egg mixture. Cook frittata until the eggs are almost completely set. Carefully flip frittata onto a plate and then slide back into the pan to finish cooking the other side, 1 to 2 minutes. Serve warm.

TIP I love this recipe because it is so versatile—empty your fridge to create your own frittata. Veggies, herbs, meats... anything goes!

Hearty Greens and Sausage Soup

Full of turkey sausage, white beans and leafy greens, this satisfying soup is filling enough to serve as a main for dinner. Remember that the most important ingredient in any soup is the stock—homemade is always best! **MAKES 4 SERVINGS**

2 tbsp (30 mL) olive oil

2 Italian-style turkey sausages, sliced

1 small onion, finely chopped

1 carrot, chopped

1 celery stalk, chopped

2 garlic cloves, chopped

1 tbsp (15 mL) chopped fresh herbs, such as sage, rosemary or thyme

¼ cup (60 mL) white wine

1 can (19 oz/540 mL) cannellini beans, drained and rinsed

4 cups (1 L) chicken stock

4 sun-dried tomatoes, finely chopped

Salt and freshly ground pepper

4 cups (1 L) chopped mixed greens, such as spinach, Swiss chard, dandelion greens and/or kale

Freshly grated Parmesan cheese, to finish

Hot pepper oil, to finish (optional)

TIP If you don't have turkey sausage, you can use regular pork sausage. For an extra layer of flavour, rub the hot crusty bread with a clove of garlic.

In a large pot, heat olive oil over medium to medium-high heat. Add sausages and cook, stirring frequently, until golden brown, 5 to 7 minutes. Add onions, carrot, celery, garlic and herbs. Cook, stirring frequently, until vegetables soften and are lightly golden brown, 3 to 4 minutes. Add wine and let reduce until almost all of the liquid has evaporated.

Mash half the beans. Stir in whole and mashed beans, stock and sun-dried tomatoes. Season with salt and pepper. Bring to a boil. Reduce heat and simmer for about 30 minutes.

If using bitter greens such as dandelion greens, blanch in boiling salted water for 1 to 2 minutes.

Add greens to soup and cook until softened, about 5 minutes. Top soup with Parmesan and a drizzle of hot pepper oil, if desired. Serve with crusty bread.

Vietnamese Chicken Noodle Soup

If you've ever tried this aromatic Vietnamese chicken soup, called *pho ga*, you'll know that it has an unforgettable broth infused with ginger, star anise and cinnamon. Finish with a combo of fresh and spicy garnishes and you have a great chicken noodle soup that will comfort you on a cold day. **MAKES 4 SERVINGS**

BOUQUET GARNI

8 to 10 slices fresh ginger

1 to 3 star anise

1 tsp (5 mL) coriander seeds

2 to 3 whole cloves

½ stick cinnamon

6 cups (1.5 L) chicken stock

1 tbsp (15 mL) sugar

1 tbsp (15 mL) fish sauce, or to taste

TO ASSEMBLE

½ package (14 oz/400 g) thin rice noodles

2 boneless, skinless chicken breasts, very thinly sliced

Handful of fresh cilantro leaves, mint leaves and/or Thai basil leaves

2 green onions, sliced

Handful of bean sprouts

Fresh Thai chilies, thinly sliced, to taste

2 limes, cut in wedges

Hoisin sauce and sriracha sauce, for serving (optional)

Make a bouquet garni: Wrap ginger slices, star anise, coriander seeds, cloves and cinnamon in a double layer of cheesecloth and tie with kitchen string.

In a large saucepan, bring chicken stock to a boil over medium-high heat. Reduce heat to a simmer. Add bouquet garni, sugar and fish sauce. Simmer for about 15 minutes.

Meanwhile, soak rice noodles in a bowl of hot water just until pliable, 5 to 10 minutes. Drain.

Stir chicken into stock. Simmer until chicken is cooked through, 1 to 2 minutes, depending on how thinly sliced the chicken is. Discard bouquet garni.

Divide noodles among serving bowls. Ladle over stock and chicken. Garnish with herb leaves, green onions, bean sprouts and chilies. Serve with lime wedges, and hoisin and sriracha sauce, if desired.

TIP This soup really is delicious as is, but you can replace the chicken with some leftover sliced flank steak.

Quick Shrimp and Corn Chowder

I always keep a bag of shrimp in the freezer—it's the perfect dinner solution in a stir-fry, pasta or soup any night of the week. This creamy chowder, topped with a crumble of crispy bacon, is simple and fast, but be warned: you'll probably be tempted to have a second bowl! MAKES 4 SERVINGS

2 tbsp (30 mL) butter

1 tbsp (15 mL) olive oil

1 small onion, chopped

2 celery stalks, diced

1 tsp (5 mL) dried thyme (or leaves from 1 sprig fresh)

2 tbsp (30 mL) all-purpose flour

About 2 cups (500 mL) diced unpeeled potatoes

1 can (19 oz/540 mL) creamed corn

4 cups (1 L) chicken or vegetable stock

Pinch of freshly grated nutmeg, or to taste

Salt and freshly ground pepper

½ lb (225 g) small to medium shrimp (thawed if frozen), peeled and deveined

2 jarred roasted red peppers, chopped

2 slices pancetta or bacon, coarsely chopped

¼ cup (60 mL) whipping cream (35%) (optional)

2 tbsp (30 mL) chopped fresh cilantro or parsley (optional)

TIP For a thicker, creamier soup, before adding the shrimp, whizz half of the soup in a blender. Stir it back into the remaining soup.

Melt butter with olive oil in a large saucepan over medium heat. Add onions, celery and thyme. Cook, stirring frequently, until veggies start to soften, 1 to 2 minutes. Add flour and cook, stirring, for 1 minute.

Add potatoes, creamed corn, stock, nutmeg, and salt and pepper to taste. Bring to a boil. Cover and reduce to a simmer. Simmer chowder until potatoes are fork-tender, about 15 minutes.

Add shrimp and roasted red peppers. Simmer until shrimp turn pink and curl, 3 to 5 minutes.

Meanwhile, cook pancetta in a small skillet over medium heat until golden and crispy.

If desired, stir in cream for a rich, creamy chowder. Reheat if needed. Serve soup garnished with pancetta and fresh herbs, if desired.

Meatloaf with Red Wine Tomato Sauce

My nonna, Angel, made the best meatloaf, and I was inspired to create one that tasted just like hers. This recipe has it all: inexpensive ingredients and loads of flavour, and it feeds a crowd. But the best part may be the sandwich you can make with the delicious leftovers! MAKES 6 TO 8 SERVINGS

RED WINE TOMATO SAUCE

2 tbsp (30 mL) olive oil

1 medium onion, finely chopped

2 carrots, finely chopped

2 celery stalks, finely chopped

½ cup (125 mL) red wine

2 ½ cups (625 mL) tomato purée (passata)

MEATLOAF

6 slices day-old white bread

Milk, for soaking bread

1 lb (450 g) ground veal

1 lb (450 g) ground beef

5 oz (140 g) thickly sliced prosciutto, diced

6 tbsp (90 mL) freshly grated Parmesan cheese, plus more for serving

1 tsp (5 mL) dried oregano

Handful of fresh Italian parsley, chopped, plus a little more for garnish

2 large eggs, lightly beaten

Salt and freshly ground pepper

3 tbsp (45 mL) olive oil

TIP Make this meatloaf extra-lean by replacing some of the veal or beef with ground chicken or turkey.

To make the tomato sauce: Heat olive oil in a large saucepan over medium heat. When oil is hot, add onions, carrots and celery. Cook, stirring occasionally, until vegetables start to soften, 3 to 5 minutes. Add red wine and tomato purée. Bring to a simmer. Gently simmer while you make the meatloaf.

Preheat oven to 400°F (200°C).

To make the meatloaf: Soak bread in milk for a few minutes to soften. Squeeze out excess milk.

In a large bowl, combine ground veal, ground beef, prosciutto, 6 tbsp (90 mL) Parmesan, oregano, parsley, soaked bread and eggs. Season with salt and pepper. Mix with your hands and shape into a loaf about 8 inches (20 cm) long and 3 inches (8 cm) wide with rounded ends.

Heat olive oil in a large nonstick skillet over medium to medium-high heat. When oil is hot, add meatloaf. Brown meatloaf on all sides, about 10 minutes.

Transfer meatloaf to a baking dish. Pour tomato sauce over and around meatloaf. Cover with foil. Bake for 25 minutes. Remove foil and continue to bake meatloaf until meat is cooked through and sauce has thickened, 15 to 20 minutes more. Let meatloaf rest for 5 to 10 minutes. Cut meatloaf into slices and serve with the sauce. Garnish with Parmesan and chopped fresh parsley.

Old-Fashioned Pot Roast

This made-in-one-pot roast, loaded with root vegetables and bathed in rich gravy, will remind you of the one that your grandma used to make. It's the perfect meal to make on a Sunday night—everyone will run to the table when this roast is served! **MAKES 8 SERVINGS**

1 beef pot roast (4 to 5 lb/1.8 to 2.25 kg), such as blade, chuck or cross rib

Salt and freshly ground pepper

3 tbsp (45 mL) olive oil

1 onion, chopped

1 carrot, chopped

2 celery stalks, chopped

2 garlic cloves, chopped

2 sprigs thyme

¼ cup (60 mL) all-purpose flour

2 tbsp (30 mL) tomato paste

3 cups (750 mL) beef stock

2 tbsp (30 mL) Worcestershire sauce

1 tbsp (15 mL) brown sugar

2 bay leaves

2 carrots, cut in 2-inch (5 cm) chunks

2 turnips, cut in 2-inch (5 cm) chunks

2 parsnips, cut in 2-inch (5 cm) chunks

1 small rutabaga, cut in 2-inch (5 cm) chunks

3 tbsp (45 mL) chopped fresh parsley, for garnish

GREEN BEANS

1 lb (450 g) green beans, trimmed

2 tbsp (30 mL) extra-virgin olive oil

Preheat oven to 325°F (160°C).

Pat pot roast dry. Season all over with salt and pepper. Heat a Dutch oven over medium-high heat. Add olive oil. When oil is hot, add pot roast and brown on all sides, 8 to 10 minutes. Remove and set aside.

If pan looks dry, add more olive oil. Add chopped onions, carrots, celery, garlic and thyme sprigs. Cook, stirring frequently, until vegetables start to soften, about 5 minutes. Sprinkle with flour. Cook, stirring constantly, another 2 minutes. Stir in tomato paste. Gradually stir in beef stock. Add Worcestershire sauce, brown sugar and bay leaves. Bring to a boil. Return roast and any juices to pot. Cover and transfer to oven. Cook, turning roast every hour, until meat starts to become tender, about 3 hours.

Add carrot, turnip, parsnip and rutabaga chunks. Cover and cook until meat is fork-tender and veggies are tender, another 1 to 1 ½ hours.

Just before pot roast comes out of the oven, make the green beans: Add green beans to a saucepan of boiling salted water. Cook until tender-crisp, 3 to 5 minutes. Drain. Season with salt and pepper, and drizzle with olive oil.

Transfer pot roast to a cutting board. Slice and arrange on a platter along with the vegetables. Pour gravy over top or serve in a gravy boat. Garnish with parsley. Serve with green beans.

Irish Stout Beef Stew

Stout beer is the secret to getting rich, complex flavour in this Irish stew. The stew is packed with hearty root veggies and finished with a hit of grainy mustard, which is an irresistible combination. Serve it piping hot with a piece of soda bread on the side and you've got a dish that will make any day feel like St. Patrick's Day!

MAKES 6 SERVINGS

2 lb (900 g) stewing beef, cut in 1-inch (2.5 cm) cubes

Salt and freshly ground pepper

3 tbsp (45 mL) butter

2 tbsp (30 mL) vegetable oil

1 medium onion, chopped

1 celery stalk, chopped

1 garlic clove, chopped

2 tbsp (30 mL) all-purpose flour

1 bottle (12 oz/355 mL) stout beer

2 ½ cups (625 mL) beef stock

1 bay leaf

2 large carrots, cut in 1 ½-inch (4 cm) pieces

2 parsnips, cut in 1 ½-inch (4 cm) pieces

1 small turnip, cut in 1 ½-inch (4 cm) pieces

5 medium potatoes, peeled and cut in 1 ½-inch (4 cm) pieces

1 tbsp (15 mL) whole-grain mustard

1 tbsp (15 mL) chopped fresh parsley or chives, to garnish

Pat stewing beef dry with paper towels. Season with salt and pepper.

In a Dutch oven or large saucepan, melt butter with oil over medium-high heat. When oil is hot, add beef in batches to avoid crowding the pan. Sear beef on all sides until well browned, about 10 minutes. Remove meat from pan. Set aside.

Reduce heat to medium. Add more oil if pan looks dry. Add onions, celery and garlic. Cook, stirring frequently, until they start to soften, about 5 minutes. Season with salt and pepper. Add flour and cook, stirring constantly, for 3 minutes. Slowly add beer, stirring to blend with flour. Increase heat and bring to a boil. Let reduce for 5 to 10 minutes. Add stock and bring to a boil again. Reduce heat to a simmer.

Return beef and any juices to pot and add bay leaf. Cover and simmer, stirring occasionally, for 1 ¼ hours. Add carrots, parsnips, turnips and potatoes. Simmer, covered and stirring occasionally, until meat and veggies are tender, about 1 hour more.

Season stew with salt and pepper. Stir in mustard. Serve garnished with parsley. Serve with soda bread, if desired.

Stefano's Big BBQ Brisket

This big beer-infused brisket is rubbed with spices and cooked low and slow in the oven for 6 hours, until the meat is fork-tender. Serve it with my homemade BBQ sauce and some mashed potatoes and you have one heck of a tasty dinner. MAKES 16 SERVINGS

BRISKET

2 tbsp (30 mL) coarse salt, such as kosher salt

2 tbsp (30 mL) freshly ground pepper

2 tbsp (30 mL) smoked paprika

2 tbsp (30 mL) garlic powder

2 tbsp (30 mL) ground cumin

2 tbsp (30 mL) brown sugar

2 tsp (10 mL) cayenne pepper, or to taste

1 beef double brisket (9 to 10 lb/ 4.1 to 4.5 kg)

1 to 2 bottles (12 oz/355 mL each) beer, preferably amber ale

BBQ SAUCE

1 tbsp (15 mL) olive oil

1 onion, minced

2 garlic cloves, minced

1 tbsp (15 mL) chili powder

1 cup (250 mL) ketchup

½ cup (125 mL) chili sauce

½ cup (125 mL) molasses

½ cup (125 mL) apple cider vinegar

¼ cup (60 mL) brewed espresso or strong coffee

1 tbsp (15 mL) Dijon mustard

1 tbsp (15 mL) Worcestershire sauce

Salt and freshly ground pepper

To make the brisket: In a small bowl, combine salt, pepper, paprika, garlic powder, cumin, sugar and cayenne. Stir to combine. Rub spice mix all over brisket. Place brisket in a large roasting pan, cover and let marinate in the fridge for at least 4 hours or up to 24 hours.

Preheat oven to 350°F (180°C).

Roast brisket, uncovered, for 1 hour.

Reduce heat to 300°F (150°C). Pour 1 bottle of beer into the roasting pan. Cover pan with foil. Slow-roast brisket, adding more beer if pan looks dry, until meat is fork-tender, 5 to 6 hours, depending on size of brisket.

While brisket is roasting, make the BBQ sauce: Heat olive oil in a medium saucepan over medium heat. When oil is hot, add onions and garlic. Cook, stirring frequently, until lightly golden brown, about 5 minutes. Add chili powder and cook,

stirring, until fragrant, about 2 minutes. Add ketchup, chili sauce, molasses, vinegar, brewed espresso, mustard, Worcestershire sauce, and salt and pepper to taste. Gently simmer, stirring frequently, until sauce thickens and flavours marry, 20 to 30 minutes. Set aside.

Transfer brisket to a cutting board, tent with foil and let rest for about 20 minutes. Reheat sauce. If desired, add some of the brisket braising liquid to flavour the sauce. Slice brisket and serve with BBQ sauce.

TIP In this recipe, you can replace the molasses with honey and the cider vinegar with white vinegar.

Breaded Veal Cutlets

Veal cutlets were in regular dinner rotation at home when I was young. I was always so amazed at how quickly my mom made them and got them on the table—they cook up in no time. Serve your cutlets with a light side dish, such as sautéed cherry tomatoes (the recipe is right here!), or put a cutlet on a bun with some marinated artichokes. Yum! **MAKES 4 SERVINGS**

BREADED VEAL CUTLETS

½ cup (125 mL) all-purpose flour

3 large eggs

2 tbsp (30 mL) milk

1 cup (250 mL) fresh or dry bread crumbs

¼ cup (60 mL) grated Parmesan cheese

2 tsp (10 mL) chopped fresh herbs, such as sage, rosemary or thyme

4 large veal cutlets, pounded ¼ inch (5 mm) thick

Salt and freshly ground pepper

2 tbsp (30 mL) butter

2 tbsp (30 mL) olive oil

SAUTÉED CHERRY TOMATOES

3 tbsp (45 mL) butter

1 ½ lb (675 g) vine-ripened cherry tomatoes

1 tsp (5 mL) sugar

Salt and freshly ground pepper

1 tbsp (15 mL) chopped fresh Italian parsley

1 tbsp (15 mL) chopped fresh marjoram

1 tbsp (15 mL) chopped fresh thyme

To make the breaded veal cutlets: Prepare a breading station by arranging 3 shallow dishes or pie plates with the following: flour in the first; eggs beaten with milk in the second; and bread crumbs, Parmesan and herbs stirred together in the third.

Season veal with salt and pepper. Dredge cutlets first in flour, then in egg mixture and lastly in bread crumb mixture.

In a large skillet over medium heat, melt butter with oil. When oil is hot, add cutlets and brown on each side, 3 to 5 minutes per side.

While cutlets are cooking, make the sautéed cherry tomatoes: In a large sauté pan, melt butter over medium-high heat. When butter is golden brown, add tomatoes. Sprinkle them with sugar and season with salt and pepper. Increase heat to high and sauté tomatoes, stirring gently, until they start to soften and skins begin to wrinkle, about 5 minutes. Add the parsley, marjoram and thyme, mix well and remove from heat.

Serve cutlets with Sautéed Cherry Tomatoes.

TIP Substitute chicken, turkey or pork in these tasty breaded cutlets. They're awesome in sandwiches!

Quick Roast Beef Quesadillas

This filling quesadilla recipe features all the flavours of a Philly cheese steak sandwich and can be made in a flash. Just keep sliced deli roast beef and provolone cheese on hand, and you'll have the ingredients of a tasty dinner on any busy weeknight. **MAKES 4 SERVINGS**

HORSERADISH DIP
¼ cup (60 mL) mayonnaise

¼ cup (60 mL) plain yogurt

1 to 2 tbsp (15 to 30 mL) creamed
   horseradish, or to taste

1 tbsp (15 mL) chopped fresh chives

QUESADILLAS
3 tbsp (45 mL) olive oil

1 small red onion, sliced

1 small sweet red pepper, sliced

1 small sweet green pepper, sliced

Salt and freshly ground pepper

4 large multi-grain or whole wheat
   flour tortillas

Dijon mustard, to taste

7 oz (200 g) thinly sliced
   deli roast beef

8 slices provolone cheese

TIP Make this recipe with leftover roast beef or even grilled flank steak. Change it up and use some grilled chicken, if you like.

To make the horseradish dip: In a small bowl, stir together mayonnaise, yogurt, horseradish and chives. Set aside.

To make the quesadillas: Heat a large skillet over medium heat. Add 2 tbsp (30 mL) olive oil. When oil is hot, add onions, red pepper and green pepper. Season with salt and pepper. Cook, stirring occasionally, until veggies are lightly golden brown, 3 to 4 minutes. Remove from heat.

Spread mustard on one half of each tortilla. Top with roast beef, cheese and veggie mixture. Fold other half over and press gently to seal.

Heat a griddle or large skillet over medium to medium-high heat. When griddle is hot, brush with a little oil. Add quesadillas. Cook until golden brown on each side and cheese starts to melt, 2 to 4 minutes per side.

Cut each quesadilla in thirds. Serve with horseradish dip.

Steak and Ale Pie

My friend Alan is British and he makes an amazing steak and ale pie infused with rich, dark beer. Tasting his dish inspired me to create a recipe of my own, but in my version, I use store-bought puff pastry and the filling can be made a day in advance. With so many shortcuts, maybe Alan will be tempted to make my recipe now! **MAKES 4 SERVINGS**

4 tbsp (60 mL) butter

1 medium onion, finely chopped

2 tbsp (30 mL) all-purpose flour

2 cups (500 mL) dark beer

3 ⅓ lb (1.5 kg) beef stewing meat or blade roast, cubed

Salt and freshly ground pepper

3 tbsp (45 mL) vegetable oil

1 cup (250 mL) beef stock

1 lb (450 g) button or cremini mushrooms, cut in half

2 tsp (10 mL) finely grated fresh horseradish (or ½ tsp/2 mL prepared horseradish)

1 sheet pre-rolled puff pastry (10 inches/ 25 cm square) or ½ lb (225 g) puff pastry, thawed if frozen

1 egg beaten with 1 tsp (5 mL) water, for egg wash

In a Dutch oven or large saucepan, melt 2 tbsp (30 mL) butter over low heat. Add onions and cook gently until softened, about 10 minutes. Add flour and cook, stirring constantly, for 2 minutes. Gradually stir in beer. Bring to a boil, then reduce heat to a bare simmer.

Meanwhile, season beef with salt and pepper. Heat a large skillet over high heat. Add oil. When oil is hot, add beef in batches, being careful not to crowd the pan. Cook beef until well browned on all sides, 8 to 10 minutes. Remove beef from pan.

Deglaze pan with beef stock, scraping the bottom of the pan with a wooden spoon to incorporate all the caramelized bits into the liquid. When liquid comes to a boil, add it to the Dutch oven. Wipe out skillet and set aside.

Add beef and any juices to stew and bring to a boil. Reduce heat and simmer, uncovered, until meat is tender and liquid has reduced by half, 1¼ to 1½ hours.

While beef is cooking, sauté the mushrooms: Melt remaining 2 tbsp (30 mL) butter in the skillet over medium-high heat. When butter starts to sizzle, add mushrooms in batches. Season with salt and pepper and sauté until golden brown, about 10 minutes.

Transfer mushrooms to an 8-cup (2 L) casserole dish. Add beef mixture and horseradish; stir well to combine. Let cool until no longer steaming, about 30 minutes, before topping with the pastry. (Filling can be covered and refrigerated overnight.)

Preheat oven to 400°F (200°C).

On a lightly floured work surface, roll out puff pastry until about 1 inch (2.5 cm) bigger than the casserole dish. Top pie with pastry. Trim and crimp edges. Brush with egg wash. Cut a few slits in the pastry to allow steam to escape. If desired, with the pastry trimmings, cut out decorative shapes, such as a leaf or beer bottle, to decorate the pie. Brush decorations with egg wash.

Bake until pastry is golden brown and filling is bubbling, about 45 minutes.

Sweet-and-Spicy Steak Tacos

Who doesn't like tacos? These ones are marinated with beer, chipotle peppers and honey, so the steak gets tender, juicy and so flavourful. This is the perfect recipe when you're on a budget and need to feed a crowd. **MAKES 8 SERVINGS**

1 bottle (330 mL) dark-style Mexican beer

Juice of 2 limes

2 tbsp (30 mL) olive oil

2 tbsp (30 mL) Worcestershire sauce

3 to 4 garlic cloves, chopped

1 to 2 chipotle peppers in adobo sauce, chopped, or to taste

1 tbsp (15 mL) honey

1 flank steak (1 ½ to 2 lb/675 to 900 g)

Salt and freshly ground pepper

8 small flour or corn tortillas or taco shells

Tomatillo salsa or fresh tomato salsa

Diced queso fresco cheese or shredded Cheddar cheese

Sliced green onions

Sliced jalapeño peppers

To marinate the flank steak: In a shallow baking dish or large resealable plastic bag, combine beer, lime juice, olive oil, Worcestershire sauce, garlic, chipotle peppers and honey. Stir to combine. Immerse flank steak in marinade. Cover (or seal bag) and refrigerate for at least 8 hours or up to 24 hours.

Preheat grill to high.

Remove steak from marinade (discard marinade). Pat dry with paper towels. Season with salt and pepper. Grill steak for 6 to 8 minutes per side for rare to medium-rare doneness, depending on thickness. Be careful not to overcook the flank steak, or it will be tough and chewy. Let steak rest for 8 to 10 minutes before slicing. Thinly slice steak across the grain.

Meanwhile, heat tortillas over medium heat in a hot dry pan or griddle until warmed and lightly toasted. Wrap tortillas in a clean kitchen towel to keep warm. (Alternatively, wrap tortillas in foil and heat for a few minutes in a 400°F/200°C oven.)

Serve warm tortillas with steak slices and salsa, queso fresco, green onions and jalapeños for topping.

Stefano's Beef Bourguignon

This traditional French comfort food may have a fancy name, but it's simply beef cubes stewed in a red wine sauce with mushrooms. Anytime you need a beautiful dish for a special occasion, serve this straight from the Dutch oven at the table with a loaf of crusty bread and some more red wine. MAKES 8 SERVINGS

2 tbsp (30 mL) olive oil

2 to 3 slices thick-cut bacon, cut in 1 ½-inch (4 cm) pieces

3 lb (1.35 kg) stewing beef, cut in 1 ½-inch (4 cm) pieces

Salt and freshly ground pepper

Flour, for dredging

4 tbsp (60 mL) butter

1 large onion, finely chopped

3 celery stalks, diced

2 garlic cloves, chopped

3 sprigs thyme

2 bay leaves

1 to 2 tbsp (15 to 30 mL) tomato paste

1 bottle dry red wine

1 cup (250 mL) beef stock

4 cups (1 L) baby button mushrooms

20 pearl onions, blanched and peeled

3 carrots, cut in 2-inch (5 cm) chunks

1 tbsp (15 mL) chopped fresh parsley, for garnish

1 tbsp (15 mL) chopped fresh chives, for garnish

Preheat oven to 350°F (180°C).

Heat a Dutch oven over medium-low to medium heat. Add 1 tbsp (15 mL) olive oil and bacon. Cook until fat renders and bacon is golden brown, 5 to 10 minutes. Transfer bacon to paper towels to drain and set aside. Leave 2 tbsp (30 mL) bacon fat in pan.

Pat beef dry with paper towels. Season with salt and pepper and lightly dredge in flour, shaking off excess flour.

Add 2 tbsp (30 mL) butter to bacon fat in pan and heat over medium-high heat. When hot, add beef in batches so you don't crowd the pan. Cook beef until well browned on all sides, 8 to 12 minutes, adding more butter if pan looks dry. Remove beef from pan.

Add 1 tbsp (15 mL) butter to pan if necessary. Add onions, celery, garlic, thyme sprigs and bay leaves. Cook, stirring frequently, until vegetables start to soften, 3 to 5 minutes.

Stir in tomato paste. Add red wine and beef stock. There should be just enough liquid to cover the meat; add additional wine or stock if needed. Bring to a boil, scraping the bottom of the pan with a wooden spoon to incorporate all the caramelized bits into the liquid. Reduce to a simmer and add the bacon and beef with any juices. Cover and put in the oven. Cook until meat is just tender, about 2 hours.

In a large skillet over medium-high heat, melt 1 tbsp (15 mL) butter with 1 tbsp (15 mL) oil. Add mushrooms and pearl onions in batches if necessary to avoid crowding the pan. Fry, stirring occasionally, until mushrooms and onions are golden brown, 5 to 7 minutes.

Add mushroom mixture and carrots to Dutch oven. Put back in oven and cook until meat is tender enough to cut with a fork and carrots are just tender, about 30 minutes. Skim excess fat, if needed. Taste and adjust seasoning. Serve garnished with parsley and chives.

Roast Beef with Fresh Herbs

Are you in a roast beef rut? Well, here is a recipe that will transform your next roast into a work of art with very little effort. Just cook the beef to your liking and roll it in a simple mix of fresh herbs. Sunday nights just got a bit more delicious! MAKES 6 TO 8 SERVINGS

1 boneless sirloin roast or prime rib roast (about 3 ⅓ lb/1.5 kg)

Salt and freshly ground pepper

¼ cup (60 mL) olive oil

1 to 2 garlic cloves

Handful of fresh basil

Handful of fresh parsley

Handful of fresh mint

Leaves from 2 sprigs rosemary

Leaves from 2 sprigs thyme

CONDIMENTS

Horseradish, mustard

Preheat oven to 425°F (220°C).

Season roast with salt and pepper. Heat a large ovenproof skillet over medium-high heat. Add olive oil. When olive oil is hot, add roast and brown on all sides.

Transfer pan to oven and cook roast for 20 minutes. Reduce heat to 325°F (160°C) and cook until internal temperature reaches 140°F (60°C) on a meat thermometer for medium-rare, 30 to 40 minutes, depending on thickness of roast. (Alternatively, cook roast until doneness is to your liking.)

While roast is cooking, finely chop garlic and herbs. Stir to combine. Transfer to a large platter or baking dish.

When roast is cooked, remove from oven and roll in herb mixture until completely covered. Tent roast with foil and let rest for 10 to 15 minutes. Slice roast and serve with horseradish and mustard, if desired.

Stefano's Tex-Mex Chili

This chunky chili is packed with meaty, smoky, spicy goodness. It's made with stewing beef, so make two or three batches—it's a great way to feed a crowd without breaking the bank. Pull this recipe out when you're entertaining a gang at a casual get-together or watching the big game—this chili is a big winner!

MAKES 6 SERVINGS

1 to 2 dried ancho chilies (or chipotle, pasilla or New Mexican chilies)

3 tbsp (45 mL) vegetable oil

2 lb (900 g) stewing beef, cut in ½-inch (1 cm) cubes

Salt and freshly ground pepper

1 onion, chopped

2 garlic cloves, finely chopped

1 ½ tsp (7 mL) ground cumin

1 tsp (5 mL) dried oregano

Pinch of cinnamon

¼ cup (60 mL) tomato paste

½ cup (125 mL) brewed coffee

2 ½ cups (625 mL) good-quality beef stock

1 tbsp (15 mL) brown sugar

1 tbsp (15 mL) Worcestershire sauce

1 tbsp (15 mL) apple cider vinegar

2 bay leaves

1 can (19 oz/540 mL) pinto beans, drained and rinsed

Hot pepper sauce, for serving (optional)

GARNISHES

Chopped green onions, crumbled cooked bacon, sliced fresh jalapeños, sour cream, shredded Cheddar cheese

TIP If you don't have pinto beans, use whatever beans you have in your pantry. You can easily replace the beef stock with vegetable stock or even water.

In a small skillet over medium heat, dry-toast ancho chilies until fragrant, 5 to 10 minutes. Chop and set aside.

Heat oil in a large Dutch oven over medium-high heat. When oil is hot, add stewing beef in batches to avoid crowding the pan. Season with salt and pepper. Brown well on all sides, about 10 minutes. Remove from pot as cooked.

Return all beef and any juices to pot. Add onions and garlic, cumin, oregano and cinnamon. Cook, stirring, until onions start to soften, about 5 minutes.

Stir in tomato paste and cook for 1 minute. Add coffee, stock, brown sugar, Worcestershire sauce, vinegar, bay leaves and chopped ancho chili. Bring to a boil. Reduce heat and simmer, covered, for 1 hour.

Stir in beans. Continue to simmer, uncovered and stirring occasionally, until beef is tender and chili is thick, about 1 hour more, depending on size of stewing beef. Taste and adjust seasoning.

Serve chili with desired garnishes. Serve with hot sauce, if desired.

Grilled Cheeseburgers with Smoky Bacon

These big, juicy burgers, made with my own special Homemade Steak Spice, are a showpiece at any barbecue. You'll have lots of steak spice left over—it gives an incredible flavour to steak. Top the burgers with a nippy slice of old Cheddar, some smoky bacon and my tangy Tomato Chutney and you've got a burger that will have people talking! **MAKES 4 SERVINGS**

HOMEMADE STEAK SPICE

3 tbsp (45 mL) kosher salt

2 tbsp (30 mL) peppercorns

2 tsp (10 mL) granulated garlic

1 tsp (5 mL) granulated onion

1 tsp (5 mL) fennel seeds

1 tsp (5 mL) mustard seeds

1 tsp (5 mL) coriander seeds

1 tsp (5 mL) dill seeds

1 tsp (5 mL) hot pepper flakes

TOMATO CHUTNEY

1 lb (450 g) ripe tomatoes

2 cooking apples, such as Cortland, peeled and grated

1 small onion, finely chopped

1 garlic clove, minced

2 tsp (10 mL) chopped fresh ginger

Grated zest and juice of 1 lime

⅔ cup (150 mL) sugar

1 tsp (5 mL) cinnamon

1 tsp (5 mL) salt

½ tsp (2 mL) white pepper

½ cup (125 mL) apple cider vinegar or white wine vinegar

CHEESEBURGERS

1 ¾ lb (790 g) medium ground beef

Homemade Steak Spice

Vegetable oil, for brushing

4 slices aged Cheddar cheese

4 burger buns

4 lettuce leaves

4 slices smoky bacon, cooked

½ onion, sliced

Tomato Chutney

To make the steak spice: In a spice grinder (or using a mortar and pestle), combine kosher salt, peppercorns, granulated garlic, granulated onion, fennel seeds, mustard seeds, coriander seeds, dill seeds and hot pepper flakes. Grind until coarsely ground. (This step can be done ahead. Store spice in an airtight container.)

To make the tomato chutney: Using a paring knife, score an X in the base of each tomato. Add to a pot of boiling water for 1 minute. Transfer to a bowl of ice water. Remove skin with paring knife. Seed tomatoes and coarsely chop.

In a large, heavy saucepan, combine apples, onions, garlic, ginger, lime zest, lime juice, sugar, cinnamon, salt, white pepper and vinegar. Bring to a gentle boil. Reduce heat to low and simmer, stirring often, until chutney is thick and has a jam-like consistency, 45 minutes to 1 hour. (This step can be done ahead. Transfer chutney to jars. Store in fridge and use within 2 weeks.)

To make the burgers: In a large bowl, combine ground beef with steak spice to taste. Mix with your hands. Divide mixture into 4 equal balls and shape into burger patties. Let stand in fridge for 10 to 15 minutes.

Preheat grill to high. Oil grill.

Brush burgers with oil and add to grill. Cook, turning once, until meat is no longer pink, 5 to 7 minutes per side, depending on thickness of burgers. Top burgers with cheese in the last few minutes of cooking to melt the cheese.

Serve burgers in buns, garnished with lettuce, bacon, onion and tomato chutney.

TIP Change the flavour combination in the burgers—make them with a mix of beef, pork and/or veal. For a chutney that is more tart, reduce the sugar to 1/3 cup (75 mL).

Oven-Baked Pork "Fried" Rice

If you like to order fried rice at a Chinese restaurant, you'll want to give this healthier baked version a try. This dish has a bit of everything, taking rice from being a side dish to the main act on the table. The tasty ground pork and shiitake mushrooms make this a one-dish wonder you'll want to make all the time!

MAKES 4 SERVINGS

2 cups (500 mL) jasmine rice

2 celery stalks, diced

1 sweet red pepper, diced

1 cup (250 mL) packed sliced
    shiitake mushroom caps

¼ to ½ lb (115 to 225 g) lean ground pork

2 tbsp (30 mL) hoisin sauce, or to taste

1 tbsp (15 mL) soy sauce, or to taste

1 tbsp (15 mL) sherry vinegar or
    rice wine vinegar

1 tbsp (15 mL) sesame oil

3 cups (750 mL) boiling water

GARNISHES

4 green onions, sliced on the diagonal

2 cups (500 mL) bean sprouts

1 cup (250 mL) diced pineapple

Sesame seeds

Soy sauce

TIP If you don't have pineapple or it's too sweet for your taste, replace it with water chestnuts. As a lighter alternative, you can make this dish with ground chicken or turkey.

Preheat oven to 350°F (180°C).

In a 2-quart (2 L) baking dish, combine rice, celery, red pepper, shiitake mushrooms, ground pork, hoisin sauce, soy sauce, vinegar and sesame oil. Stir to combine. Add boiling water. Cover tightly with foil or lid. Bake until rice is tender and meat is cooked, 45 minutes to 1 hour. Let rest, covered, for 5 to 10 minutes.

Fluff rice with a fork and stir to mix. Serve with desired garnishes.

Fennel Pork Chops

Fennel seeds and garlic add outstanding flavour to these grilled pork chops. They're easy to prepare, cook up quickly and can be a lifesaver when you have last-minute dinner guests. **MAKES 4 SERVINGS**

4 thick-cut bone-in pork chops

Salt and freshly ground pepper

2 tbsp (30 mL) fennel seeds, crushed

2 garlic cloves, finely chopped

About ¼ cup (60 mL) olive oil

Preheat grill to medium-high.

Season pork chops with salt and pepper and evenly coat with fennel seeds and garlic. Drizzle chops with olive oil.

Add pork chops to grill. Cover and grill chops for 4 to 5 minutes. Flip and cook until just a hint of pink remains in centre, another 4 to 5 minutes, depending on thickness of chops.

Sweet-and-Sour Pineapple Pork

This Chinese favourite can be made faster than your takeout is delivered. Who can resist all that crispy stir-fried pork tenderloin and the pineapple chunks, slathered in the sticky sweet-and-sour sauce? I sure can't! MAKES 4 SERVINGS

PINEAPPLE PORK

1 large egg, beaten

½ cup (125 mL) all-purpose flour

⅓ cup (75 mL) pineapple juice

½ tsp (2 mL) salt

Peanut oil or vegetable oil, for frying

1 small pork tenderloin (¾ to 1 lb/340 to 450 g), cut in large cubes

SWEET-AND-SOUR SAUCE

1 cup (250 mL) pineapple juice

¼ cup (60 mL) brown sugar

¼ cup (60 mL) white vinegar

¼ cup (60 mL) tomato purée (passata)

2 tbsp (30 mL) cornstarch

1 tbsp (15 mL) molasses

TO ASSEMBLE

1 tbsp (15 mL) peanut oil

1 small onion, cubed

½ sweet red pepper, cubed

½ sweet green pepper, cubed

1½ cups (375 mL) fresh pineapple cubes

1 to 2 tbsp (15 to 30 mL) sesame seeds, for garnish

3 green onions, chopped, for garnish

To make the coating for the pineapple pork: Combine egg, flour, pineapple juice and salt in a bowl. Whisk to blend. Set aside.

Pour enough oil into a deep saucepan or wok to come about 1½ inches (4 cm) up the sides of the pan. Heat oil to 350°F (180°C) over medium heat.

Toss pork in coating. Working in batches to avoid crowding the pan if needed, add pork to hot oil. Fry pork, turning once, until coating is golden and meat is just cooked through, about 3 minutes. Drain on paper towels. Drain wok, if using.

To make the sweet-and-sour sauce: In a medium bowl, combine pineapple juice, brown sugar, vinegar, tomato purée, cornstarch and molasses. Whisk to blend.

Heat 1 tbsp (15 mL) peanut oil in wok or a large skillet over medium-high heat. When oil is hot, add onions, red and green peppers and pineapple cubes; stir-fry for 2 to 3 minutes. Add sweet-and-sour sauce. Bring to a boil and cook until sauce starts to thicken, 1 to 2 minutes. Add pork and stir-fry until meat is heated through. Serve garnished with sesame seeds and green onions. Serve over steamed rice.

Double-Pork Cheeseburgers

This ain't no diet burger, guys. When you want to indulge a little, make a batch of these double-pork burgers. The ribbons of prosciutto give an extra layer of meaty flavour to the pork patties. Top them with slices of creamy Camembert and mayo—it's a burger that's worth the splurge! MAKES 4 SERVINGS

1 lb (450 g) ground pork

2 slices prosciutto, finely diced

½ small onion, finely chopped

4 sun-dried tomatoes packed in oil, finely chopped

2 tbsp (30 mL) freshly grated Parmesan cheese

2 tsp (10 mL) finely chopped fresh thyme

½ tsp (2 mL) dried oregano

1 large egg, lightly beaten

1 to 2 tbsp (15 to 30 mL) fresh or dry bread crumbs

Salt and freshly ground pepper

Oil, for brushing

8 slices Camembert cheese

4 burger buns

4 small handfuls of arugula

4 tsp (20 mL) mayonnaise

Tomato slices

Onion slices

TIP Try this burger with a mix of beef and pork for added flavour. Replace the prosciutto with regular ham. A nice aged Cheddar can stand in for the Camembert.

In a large bowl, combine pork, prosciutto, onions, sun-dried tomatoes, Parmesan, thyme, oregano, egg and 1 tbsp (15 mL) bread crumbs. Season with salt and pepper. Mix with your hands. If burger mixture is too moist to hold together, add remaining 1 tbsp (15 mL) bread crumbs. Cover and let mixture rest in the fridge for 2 to 4 hours. The burgers will be more flavourful and hold together better on the grill.

Divide mixture into 4 balls and shape into 4 patties. Cover and return to fridge for 30 more minutes.

Meanwhile, preheat grill to high. Oil grill.

Brush burger patties with oil and add to grill. Cook burgers, turning once, for 5 to 6 minutes per side. Turn off one side of the grill and finish cooking burgers over indirect heat, until meat is no longer pink in the centre, 4 to 5 minutes. Top burgers with Camembert cheese in the last few minutes of cooking to melt the cheese.

Sandwich burgers in buns and top with arugula, mayo, tomato and onion.

Stefano's Pork Souvlaki

This family-friendly dinner brings the popular Greek takeout dish to your table. Just marinate your pork before you go to work, and when you get back home, grill it up. Serve it with some warm pita bread and some fresh tzatziki and everyone will say "Opa!" *MAKES 4 SERVINGS*

¼ cup (60 mL) olive oil

Grated zest and juice of ½ lemon

2 large garlic cloves, chopped

2 tsp (10 mL) dried oregano

2 small pork tenderloins (about ¾ lb/340 g each)

Salt and freshly ground pepper

4 Greek-style pitas

Tzatziki, for serving

To make the marinade: In a large bowl, combine olive oil, lemon zest, lemon juice, garlic and oregano. Whisk to combine.

Cut pork into 1½-inch (4 cm) cubes. Add to marinade. Cover and let marinate in the fridge for 1 to 2 hours.

Preheat the grill to medium-high.

Thread pork cubes evenly on 4 large metal skewers. Season pork with salt and pepper. Add souvlaki to grill. Cook, turning once, until pork is just cooked through, with just a hint of pink in the centre, 5 to 6 minutes per side. Serve with pita bread and tzatziki.

TIP Obviously, I made my pork souvlaki with pork, but you can use chicken, turkey, lamb or veal.

Saucy Garlic BBQ Ribs

BBQ ribs are always a favourite, so I'm sharing one of my very best rib recipes with you. They're coated in a rich Italian-inspired BBQ sauce—you won't want to waste a drop! **MAKES 4 SERVINGS**

RUB

¼ cup (60 mL) olive oil

4 garlic cloves, chopped

2 tbsp (30 mL) hot pepper flakes

2 tbsp (30 mL) chopped fresh sage

2 tbsp (30 mL) chopped fresh rosemary

1 tsp (5 mL) salt

1 tsp (5 mL) freshly cracked black pepper

3 lb (1.35 kg) spareribs

BBQ SAUCE

¼ cup (60 mL) olive oil

4 garlic cloves, chopped

2 cups (500 mL) tomato sauce

1 tbsp (15 mL) Worcestershire sauce

1 tsp (5 mL) hot pepper sauce

Salt and freshly ground pepper

To marinate the ribs: Stir together olive oil, garlic, hot pepper flakes, sage, rosemary, salt and pepper. Spread rub mixture evenly over both sides of ribs. Cover with plastic wrap and marinate in the fridge for at least 2 hours or up to 24 hours.

To make the BBQ sauce: Heat olive oil in a heavy, medium saucepan pan over medium-low heat. Gently cook garlic, stirring occasionally, until soft, 3 to 5 minutes. Add tomato sauce, Worcestershire sauce and hot pepper sauce. Season with salt and pepper. Bring to a boil, then reduce heat to a simmer. Cook sauce, stirring frequently, until reduced to a dry, thick paste and no liquid remains, about 30 minutes.

Meanwhile, preheat oven to 325°F (160°C). Line a baking sheet with a double layer of foil with enough overhang to wrap foil around the ribs.

Lay ribs bone side down on the foil-lined baking sheet. Spoon sauce evenly over ribs. Wrap foil around ribs and seal. Bake until ribs are tender when poked with a knife, about 2 hours. Remove ribs from sauce, shaking off excess sauce and reserving sauce for basting. (This step can be done the day before. Reserve ribs and sauce separately, covered and refrigerated.)

Preheat grill to medium.

Grill ribs, turning and basting with sauce every 5 minutes, until browned and heated through, about 20 minutes total.

Hearty Cassoulet

This famous French stew, made with a variety of meats, hearty root vegetables and beans, is ideal for warming your belly on a cold day. This is truly one of the great recipes for entertaining—it may take a little time to prepare, but trust me, it is well worth the effort. **MAKES 8 TO 10 SERVINGS**

CASSOULET

6 cups (1.5 L) navy beans

5 garlic cloves

2 onions

4 bay leaves

3 sprigs thyme

5 cloves

12 peppercorns

About 8 cups (2 L) chicken stock or water

4 carrots, cut in thirds

2 celery stalks

1 small ham hock

4 oz (115 g) thick-cut bacon,
    cut in 1 ½-inch (4 cm) strips

4 duck legs

1 tbsp (15 mL) chopped fresh thyme

4 pork sausages, cut in half or quarters

1 cup (250 mL) white wine

BREAD CRUMB TOPPING

1 ½ cups (375 mL) fresh bread crumbs

¼ cup (60 mL) olive oil

2 tbsp (30 mL) chopped fresh parsley

1 tbsp (15 mL) chopped fresh thyme

Salt and freshly ground pepper

Soak beans in enough water to cover overnight.

Chop 4 of the garlic cloves; set aside. Peel remaining garlic clove, leaving whole; set aside. Chop 1 onion; set aside. Peel remaining onion, leaving whole; set aside.

Make a bouquet garni: Wrap bay leaves, thyme, cloves and peppercorns in cheesecloth and tie with kitchen string.

Drain and rinse beans. Transfer to a large saucepan. Add enough chicken stock to cover beans. Add bouquet garni, reserved whole onion, carrots, celery and ham hock. Bring to a boil, reduce heat and simmer until beans are just tender, 45 minutes to 1 hour.

Remove ham hock and shred or chop the meat. Set aside.

Drain beans, reserving beans, bean liquid and carrots separately. Set aside. Discard onions and celery.

In a large skillet over medium-low heat, cook bacon until lightly golden, 5 to 8 minutes. Drain on paper towels. Set aside.

Remove all but 2 tbsp (30 mL) of the bacon fat from pan. Increase heat to medium. Add duck legs and cook until browned on all sides, about 10 minutes. Remove from pan and set aside. Pour all but 1 tbsp (15 mL) of the duck fat into a small bowl. Set aside.

Add reserved chopped onions and garlic to skillet and cook, stirring frequently, until vegetables are soft, 3 to 5 minutes. Remove from pan and set aside.

Preheat oven to 325°F (160°C).

Rub the inside of a large Dutch oven or deep casserole dish with reserved whole clove of garlic. Leave garlic clove in the pot.

Add reserved duck fat to the pot. Start layering the ingredients in the pot. It doesn't have to be perfect or pretty as long as you get everything in the pot. Layer about one-sixth of the beans, shredded ham hock, more beans, whole duck legs, beans, onions, carrots, thyme, beans, bacon, beans, sausages and a final layer of beans. Pour in white wine and enough reserved bean liquid to just cover the beans. Cover and bake until all the meat is cooked and the duck is tender, 2 to 2 ½ hours.

Meanwhile, make the bread crumb topping: In a small bowl, combine bread crumbs, olive oil, parsley, thyme, and salt and pepper to taste.

Preheat broiler.

Sprinkle bread crumb topping over cassoulet. Broil until golden, 3 to 4 minutes. If desired, serve with Frisée, Fennel and Apple Salad (page 133) and, for dessert, French Lemon Tart (page 347).

(photo on next page)

TIP This is a perfect dish for a special meal because you can assemble it the night before and cook it right before your guests arrive. For an extra-smoky flavour, use double-smoked bacon—it's already a decadent dish, so why not? Use confit duck legs for a more traditional cassoulet.

Family-Style Calzone

The bigger, the better! If your family likes to make pizza, you'll love this fun, giant-size take on a calzone, or pizza turnover. It's a half-moon-shaped envelope of soft dough stuffed with tasty sauce, cheese and meat. The kids will definitely want to help make this one! MAKES 4 SERVINGS

1 cup (250 mL) tomato sauce

6 to 8 slices ham, chopped

1 small sweet red pepper, sliced and sautéed (or 1 roasted red pepper)

1 cup (250 mL) sautéed sliced mushrooms

About 2 cups (500 mL) shredded mozzarella cheese

12 oz (340 g) whole wheat pizza dough

Olive oil, for brushing

Preheat oven to 425°F (220°C). Oil a pizza pan or baking sheet.

To make the filling: In a medium bowl, combine tomato sauce, ham, red pepper, mushrooms and mozzarella. Stir to mix. Set aside.

Sprinkle work surface with a little flour. Roll out dough into a rough 12-inch (30 cm) circle about ½ inch (1 cm) thick.

Transfer dough to oiled pizza pan. Spoon filling onto one side of dough, leaving a 1-inch (2.5 cm) border. Fold other half over filling. Seal edges by crimping the dough with your fingertips. Roll edges up to further seal the dough. Cut a few steam vents in the top of the calzone with a paring knife. Brush with oil.

Bake until calzone is golden brown and sounds hollow when you tap the bottom, 25 to 30 minutes. Let cool for 5 minutes. Slice and serve.

Classic Margherita Pizza

Guys, you don't get any more classic than this simple, delicious Neapolitan-style thin-crust pizza. Originally a pizza made for a queen, celebrating the colours of the Italian flag, this tomato, mozzarella and basil pizza shows that you don't need many ingredients to make magic in the kitchen! **MAKES TWO 10-INCH (25 CM) PIZZAS**

PIZZA DOUGH

2 ¾ to 3 cups (675 to 750 mL) all-purpose flour

1 tbsp (15 mL) salt

1 cup (250 mL) warm water

1 tbsp (15 mL) sugar

1 package (2 ¼ tsp/8 g) active dry yeast

TO ASSEMBLE

Handful of cornmeal

⅔ cup (150 mL) tomato purée (passata) or tomato sauce

2 balls (3 ½ oz/100 g each) buffalo mozzarella, sliced

Leaves from 1 small bunch basil

Extra-virgin olive oil, for drizzling

Hot pepper oil, to finish (optional)

To make the pizza dough: In a large bowl, stir together 2 ¾ cups (675 mL) flour and salt. In a small bowl, stir sugar and yeast into warm water. Let sit until yeast starts to foam, 5 to 10 minutes.

Add yeast mixture to flour mixture. Stir or work with your hands until dough starts to form into a ball. On a lightly floured work surface, knead dough until smooth and elastic, 7 to 8 minutes, adding more flour if dough is sticky.

Transfer dough to an oiled bowl and cover with plastic wrap. Let rise in a warm place until it doubles in volume, 30 to 40 minutes.

Meanwhile, preheat oven to 450°F (230°C). Sprinkle cornmeal onto 2 pizza pans. (Alternatively, heat a pizza stone according to manufacturer's instructions. Sprinkle cornmeal on a pizza peel so the pizza will easily slide onto the hot stone.)

To assemble the pizzas: Punch down dough. Cut in half. On a lightly floured work surface, roll out each half into a 10-inch (25 cm) round. Transfer dough to pizza pans or pizza peel.

Top pizzas with tomato purée, mozzarella and basil. Drizzle with a little olive oil.

For best results, bake pizzas one at a time. Cook until crust is golden brown and crisp and cheese is bubbly, 10 to 15 minutes.

Finish with another drizzle of extra-virgin olive or hot pepper oil, if desired.

Quick Chicken Taco Salad

Deli roasted chicken, store-bought barbecue sauce and prepared coleslaw mix make this taco salad a quick dinner fix any night of the week. You'll love it because it's so easy to make, and the kids will love it because they can eat the bowl! **MAKES 4 SERVINGS**

TACO BOWLS

4 large flour tortillas

2 tbsp (30 mL) olive oil

PULLED-CHICKEN MIX

1 small deli roasted chicken

1 tbsp (15 mL) olive oil

1 garlic clove, chopped

1 to 1 ½ cups (250 to 375 mL)
   barbecue sauce

Sliced pickled jalapeño peppers

COLESLAW

1 bag (14 oz/398 g) shredded
   green cabbage (or ½ large green
   cabbage, shredded)

3 tbsp (45 mL) chopped fresh cilantro

Juice of 2 limes

Pinch of sugar

⅓ cup (75 mL) olive oil

Salt and freshly ground pepper

GARNISHES

½ cucumber, sliced or diced

1 tomato, diced

1 avocado, diced

½ red onion, sliced

3 tbsp (45 mL) chopped fresh
   cilantro or cilantro leaves

1 cup (250 mL) shredded
   Cheddar cheese

Sour cream

1 lime, cut in wedges

Preheat oven to 400°F (200°C).

To make the tortilla bowls: Lightly brush tortillas with oil. Nestle each tortilla between 2 ovenproof bowls. Bake until tortilla takes on bowl shape, about 15 minutes. For extra-crispy shells, remove from bowls and bake on oven rack until golden and crispy, another 5 minutes. Let cool.

To make the pulled-chicken mix: Remove chicken from bones and shred or chop meat. Set aside.

Heat a large skillet over medium heat. Add olive oil. When oil is hot, add garlic. Cook, stirring frequently, for 1 to 2 minutes. Add barbecue sauce, adjusting amount used depending on how saucy you like your pulled chicken. Bring to a

boil. Add chicken and pickled jalapeños to taste. Stir. Cover and cook until chicken is heated through, 8 to 10 minutes. Remove from heat.

To make the coleslaw: In a large bowl, combine cabbage, cilantro, lime juice, sugar and olive oil. Toss to mix. Season with salt and pepper; toss again.

To assemble salads: Divide coleslaw among taco bowls. Top with pulled-chicken mix. Serve with desired garnishes.

TIP Make this salad with leftover beef or pork tenderloin. Make miniature taco bowls for your backyard barbecue using small tortillas and smaller bowls to form the tacos. Just make sure you use heatproof bowls on the grill!

Everyday Skillet Chicken Biryani

This is a quick-and-easy take on the traditional Indian rice dish. This biryani is impressive enough to serve at a dinner party, but simple enough that you can make it any night of the week. It's a tasty new way to bring chicken to the table! **MAKES 4 TO 6 SERVINGS**

1 ½ cups (375 mL) basmati rice

1 tbsp (15 mL) vegetable oil

3 small boneless, skinless chicken breasts, cut in large cubes

Salt and freshly ground pepper

3 tbsp (45 mL) butter

1 large carrot, diced

1 large onion, thinly sliced

2 garlic cloves, chopped

1 fresh green chili, or to taste, chopped (optional)

1 tbsp (15 mL) chopped fresh ginger

1 to 2 tbsp (15 to 30 mL) garam masala

1 tbsp (15 mL) turmeric

¼ cup (60 mL) raisins

3 cups (750 mL) chicken stock

¼ cup (60 mL) chopped fresh cilantro

½ cup (125 mL) sliced almonds or cashews

2 tbsp (30 mL) chopped fresh mint

Plain yogurt, for serving (optional)

1 lime, cut in wedges, for serving (optional)

TIP If you don't have turmeric, use some saffron and a little cumin.

Soak basmati rice in water for 30 minutes. Drain. (If you are pressed for time, you can omit this step.)

Heat oil in a large saucepan or skillet over medium to medium-high heat. Add chicken. Season with salt and pepper. Cook, stirring occasionally, until chicken starts to brown on all sides, 5 to 6 minutes. Remove chicken from pan and set side.

Add butter, carrots, onions, garlic, chili, ginger and garam masala to pan. Cook, stirring frequently, until onions are golden and spices are fragrant, 5 to 10 minutes.

Add rice and turmeric to pan. Stir, and let rice toast for 1 to 2 minutes. Stir in raisins, stock and chicken with any juices. Bring to a boil. Reduce heat to low, cover and cook until liquid has evaporated and rice is tender, 18 to 20 minutes. Remove from heat and let rest, covered, 5 to 10 minutes. Fluff rice with a fork.

Garnish biryani with cilantro, almonds and mint. Serve with yogurt and lime wedges, if desired. (Alternatively, to serve biryani more formally, mould in buttered serving bowls. Invert onto serving plates and then garnish.)

Portuguese Grilled Chicken

Fire up the grill and make a big platter of this tasty classic Portuguese-inspired chicken. Once you have a bite of this slightly spicy flame-broiled chicken, you'll understand why it's one of the world's most popular chicken dishes. Serve it with some spicy piri-piri dipping sauce for added kick. **MAKES 4 SERVINGS**

DIPPING SAUCE

3 tbsp (45 mL) olive oil

1 small onion, finely chopped

2 garlic cloves, finely chopped

2 fresh red finger chilies, or to taste, finely chopped

¾ cup (175 mL) tomato purée (passata)

¼ cup (60 mL) white vinegar

¼ cup (60 mL) sugar

Salt and freshly ground pepper

Piri-piri sauce, to taste

GRILLED CHICKEN

2 garlic cloves, minced

1 cup (250 mL) dry white wine

3 tbsp (45 mL) extra-virgin olive oil

1 tbsp (15 mL) dried oregano

1 tbsp (15 mL) chopped fresh Italian parsley

1 tbsp (15 mL) chopped fresh rosemary

1 tsp (5 mL) piri-piri sauce, sambal oelek or Louisiana-style hot pepper sauce

1 tsp (5 mL) salt

1 tsp (5 mL) freshly ground pepper

1 chicken (3 to 4 lb/1.35 to 1.8 kg), cut in 10 pieces

To make the dipping sauce: Heat oil in a small saucepan over medium heat. Add onions, garlic and chilies. Cook, stirring frequently, until onions start to soften, 3 to 5 minutes.

Add tomato purée, vinegar, sugar, and salt and pepper to taste. Bring to a boil. Reduce heat and simmer until slightly thickened, 15 to 20 minutes. If desired, purée until smooth. Add piri-piri sauce. Set aside.

To marinate the chicken: In a large bowl, combine garlic, wine, olive oil, oregano, parsley, rosemary, piri-piri sauce, salt and pepper. Mix well. Add chicken pieces and toss to coat well. Cover or transfer to a large resealable bag. Marinate chicken in the fridge for at least 2 hours or up to 24 hours.

Preheat grill to high.

Remove chicken from marinade (discard marinade). Add chicken to grill. Reduce heat to medium. Grill chicken, turning frequently, until juices run clear and meat is no longer pink inside, 25 to 35 minutes, depending on thickness of chicken. Serve with dipping sauce.

Chicken Scaloppine with Lemon and Capers

If you haven't made scaloppine before, this is a great recipe to try. The chicken is flattened and lightly dredged in flour—that means it cooks up fast with a nice breaded exterior. The lemon and caper sauce really elevates the recipe and makes it versatile enough to serve when entertaining or on busy weeknights. **MAKES 2 SERVINGS**

2 boneless, skinless chicken breasts

Salt and freshly ground pepper

Flour, for dredging

¼ cup (60 mL) olive oil

Juice of 1 lemon

1 to 1 ¼ cups (250 to 300 mL) chicken stock

Leaves from 3 to 4 sprigs thyme, finely chopped

2 tbsp (30 mL) capers

1 tbsp (15 mL) unsalted butter

1 tbsp (15 mL) grated lemon zest

TIP Make this recipe with veal or turkey instead of chicken. You can also use vegetable stock in place of chicken stock.

Cut chicken breasts in half lengthwise. Lightly pound between sheets of plastic wrap to an even ½-inch (1 cm) thickness. Season with salt and pepper and dredge in flour, shaking off any excess flour.

In a large skillet, heat olive oil over high heat. When oil is hot, fry chicken until golden brown on each side, about 2 minutes per side. Deglaze pan with lemon juice and cook until almost all the juice has evaporated. Add chicken stock. Reduce heat to medium and cook chicken until just cooked through, 5 to 7 minutes. Transfer chicken to plates and cover with foil to keep warm.

Add chopped thyme and capers to pan. If pan looks dry, add a little more chicken stock. Gently whisk in butter. Pour sauce over chicken. Garnish with freshly grated lemon zest.

Brie-Stuffed Chicken with Cranberry Sauce

Whenever you need an easy but impressive main for your next fancy dinner party, make this Brie-and-prosciutto-stuffed chicken. Your guests will be wowed when they cut into the tender, juicy chicken and find the tasty surprise inside. Use the roasted cranberry sauce with turkey, too—you can enjoy the flavours of the holidays anytime! **MAKES 4 SERVINGS**

About 4 oz (115 g) Brie, cut in 4 slices

4 thin slices prosciutto

4 boneless, skin-on chicken breasts

Salt and freshly ground pepper

2 tbsp (30 mL) olive oil

2 tbsp (30 mL) butter

1 shallot, chopped

1 cup (250 mL) fresh or frozen cranberries

1 firm-ripe pear, such as Bosc or Anjou, peeled and chopped

Leaves from 1 sprig sage, coarsely chopped if large

¼ cup (60 mL) brandy or white wine

½ cup (125 mL) chicken stock

3 tbsp (45 mL) honey

2 tbsp (30 mL) chopped fresh parsley, for finishing

Preheat oven to 400°F (200°C).

Wrap each slice of Brie with a slice of prosciutto to create a little package, trimming prosciutto if needed. Set aside.

Using a paring knife, cut a lengthwise pocket for the Brie package in each chicken breast. Gently push a Brie package into each pocket and close the pocket with toothpicks. Season chicken with salt and pepper.

Heat a large ovenproof skillet over medium-high heat. Add olive oil and butter. When butter has melted and oil is hot, add stuffed chicken breasts, skin side down. Cook until chicken starts to brown, 2 to 3 minutes. Flip chicken and add shallot, cranberries, pear and sage.

Transfer to oven. Bake until chicken is cooked through, 10 to 12 minutes, depending on thickness of chicken breast. Transfer chicken to a cutting board and cover with foil to keep warm.

Heat skillet over medium heat. (Remember, the handle will be hot!) Add brandy, chicken stock and honey. Cook, stirring occasionally, until sauce is slightly syrupy, 3 to 5 minutes.

Remove toothpicks from chicken. Slice chicken and transfer to plates. Spoon pan sauce over or around chicken. Garnish with chopped parsley. Serve with steamed asparagus, if desired.

TIP The Brie in this recipe can be replaced with Camembert, and the prosciutto with ham.

Lemon Yogurt Chicken Kabobs

Here's a great recipe for your next barbecue—a tasty, tangy chicken dish that the whole family will love. Each kabob has the perfect combination of tender meat, veggies and fruit, and the amazing yogurt and lemon mixture does double duty as both a marinade for the chicken and a dip for your skewers. **MAKES 4 SERVINGS**

YOGURT MARINADE AND DIP

2 cups (500 mL) plain yogurt

2 garlic cloves, finely chopped

Grated zest of 1 lemon

2 tbsp (30 mL) lemon juice

¼ cup (60 mL) chopped fresh cilantro

2 tbsp (30 mL) olive oil

2 tsp (10 mL) ground cumin

2 tsp (10 mL) ground coriander

2 tsp (10 mL) paprika

1 tsp (5 mL) hot pepper flakes, or to taste

Salt and freshly ground pepper

Extra-virgin olive oil, for drizzling

KABOBS

8 boneless, skinless chicken thighs, cut in 1½-inch (4 cm) cubes

16 cherry tomatoes

1 red onion, cut in 1½-inch (4 cm) cubes

1 large sweet red pepper, cut in 1½-inch (4 cm) cubes

1 large sweet green pepper, cut in 1½-inch (4 cm) cubes

¼ pineapple, peeled and cut in 1½-inch (4 cm) cubes

To make the yogurt marinade and dip: In a large bowl, combine yogurt, garlic, lemon zest, lemon juice, cilantro, olive oil, cumin, coriander, paprika, hot pepper flakes, and salt and pepper to taste. Stir until well mixed. Set aside 1 cup (250 mL) yogurt mixture for serving as a dip.

To make the kabobs: Add chicken to remaining yogurt marinade and toss to coat. Cover and let marinate in the fridge for 4 to 8 hours.

Preheat grill to medium-high. Oil grill. (Alternatively, use a grill pan to cook kabobs.)

Thread chicken onto 8 large metal skewers, alternating with cherry tomatoes, red onion, red and green pepper, and pineapple.

Add skewers to grill. Cook, turning once, until chicken is cooked all the way through but still juicy, 10 to 15 minutes.

Drizzle reserved yogurt dip generously with olive oil. Serve kabobs with yogurt dip and steamed rice, if desired.

Thai Chicken Stir-Fry

This Thai chicken stir-fry is quick to make and tastes better than takeout! It's a recipe that shows you what the "four S's" of Thai food are all about—the perfect balance of sweet, sour, salty and spicy flavours. It's a quick and tasty dinner the whole family will enjoy. **MAKES 4 SERVINGS**

½ package (14 oz/400 g) rice noodles, preferably medium-sized flat noodles

⅓ cup (75 mL) water

2 tbsp (30 mL) soy sauce

2 tbsp (30 mL) oyster sauce

2 tbsp (30 mL) fresh lime juice

1 tbsp (15 mL) sugar

3 tbsp (45 mL) canola oil

2 boneless, skinless chicken breasts, cubed

2 garlic cloves, crushed

1 tbsp (15 mL) chopped fresh ginger

1 whole fresh Thai bird's eye chili, or to taste

⅔ cup (150 mL) shiitake mushroom caps, sliced

½ sweet red pepper, diced

4 cobs fresh or canned baby corn, cut in half crosswise

Handful of snow peas, trimmed

2 green onions, cut in 1-inch (2.5 cm) pieces

4 baby bok choy, cut in quarters

4 to 6 Thai basil leaves, chopped, for garnish

¼ cup (60 mL) chopped raw cashews, for garnish

Pour boiling water over rice noodles in a bowl and soak for 20 minutes. Drain and set aside.

To make the stir-fry sauce: In a small bowl, combine water, soy sauce, oyster sauce, lime juice and sugar. Stir well to dissolve sugar. Set aside.

In a large wok or skillet, heat canola oil over medium-high heat. When oil is hot, add chicken, garlic, ginger and Thai chili. Stir-fry until chicken is golden brown, 1 to 2 minutes.

Increase heat to high and add mushrooms, red pepper, baby corn, snow peas and green onions. Stir-fry for 2 to 3 minutes. Add bok choy and stir-fry for 1 minute more.

Stir in reserved sauce. When sauce comes to a boil, add reserved noodles. Add 1 to 2 tbsp (15 to 30 mL) water if sauce looks too thick or wok looks dry. Continue to stir-fry until bok choy is just tender and noodles are heated through, 2 to 3 minutes. Remove chili before serving. Garnish with Thai basil and cashews. Serve immediately.

TIP Use sliced flank steak instead of chicken. If snow peas aren't available, replace with sweet peas or edamame.

Oven-Roasted Beer Can Chicken

You may have seen beer can chicken made on the barbecue, but this easy oven-roasted version can be made indoors any time of year. The beer makes the chicken incredibly moist, tender and flavourful. Just be sure to set aside a beer for the cook to enjoy! MAKES 4 TO 6 SERVINGS

2 tsp (10 mL) dried thyme

2 tsp (10 mL) smoked paprika

1 tsp (5 mL) garlic powder

1 tsp (5 mL) dry mustard

1 tsp (5 mL) onion powder

1 tsp (5 mL) ground celery seeds

Pinch of cayenne pepper (optional)

Salt and freshly ground pepper

1 chicken (2 ½ to 3 lb/1.125 to 1.35 kg)

2 tbsp (30 mL) olive oil

1 can amber ale

1 large red onion, cut in quarters

2 heads garlic, cut in half horizontally

TIP To make a pan sauce to serve with the chicken: Pour beer remaining in can into pan juices in roasting pan. Cook over medium heat, stirring to incorporate pan juices into the sauce, 5 to 10 minutes.

Preheat oven to 425°F (220°C).

To make the spice rub: In a small bowl, combine thyme, paprika, garlic powder, dry mustard, onion powder, celery seeds, cayenne (if desired), and salt and pepper to taste. Stir well.

Pat chicken dry with paper towels. Rub spices all over chicken and inside cavity. Rub olive oil over chicken.

Open can of beer and pour out about a quarter of it. (Removing some of the beer means the liquid will heat faster and therefore create more steam as the chicken roasts.) Slide chicken over beer can. Transfer to a roasting pan, making sure the legs are in front of the can to support the chicken. Tuck wings behind back. Add onion and garlic to pan.

Roast chicken until juices run clear and meat is no longer pink, about 1 hour, depending on size of chicken. Tent chicken loosely with foil and let rest in roasting pan for 15 to 20 minutes.

Carefully remove chicken from beer can (can will still be hot). Carve chicken and serve with roasted onions and pan juices. Serve with boiled or grilled corn on the cob, if desired.

Roast Chicken with Herbs

It is possible to roast a whole chicken in less than an hour. When we made this spatchcocked, or flattened, chicken on *In the Kitchen*, our studio audience was amazed at how quickly it cooked and how delicious it was. Everyone left the show excited about having their new go-to roast chicken recipe—I hope you're excited, too! MAKES 4 TO 6 SERVINGS

6 garlic cloves, peeled

¼ cup (60 mL) chopped fresh Italian parsley

2 tbsp (30 mL) chopped fresh rosemary

2 tbsp (30 mL) chopped fresh thyme

1 tbsp (15 mL) hot pepper flakes, or to taste

Grated zest of 1 lemon

⅓ cup (75 mL) extra-virgin olive oil, plus more for brushing

1 chicken (3 to 3 ½ lb/1.35 to 1.5 kg)

Salt and freshly ground pepper

1 small onion, chopped

1 carrot, chopped

1 celery stalk, chopped

1 cup (250 mL) chicken stock

2 tbsp (30 mL) butter

Preheat oven to 425°F (220°C).

In a mini food processor, combine garlic, parsley, rosemary, thyme, hot pepper flakes, lemon zest and olive oil. Pulse mixture to a smooth paste. (Alternatively, use a mortar and pestle.)

To spatchcock the chicken, place chicken breast side down on a cutting board. Using kitchen shears, cut along each side of the backbone. Discard backbone. Turn chicken breast side up. Press firmly on breastbone to flatten the chicken. Tuck wings behind back.

Gently slide your fingers under the skin of each breast, separating skin from flesh and being careful not to tear the skin. Insert the herb paste evenly under the skin. Rub chicken with a little olive oil. Season with salt and pepper.

Scatter onion, carrot and celery in a roasting pan. Place spatchcocked chicken breast side up on the bed of vegetables. Roast chicken until skin is golden and crisp, juices run clear and meat is no longer pink, 45 minutes to 1 hour, depending on size of chicken.

Transfer chicken to a cutting board and let rest 15 minutes before carving.

Meanwhile, add chicken stock to vegetables in roasting pan. Over medium-high heat, bring stock to a boil. Let pan juices reduce until slightly syrupy. Remove vegetables and serve with chicken, if desired. Remove roasting pan from heat and whisk in butter to thicken pan juices. Serve pan sauce with chicken.

TIP A delicious roast chicken starts with a good-quality bird. Buy the best quality chicken possible, organic free-range if you can. Add different root vegetables into the mix, such as sweet potato or celeriac (celery root).

Asian Chicken Salad Cups

If you're looking to eat a bit lighter, try this carb-free main. These delicious little cups may be lower in fat, but that doesn't mean they hold back in the flavour department. It's fun to use the iceberg lettuce leaves as an edible bowl—a great way to add some crunch and texture to a low-fat main. **MAKES 4 SERVINGS**

CHICKEN FILLING

1 tbsp (15 mL) vegetable oil

1 lb (450 g) ground chicken

Salt and freshly ground pepper

Handful of shiitake mushrooms, woody stems removed, sliced

Handful of cremini or button mushrooms, sliced

2 garlic cloves, chopped

1 tbsp (15 mL) chopped fresh ginger

1 to 2 tsp (10 mL) curry powder, or to taste

Handful of canned water chestnuts, diced

2 tbsp (30 mL) rice wine vinegar

2 tbsp (30 mL) oyster sauce

1 tbsp (15 mL) sesame oil

Soy sauce

1 tbsp (15 mL) chopped fresh cilantro

TO ASSEMBLE

1 head iceberg lettuce, leaves separated

Sweet chili sauce

GARNISHES

⅓ cup (75 mL) chopped toasted unsalted peanuts

2 green onions, sliced

4 radishes, thinly sliced

1 carrot, julienned

1 cucumber, julienned

1 to 2 fresh red chilies, sliced

To make the chicken filling: Heat a large skillet over medium-high heat. Add oil. When oil is hot, add ground chicken. Season with salt and pepper. Cook, stirring occasionally, until meat starts to brown, about 5 minutes. Add mushrooms, garlic, ginger and curry powder. Cook, stirring frequently, until mushrooms are golden brown. Add water chestnuts, rice wine vinegar, oyster sauce, sesame oil and soy sauce to taste. Cook until chicken is cooked through and mixture is dry, about 5 minutes. Remove from heat and stir in cilantro.

To assemble the salad cups: Spoon chicken filling onto large lettuce leaves. Drizzle with sweet chili sauce to taste. Garnish as desired.

Stefano's Buttermilk Fried Chicken

One of my guilty pleasures is definitely fried chicken. There is nothing better than a big basket of juicy southern-inspired chicken covered in a crispy coating. In this recipe, the extra-crispy skin comes from dredging the pieces in flour twice. This is one time that I'll encourage you to double-dip! **MAKES 4 TO 6 SERVINGS**

3 cups (750 mL) buttermilk

1 tbsp (15 mL) Worcestershire sauce

Hot pepper sauce

1 chicken, cut in 8 or 10 pieces

2 ¼ cups (550 mL) flour

Pinch of cayenne, or to taste

Salt and freshly ground pepper

Peanut oil or vegetable oil, for frying

In a large bowl, combine buttermilk, Worcestershire sauce and a few dashes of hot sauce to taste. Stir. Add chicken to buttermilk. Turn to coat. Cover and let marinate in the fridge for at least 6 hours or overnight.

Combine flour, cayenne, and salt and pepper to taste. Remove chicken pieces from marinade (reserving marinade) and dredge in flour mixture, coating well. Dip chicken back into marinade and then dredge once again in flour. Shake off any excess flour. Discard marinade.

Pour enough oil into a large cast-iron skillet to come 1 to 2 inches (2.5 to 5 cm) up the side of the pan. Heat oil over medium heat. When oil is hot, add chicken. Fry chicken until juices run clear and meat is no longer pink, turning once and reducing heat to medium-low if chicken is browning too fast. Depending on thickness of chicken pieces, total cooking time will be 20 to 30 minutes. Drain chicken on a rack or on paper towels. Serve hot or cold.

Alternatively, preheat oven to 350°F (180°C). Fry chicken until golden brown, 7 to 8 minutes per side, then transfer to oven and bake until juices run clear and meat is no longer pink, 10 to 15 minutes.

TIP The best way to test your oil's temperature is with a deep-fry thermometer.

Chicken Burritos

This classic Mexican main is an awesome way to use up leftover chicken. Kids and adults always love the big flavours and textures in each tasty tortilla—and who doesn't get excited when they can dress it up however they like? Be sure to have lots of sour cream, salsa and guacamole ready to serve with them.

MAKES 8 SERVINGS

CHICKEN BURRITO FILLING

1 tbsp (15 mL) olive oil

½ cup (125 mL) chopped onion

1 garlic clove, minced

1 to 2 tbsp (15 to 30 mL) chili powder

1 tsp (5 mL) ground cumin

1 cup (250 mL) canned or cooked red kidney beans, drained and rinsed if canned

3 large ripe tomatoes, cored and coarsely chopped

¼ cup (60 mL) water

About 1 cup (250 mL) shredded cooked chicken

2 tbsp (30 mL) chopped fresh cilantro

TO ASSEMBLE

8 small flour tortillas

Shredded Cheddar cheese

GARNISHES

Guacamole (page 51), shredded lettuce, sour cream, tomato salsa

TIP If you want to skip the baking step, warm tortillas and spoon about ⅓ cup (75 mL) chicken mixture onto the centre of each tortilla. Top with cheese, lettuce and sour cream. Roll up tortillas and serve with salsa and guacamole.

To make the burrito filling: In a medium saucepan, heat olive oil over medium-high heat. When oil is hot, add onions and garlic. Cook, stirring frequently, until onions are softened, 3 to 4 minutes. Stir in chili powder and cumin. Continue to cook, stirring, until fragrant, about 1 minute.

Add kidney beans, tomatoes and water. Bring to a boil. Reduce heat to medium-low and simmer, until mixture is thickened, about 20 minutes.

Stir in shredded chicken. When chicken is heated through, stir in cilantro and remove from heat.

Preheat oven to 375°F (190°C). Oil a 13- × 9-inch (3 L) baking dish.

Arrange tortillas on work surface. Spoon ⅓ cup (75 mL) chicken mixture onto the centre of each tortilla. Sprinkle with a little Cheddar. Fold in sides, then fold in top and bottom to seal in filling. Place burritos seam side down in baking dish. Sprinkle with additional Cheddar. Bake until cheese melts and is lightly golden brown, 5 to 10 minutes. Serve with desired garnishes.

Stefano's Jerk Chicken

I've always loved the spicy, complex flavours in jerk chicken. There's something about the combination of spicy peppers, warm spices and tender chicken that takes me to the islands with the first bite. Here's my version of this classic dish—save the cost of a plane ticket to Jamaica and make a big batch!

MAKES 4 TO 6 SERVINGS

1 chicken, cut in 8 pieces

JERK MARINADE
1 Scotch bonnet or jalapeño pepper
8 green onions, coarsely chopped
4 garlic cloves, chopped
About ¼ cup (60 mL) chopped fresh thyme
2 tbsp (30 mL) chopped fresh ginger
2 tbsp (30 mL) brown sugar

2 tbsp (30 mL) ground allspice
2 tsp (10 mL) cinnamon
½ tsp (2 mL) nutmeg
½ tsp (2 mL) ground cloves
Juice of 6 limes
¼ cup (60 mL) vegetable oil
Salt and freshly ground pepper

To make the jerk marinade: In a food processor, combine Scotch bonnet pepper, green onions, garlic, thyme, ginger, brown sugar, allspice, cinnamon, nutmeg, cloves, lime juice, vegetable oil, and salt and pepper to taste. Pulse until smooth.

If making Mango Cabbage Slaw, set aside 1 to 2 tsp (5 to 10 mL) jerk marinade in fridge. Scrape remaining marinade into a large non-aluminum bowl or resealable plastic bag.

Cut a few incisions into each piece of chicken. Scoring the chicken allows the marinade to penetrate the meat. Add chicken to marinade and toss to coat. Cover and let marinate in the fridge for at least 4 hours or up to 24 hours, tossing chicken occasionally so it marinates evenly.

Preheat grill to medium-high. Oil grill.

Add chicken to grill. Cover and reduce heat to medium. Grill chicken, turning frequently, until juices run clear and meat is no longer pink, 25 to 35 minutes, depending on thickness of chicken. Serve jerk chicken with Island Rice and Peas (page 173) and Mango Cabbage Slaw (page 142), if desired, for a complete Caribbean feast.

Stefano's Chicken Parmigiana

Chicken parmigiana may not be an authentic Italian dish, but man, is it ever good. Lightly breaded pieces of juicy, tender chicken are topped with a fresh tomato sauce and melted cheese—nothing's wrong with that! Serve with Spaghetti with Tomato Sauce and Pancetta, or simply use some of the leftover sauce for the topping. MAKES 4 SERVINGS

1 cup (250 mL) all-purpose flour

2 eggs, beaten

1 ½ cups (375 mL) fresh or dry bread crumbs

1 to 1 ½ cups (250 to 375 mL) grated Parmesan cheese

1 tbsp (15 mL) chopped fresh parsley

1 garlic clove, minced

4 boneless, skinless chicken breasts

Salt and freshly ground pepper

2 tbsp (30 mL) butter

2 tbsp (30 mL) olive oil

Sauce from Spaghetti with Tomato Sauce and Pancetta (page 102)

1 cup (250 mL) shredded mozzarella cheese, for topping

TIP These chicken cutlets can easily be replaced with veal. Use whatever good melting cheese you prefer.

Preheat oven to 350°F (180°C). Line a baking sheet with parchment paper.

Prepare a breading station by arranging 3 shallow dishes or pie plates with the following: flour in the first; beaten eggs in the second; and bread crumbs, ½ to 1 cup (125 to 250 mL) Parmesan, parsley and garlic in the third.

Season chicken with salt and pepper. Dredge chicken first in flour, then in egg mixture and lastly in bread crumb mixture.

Heat a large skillet over medium heat. Add butter and oil. When butter has melted and oil is hot, add chicken and cook until golden brown on each side, 2 to 3 minutes per side.

Transfer chicken to baking sheet. Top each with a spoonful of tomato sauce, about ¼ cup (60 mL) shredded mozzarella and 2 tbsp (30 mL) grated Parmesan.

Bake until chicken is cooked through, 12 to 15 minutes, depending on thickness.

Chicken Cacciatore

If I had to pick my favourite chicken recipe, chicken cacciatore would be it. I can still remember my grandma preparing it for dinner—all that rich tomato sauce and the tender pieces of chicken. In my version, I've added loads of olives and roasted red peppers to the mix. But it's still cooked in one pot, making it perfect for doubling or even tripling when you need to feed a crowd. **MAKES 4 SERVINGS**

4 chicken drumsticks

4 chicken thighs

Salt and freshly ground pepper

3 tbsp (45 mL) extra-virgin olive oil

1 small onion, chopped

2 garlic cloves, chopped

Leaves from 1 sprig each sage, rosemary and thyme, chopped

Handful of pitted black olives

Handful of pitted green olives

1 to 2 tbsp (15 to 30 mL) tomato paste

¾ cup (175 mL) dry white or red wine

3 to 4 jarred roasted red peppers, sliced

1 can (28 oz/796 mL) diced tomatoes

1 cup (250 mL) chicken stock

2 tbsp (30 mL) chopped fresh Italian parsley, for garnish

Preheat oven to 350°F (180°C).

Season chicken drumsticks and thighs with salt and pepper. Heat a Dutch oven or large ovenproof skillet over medium heat. Add olive oil. When oil is hot, add chicken. Cook until chicken is browned on all sides, about 5 minutes per side.

Add onions, garlic and herbs. Cook, stirring frequently, until vegetables start to soften, 2 to 3 minutes. Stir in olives and cook for 1 to 2 minutes. Stir in tomato paste and cook for 1 to 2 minutes. Stir in wine and bring to a boil. Let reduce for 5 minutes. Add roasted peppers, tomatoes and chicken stock. Bring to a boil.

Cover and transfer to oven. Bake, stirring occasionally, until chicken is cooked through and sauce has thickened slightly, 35 to 40 minutes. Taste and adjust seasoning. Serve garnished with chopped parsley.

Stefano's Ultimate Pad Thai

If you love eating this classic dish in a Thai restaurant, you'll be happy to know it's easy to make at home. This recipe has the perfect combination of tofu, shrimp and chicken, served up with rice noodles and an irresistible sweet-and-tangy sauce. Garnish as you like with peanuts, bean sprouts and cilantro and dig in!

MAKES 4 SERVINGS

¾ package (14 oz/400 g) flat rice noodles, preferably ¼ inch (5 mm) wide

¼ cup (60 mL) ketchup

3 tbsp (45 mL) sugar

3 tbsp (45 mL) lime juice

3 tbsp (45 mL) fish sauce

½ cup (125 mL) vegetable oil

½ package (14 to 16 oz/400 to 450 g) extra-firm pressed tofu, diced (or about 1 cup/250 mL diced tofu)

2 small boneless, skinless chicken breasts, thinly sliced

Salt

20 small to medium shrimp, peeled, deveined, tails removed

2 shallots, finely chopped

2 Thai chilies, or to taste, finely chopped

1 heaping tbsp (18 mL) finely chopped fresh ginger

1 heaping tbsp (18 mL) finely chopped garlic

3 eggs, lightly beaten

¾ cup (175 mL) unsalted peanuts, toasted and coarsely chopped

3 green onions, sliced on the diagonal

2 handfuls of bean sprouts

Large handful of fresh cilantro, chopped

3 limes, cut into wedges

Pour boiling water over rice noodles in a bowl and soak for about 1 minute. Drain and set aside. (Alternatively, let soak in room-temperature water until pliable, about 1 hour. Or soak in cold water and store in fridge 1 day in advance.)

To make the sauce: In a small bowl, combine ketchup, sugar, lime juice, and fish sauce. Whisk to combine. Set aside.

Heat vegetable oil in a wok over medium heat. Fry tofu until golden, 1 to 2 minutes. Drain on paper towels. (This step can be done the day before.)

Remove 3 tbsp (45 mL) oil from wok. Increase heat to high. Add chicken and season with salt. Stir-fry for 1 to 2 minutes. Add shrimp and stir-fry until both chicken and shrimp are just cooked, about 2 minutes. Transfer to a plate.

Add shallots, chilies, ginger and garlic to wok; stir-fry until lightly golden, about 30 seconds. Add eggs; fry, stirring, for 1 minute.

Add reserved noodles and sauce; stir-fry for 1 to 2 minutes. Return chicken and shrimp to wok. Cook until heated through, 1 to 2 minutes.

Serve pad thai garnished with peanuts, green onions, bean sprouts, cilantro and lime wedges.

Tuna and White Bean Pasta Salad

If you're like me, you always have pasta, canned beans and canned tuna in your pantry. Here I've brought those three staples together as a base for this beautiful salad. Add a combination of colourful radicchio, licorice-flavoured fennel and some fruity olives and you have a healthy, hearty dinner in minutes.

MAKES 4 SERVINGS

½ lb (225 g) fusilli

1 small fennel bulb, thinly sliced crosswise

1 tbsp (15 mL) chopped fennel fronds

½ head radicchio, sliced

Handful of pitted green olives, sliced

1 cup (250 mL) canned white beans, drained and rinsed

½ red onion, sliced

⅓ cup (75 mL) white wine vinegar

½ cup (125 mL) extra-virgin olive oil

Salt and freshly ground pepper

2 cans (6 ½ oz/184 g each) tuna, preferably packed in olive oil, drained

2 handfuls of arugula

TIP Do your best to use a good-quality tuna in this salad. For the beans, use whatever kind you have on hand in your pantry. If you do not have beans, you can use chickpeas instead.

Bring a large pot of water to a boil. Generously salt. Add pasta and cook until al dente.

Drain pasta and run under cool water. Drain again and transfer to a large bowl.

Add fennel, fennel fronds, radicchio, green olives, white beans and red onion. Add vinegar and olive oil. Season with salt and pepper. Toss. Add tuna and arugula. Lightly toss. Serve.

Brown Rice, Salmon and Asparagus Salad

Who knew that healthy could be so filling and delicious? When I made this recipe on the show, it was an instant hit. The audience (and crew!) oohed and aahed as I drizzled the layers of earthy brown rice, fresh asparagus and tender salmon with my tangy citrus dressing. I can taste it now! **MAKES 4 SERVINGS**

DRESSING

1 shallot, chopped

1 garlic clove, minced

½ cup (125 mL) extra-virgin olive oil

¼ cup (60 mL) fresh orange juice

¼ cup (60 mL) balsamic vinegar

1 tbsp (15 mL) Dijon mustard

1 tbsp (15 mL) honey

Salt and freshly ground pepper

SALAD

1 cup (250 mL) brown and wild rice blend
   (or use all brown rice)

Salt and freshly ground pepper

2 cups (500 mL) frozen shelled edamame

12 spears asparagus (about 1 bunch),
   trimmed

4 skin-on salmon fillets (5 oz/140 g each)

1 tbsp (15 mL) extra-virgin olive oil

2 tbsp (30 mL) chopped fresh chives

Grated orange zest, for garnish

To make the dressing: In a small bowl, combine shallot, garlic, olive oil, orange juice, balsamic vinegar, mustard and honey. Whisk until emulsified. Season with salt and pepper. Adjust seasoning and acidity to taste. Set aside.

In a medium saucepan, cover rice with 2 cups (500 mL) cold water and add a pinch of salt. Bring to a boil. Reduce heat to low, cover and cook until rice is tender and water is absorbed, 40 to 50 minutes, depending on the rice blend you are using. Let sit, covered, about 10 minutes. Fluff with a fork and transfer to a large bowl.

While rice sits, add edamame to a saucepan of boiling salted water and cook until tender, 4 to 5 minutes. Drain and add to rice in bowl.

Preheat grill to high. Oil grill.

Drizzle asparagus and salmon with olive oil and season with salt and pepper. Add asparagus and salmon, skin side down, to grill. Reduce heat to medium-high. Grill asparagus, turning as needed, until tender-crisp, 2 to 3 minutes. Grill salmon, turning once, until opaque and just cooked through, 3 to 5 minutes per side, depending on thickness of fish. (Asparagus and salmon may be served hot, warm or at room temperature.)

Whisk dressing again if needed. Toss rice and edamame with about three-quarters of the dressing.

Cut asparagus into 2-inch (5 cm) pieces and toss with salad. Break salmon into bite-size pieces. Gently fold salmon and chives into salad. Drizzle salad with more dressing. Garnish with orange zest. Serve warm or at room temperature.

TIP The brown rice can be replaced with basmati rice. Try this recipe with canned salmon or tuna for a quick lunch.

Grilled Tuna Niçoise Salad

This recipe is my take on a classic French salade niçoise, which combines tuna, boiled new potatoes, steamed green beans and salty, cured niçoise olives. Just grill up a big beautiful piece of ahi tuna, lay it on a bed of mixed greens and veggies and drizzle it with my special olive tapenade dressing. It's a light, impressive addition to any lunch, brunch or dinner. **MAKES 4 SERVINGS**

OLIVE TAPENADE DRESSING

About ⅓ cup (75 mL) pitted black olives, such as niçoise or kalamata

1 tbsp (15 mL) capers

1 garlic clove, minced

2 tbsp (30 mL) chopped fresh parsley

2 tsp (10 mL) chopped fresh thyme

3 tbsp (45 mL) white wine vinegar

½ to ⅔ cup (125 to 150 mL) extra-virgin olive oil

Salt and freshly ground pepper

SALAD

1 lb (450 g) red new potatoes (unpeeled), scrubbed

½ lb (225 g) green beans, trimmed

1 ¼ lb (565 g) sushi-grade ahi tuna steaks

4 handfuls of mixed greens

Mixed heirloom tomatoes, sliced or cut in wedges

To make the olive tapenade dressing: In a food processor, combine olives, capers, garlic, parsley, thyme, vinegar and ½ cup (125 mL) olive oil. Pulse until smooth, adding more olive oil, if needed, to make a pourable dressing. Season with salt and pepper. Set aside.

To make the salad: In a large saucepan, cover potatoes with cold water. Generously salt. Bring to a boil and cook potatoes until just tender, 15 to 20 minutes, depending on size of potatoes. Drain and set aside.

Meanwhile, cook green beans in boiling salted water until tender-crisp, 3 to 4 minutes. (You can cook the beans in the last 4 minutes with the potatoes, if desired.) Drain and set aside.

Preheat grill to high. Clean grill and brush with oil.

Season tuna with salt and brush with olive oil. Sear on all sides, 2 to 3 minutes total, depending on thickness. Let tuna rest for 5 to 7 minutes before slicing.

Arrange on a platter: mixed greens, potatoes, green beans, tomatoes, and tuna slices. Drizzle with the dressing. Serve.

Grilled Scallop Salad with Fennel and Grapefruit

If you like scallops, you'll love the fresh, delicate flavour of this salad. Grilling the scallops gives them a subtle smoky flavour, and the combination of licorice-laced fennel and the tangy grapefruit is a match made in heaven. This is a perfect summertime dinner. *MAKES 4 SERVINGS*

1 red onion, thinly sliced

Juice of 1 lemon + 1 tbsp (15 mL) fresh lemon juice

1 tbsp (15 mL) sugar

1 tsp (5 mL) salt

1 small fennel bulb, thinly sliced crosswise

1 pink grapefruit, segmented

1 small bunch chives, finely chopped

2 tbsp (30 mL) white balsamic or white wine vinegar

¼ cup (60 mL) extra-virgin olive oil

Salt and freshly ground pepper

12 fresh sea scallops

Olive oil, for brushing

Fennel fronds, for garnish

TIP This salad is also delicious served with orange segments instead of grapefruit.

In a medium bowl, combine red onion, juice of 1 lemon, sugar and salt. Let pickled red onion marinate for 30 to 60 minutes.

Meanwhile, preheat grill to high or heat an indoor grill pan over high heat. Oil grill.

Combine fennel, grapefruit segments and chives in a large bowl. Add vinegar, 1 tbsp (15 mL) lemon juice and olive oil. Season with salt and pepper. Toss to combine. Taste and adjust dressing by drizzling with a little more olive oil or lemon juice. Set aside.

Pat scallops dry with paper towels. Brush scallops with olive oil and season with salt and pepper. Sear scallops on grill, turning once, until they just turn opaque, 1 to 2 minutes per side. Do not overcook or scallops will be rubbery.

Divide fennel salad among 4 plates. Top each serving with 3 grilled scallops. Garnish with pickled red onions and fennel fronds.

Olive-Oil-Poached Halibut

This beautiful main dish will wow your guests. Poaching the halibut in olive oil really seals in its juices, resulting in the most tender, moist and luxurious texture. Serve the fish on top of some herb-infused vegetables for a dish that's close to perfection! **MAKES 4 SERVINGS**

OLIVE-OIL-POACHED HALIBUT

4 cups (1 L) virgin olive oil

8 small shallots, peeled

Peel of 1 lemon (removed with a vegetable peeler)

1 tbsp (15 mL) four-peppercorn mix

2 sprigs thyme

16 to 20 grape tomatoes

4 halibut fillets (5 to 6 oz/ 140 to 170 g each)

Salt and freshly ground pepper

SALAD

¼ cup (60 mL) sherry vinegar

1 tsp (5 mL) Dijon mustard

1 bunch radishes, cut in half or quarters, blanched until tender-crisp

4 large handfuls of sugar snap peas, trimmed, blanched until tender-crisp

Chervil sprigs or micro greens, for garnish

To make the olive-oil-poached halibut: In a medium saucepan, heat olive oil over medium heat. Add shallots, lemon peel, peppercorns, thyme sprigs and grape tomatoes. Warm oil to 115°F to 130°F (46°C to 55°C). It should be hot to the touch but not burning. Let flavours infuse into oil, about 15 minutes.

Season both sides of halibut with salt and pepper. Place fish in the oil. The oil should cover the fish. Poach until fish is just cooked through, 10 to 15 minutes. Carefully remove fish, grape tomatoes and shallots; set aside. Reserve olive oil.

To make the salad: In a small bowl, combine sherry vinegar, ½ cup (125 mL) warm olive oil, mustard, and salt and pepper to taste. Whisk until emulsified. In a bowl, toss a little of the dressing with the blanched radishes and peas.

Plate each piece of fish with some grape tomatoes, shallots, radishes and peas. Garnish with a drizzle more of the dressing and sprigs of chervil or micro greens.

TIP This is a great technique to cook almost any fish fillet. It keeps the fish nice and moist. Try it with salmon, trout or cod.

Salmon Stuffed with Spinach and Feta

The next time you're invited to a potluck, offer to bring this show-stopping main dish—it's one that will make you look like a star. Just stuff the salmon ahead of time, bring it to the party and cook it on the spot. It's easy to make and an impressive addition to any table. **MAKES 4 TO 6 SERVINGS**

4 tbsp (60 mL) olive oil

5 oz (140 g) baby spinach (about 3 cups/750 mL)

2 garlic cloves, finely chopped

1 large shallot, finely chopped

2 tbsp (30 mL) chopped fresh dill

2 tsp (10 mL) grated lemon zest (optional)

4 to 5 oz (115 to 140 g) feta cheese, crumbled (about ½ cup/125 mL)

Salt and freshly ground pepper

1 side of salmon (about 2 lb/900 g)

½ lemon, thinly sliced, each slice cut in half

DILL AND CAPER SAUCE

1 cup (250 mL) plain yogurt

2 tbsp (30 mL) extra-virgin olive oil

2 tbsp (30 mL) chopped fresh dill

2 tbsp (30 mL) capers

1 tsp (5 mL) Dijon mustard

1 tsp (5 mL) honey

Squeeze of fresh lemon juice

Salt and freshly ground pepper

TIP Instead of spinach, use Swiss chard. For a totally different dish, replace the feta with goat cheese.

To make the stuffed salmon: Heat 1 tbsp (15 mL) olive oil in a large sauté pan over medium-high heat. Add spinach and sauté just until it starts to wilt. Transfer to a colander and let cool. Squeeze out excess liquid. In a medium bowl, combine spinach, garlic, shallot, dill, lemon zest, feta and 2 tbsp (30 mL) olive oil. Stir to combine. Season with salt and pepper.

Preheat oven to 400°F (200°C). Line a baking sheet with parchment paper.

Cut salmon crosswise into 2 pieces of equal length. Score the skin side of one piece in 1 ½-inch (4 cm) intervals. Set aside.

Set the other salmon piece skin side down on the baking sheet. Spread evenly with the spinach and feta stuffing. Cover with the reserved salmon piece, scored side up, with the thinner end of the top piece over the thicker end of the bottom piece. Fill score marks with lemon slices. Season with salt and pepper and drizzle with remaining 1 tbsp (15 mL) olive oil.

Bake until internal temperature reaches 140°F (60°C), 15 to 20 minutes, depending on thickness of fish.

While salmon bakes, make the dill and caper sauce: In a medium bowl, combine yogurt, olive oil, dill, capers, mustard, honey, lemon juice, and salt and pepper to taste. Stir to combine. Taste and adjust seasoning.

Serve salmon with dill and caper sauce.

Maple-Bacon-Wrapped Salmon

If you're new to cooking, this is the perfect salmon recipe to make. It brings together three of my favourite ingredients—salmon, bacon and maple syrup—and the method is almost too easy. To the young guys out there, this is a great one to make for your next date night . . . trust me! **MAKES 4 SERVINGS**

4 skinless salmon fillets (about 5 oz/
    140 g each)

Salt and freshly ground pepper

2 sprigs tarragon, cut in half

Grated zest of 1 lemon

8 slices maple-smoked bacon

2 tbsp (30 mL) butter

1 tbsp (15 mL) olive oil

2 tbsp (30 mL) maple syrup

Preheat oven to 375°F (190°C).

Season salmon with salt and pepper. Place a piece of tarragon and some lemon zest on top of each fillet of salmon. Wrap 2 slices of bacon around each fillet, securing with toothpicks or wooden skewers.

Heat butter and olive oil in a large ovenproof skillet over medium-high heat. When butter is melted, add salmon. Fry salmon, turning once, until golden brown on each side, 2 to 3 minutes per side. Brush each fillet with some maple syrup and transfer skillet to oven. Cook until salmon is just cooked through and begins to flake when tested with a fork, about 7 minutes, depending on thickness of fish.

TIP Replace the salmon with fresh halibut. Use sage instead of tarragon.

California Roll Salmon Burgers

When I say these burgers are good, I mean they are GOOD! Top these moist, flavourful salmon patties with whatever toppings you like, but, for a mind-blowing burger, try my "California roll" combo. Avocado, cucumber, pickled ginger and a hint of my wasabi mayo make this sushi-inspired burger an unforgettable meal. MAKES 6 SERVINGS

SALMON BURGERS

1 side of salmon (about 2 lb/900 g), skin removed, coarsely cut into cubes

2 large eggs, lightly beaten

2 tbsp (30 mL) mayonnaise

1 cup (250 mL) panko bread crumbs

3 green onions, finely chopped

1 tbsp (15 mL) chopped fresh ginger

3 tbsp (45 mL) soy sauce, or to taste

2 tbsp (30 mL) sesame oil

1 tbsp (15 mL) sugar

1 tbsp (15 mL) rice wine vinegar

Pinch of salt

2 to 3 tbsp (30 to 45 mL) vegetable oil

TO ASSEMBLE

Mayonnaise

Wasabi paste, to taste

6 sesame burger buns, toasted if desired

Avocado slices, pickled ginger, cucumber slices, red onion slices, sprouts

TIP For another great flavour, make these burgers with lump crabmeat instead of salmon. If you cannot find panko crumbs, just use plain dry bread crumbs.

To make the salmon burgers: Working in batches, pulse cubed salmon in a food processor just until finely chopped. Be careful not to over-process. Transfer chopped salmon to a large bowl. Add eggs, mayonnaise, bread crumbs, green onions, ginger, soy sauce, sesame oil, sugar, rice wine vinegar and salt. Mix with your hands. Divide mixture into 6 even portions and shape each portion into a patty about 1 inch (2.5 cm) thick.

Heat a large nonstick skillet over medium heat. Add vegetable oil. When oil is hot, add burgers in batches, if needed, to avoid crowding the pan. Fry, turning once, until burgers are just cooked through, 2 to 4 minutes per side.

Combine mayonnaise and wasabi paste to taste.

Serve salmon burgers in buns and garnish with wasabi mayonnaise and desired toppings.

Crispy Fish Burgers with Tartar Sauce

I've heard from a few of our viewers that these are the best fish burgers they've ever had—I'm so glad! If your family likes fish fingers, I bet they'll love these crispy fish burgers, too. My tartar sauce is creamy and tangy, a tasty condiment that you'll want to pair with any fish or seafood dish. **MAKES 6 SERVINGS**

TARTAR SAUCE

6 tbsp (90 mL) mayonnaise

1 tbsp (15 mL) capers, drained and rinsed, finely chopped

2 or 3 gherkins, finely chopped

½ garlic clove, finely chopped

½ tsp (2 mL) grated lemon zest

1 ½ tsp (7 mL) lemon juice

Salt and freshly ground pepper

FISH BURGERS

1 sprig rosemary

1 lb (450 g) skinless fresh cod fillets

12 oz (340 g) Yukon Gold potatoes, boiled and mashed

2 tbsp (30 mL) finely chopped fresh Italian parsley

2 tbsp (30 mL) grated Parmesan cheese

Salt and freshly ground pepper

1 egg

1 ½ to 2 cups (375 to 500 mL) panko bread crumbs

Olive oil, for frying

6 burger buns

Tomato slices, cucumber slices and lettuce leaves

To make the tartar sauce: Mix together all sauce ingredients. Taste and adjust seasoning. Chill until needed.

Preheat oven to 200°F (100°C).

To make the fish burgers: Place the cod in a large saucepan and add enough water to cover. Remove cod and set aside. Add rosemary sprig to water and bring to a boil. When the water boils, remove rosemary. Add cod and reduce heat to a simmer. Poach cod until just cooked through and flesh flakes when tested with a fork, 5 to 7 minutes.

Strain cod and transfer to a large bowl. Flake with a fork. Add mashed potatoes, parsley and Parmesan. Mix well and season with salt and pepper.

In a shallow dish or pie plate, beat the egg. Place panko crumbs in a second dish. Divide fish mixture into 6 balls and shape into 6 patties. Coat patties in beaten egg and then dredge in bread crumbs, coating well. For a crispier coating, repeat this breading step.

Pour enough oil into a deep skillet to come about 1 inch (2.5 cm) up the side of the pan. Heat over medium heat. Test that the oil is at the right temperature by dipping the handle of a wooden spoon in the oil. If the handle releases a steady stream of small bubbles, the oil is ready for frying. Add burgers to oil, working in batches if needed to avoid crowding the pan. Cook burgers, turning once, until golden brown on each side, 3 to 5 minutes per side. Drain burgers on paper towels. Keep warm in oven while you fry the remaining burgers.

Serve burgers in buns and garnish with tartar sauce, tomato, cucumber and lettuce.

TIP You can make this recipe with salmon. Shape the fish mixture into bite-size croquettes, fry them in oil and serve them buffet-style with the tartar sauce for dipping.

Pan-Fried Trout with Anchovy Butter

This recipe was inspired by fishing trips with my buddies. We catch fresh trout and, minutes later, we're pan-frying them over an open fire with a little bit of anchovy-infused butter. (Yes, I take anchovies on my fishing trips!) The good news is, you don't need a fire pit to make this delicious trout recipe at home. **MAKES 4 SERVINGS**

ANCHOVY BUTTER

8 to 12 anchovy fillets (or 1 tbsp/
    15 mL anchovy paste)

Grated zest and juice of ½ lemon

2 tsp (10 mL) chopped fresh thyme

1 garlic clove

Salt and freshly ground pepper

1 cup (250 mL) unsalted butter,
    at room temperature

PAN-FRIED TROUT

4 rainbow trout fillets (5 to 6 oz/
    140 to 170 g each)

2 tbsp (30 mL) grapeseed or peanut oil

1 lb (450 g) green beans, trimmed
    and blanched

To make the anchovy butter: In a food processor, combine anchovies, lemon zest, lemon juice, thyme, garlic, and salt and pepper to taste. Pulse to combine. Add butter and pulse until combined. (Alternatively, chop and mix by hand.)

To make the pan-fried trout: Pat trout dry with paper towels. Season with salt and pepper.

Heat a large, heavy or nonstick skillet over medium-high heat. Add oil. When oil is hot, add trout skin side down. Cook in two batches if all 4 fillets don't fit in the pan. Cook until skin browns, 4 to 5 minutes. Flip the fish and continue cooking for an additional 1 to 2 minutes. (Alternatively, to prevent skin from curling, place fillets in cold pan with oil. Turn heat to medium-high. Proceed as above, cooking the fish for a few minutes longer before flipping.)

Transfer fish to plates. Reduce heat to medium and add 6 tbsp (90 mL) anchovy butter to pan. When the butter has just melted, spoon 1 tbsp (15 mL) over each fillet. Add green beans to the pan and toss with remaining butter. Serve fish with green beans.

TIP This recipe makes more anchovy butter than you need. Roll the remaining butter into a log in plastic wrap. Keep in fridge for 2 to 3 days or freeze for up to 1 month. Cut into coins and use over steaks, chicken or veggies.

Pecan-Crusted Baked Fish

If you're looking for a healthy alternative on your family's fish and chips night, give this baked fish recipe a try. Instead of a fried batter, these fillets are coated in a pecan and bread crumb crust. The haddock bakes up crispy on the outside, tender on the inside. I think the baked version may just be better than deep-fried! **MAKES 4 SERVINGS**

Tartar Sauce (page 284)

1½ tbsp (20 mL) Dijon mustard

2 tbsp (30 mL) chopped fresh basil

Hot pepper sauce

½ cup (125 mL) all-purpose flour

2 eggs, beaten

About 2 cups (500 mL) fresh bread crumbs

¼ cup (60 mL) finely ground pecans

Leaves from 1 sprig thyme, chopped

Pinch of cayenne pepper, or to taste

Salt and freshly ground pepper

4 haddock fillets (about 6 oz/170 g each) or any white-fleshed fish

1 to 2 tbsp (15 to 30 mL) olive oil

Lemon wedges, for serving

TIP If you do not have pecans in your pantry, use ground almonds or hazelnuts in the crust. You can also substitute a few drops of hot pepper sauce for the cayenne.

Make the tartar sauce, adding Dijon mustard, chopped fresh basil and hot sauce to taste. Chill until needed.

Preheat oven to 425°F (220°C).

Prepare a breading station by arranging 3 shallow dishes or pie plates with the following: flour in the first; beaten eggs in the second; and bread crumbs, pecans, thyme, cayenne, and salt and pepper to taste stirred together in the third.

Season haddock with salt and pepper. Dredge fish first in flour, then in egg and lastly in bread crumb mixture, coating well.

Heat a baking sheet in the oven for 5 minutes. When pan is hot, drizzle with olive oil. Add fish and drizzle a little olive oil on top of it, too. Bake, turning once, until fish just starts to flake when tested with a fork, 10 to 12 minutes, depending on thickness. Serve with lemon wedges and Tartar Sauce (page 284).

Thai Coconut Shrimp Curry

Grab a can of coconut milk from the pantry and a bag of shrimp from the freezer—you'll have an easy, decadent curry in no time flat. Depending on how spicy you like it, you can use less or more Thai curry paste, but I dare you to kick up the heat! **MAKES 4 SERVINGS**

1 to 2 tbsp (15 to 30 mL) coconut oil or vegetable oil

1 sweet red pepper, chopped

1 medium shallot, finely chopped

1 garlic clove, finely chopped

2 tsp (10 mL) chopped fresh ginger

1 to 2 tbsp (15 to 30 mL) Thai red curry paste, or to taste

1 can (14 oz/398 mL) diced tomatoes

1 can (14 oz/400 mL) coconut milk

Salt and freshly ground pepper

About 20 large shrimp, peeled and deveined

Juice of 1 lime

¼ cup (60 mL) chopped fresh cilantro or Thai basil

½ cup (125 mL) unsweetened coconut, toasted, for garnish

Heat a large skillet over medium to medium-high heat. Add oil. When oil is hot, add red pepper and shallot. Cook, stirring, until vegetables start to soften, about 2 minutes. Add garlic and ginger. Cook, stirring, until soft, another minute. Add curry paste. Cook, stirring, for 1 to 2 minutes.

Add tomatoes and coconut milk. Season with salt and pepper. Bring to a boil, then reduce heat to a simmer. Cook until sauce reduces and thickens, 5 to 10 minutes.

Add shrimp and stir. Cook until shrimp start to turn pink and curl and are just cooked through, 4 to 5 minutes, depending on size of shrimp. Do not overcook or shrimp will be rubbery.

Add lime juice and cilantro and stir. Serve garnished with toasted coconut. Serve with steamed jasmine rice.

Shrimp Po' Boy Sandwich

The classic po' boy (or poor boy) is a traditional submarine sandwich from Louisiana and a casual street food in New Orleans. It's one of my favourites. If you can't take a quick trip to the Big Easy, make my shrimp po' boy, topped with lettuce, tomato, mayo and a little hot sauce. It's like a Mardi Gras in your mouth! MAKES 4 SERVINGS

1 cup (250 mL) all-purpose flour

1 tbsp (15 mL) Cajun seasoning, or to taste

Salt and freshly ground pepper

3 eggs, beaten

2 cups (500 mL) cornmeal

2 cups (500 mL) panko or dry bread crumbs

Peanut oil, for deep-frying

20 medium to large shrimp, peeled, deveined, tails removed

4 soft-style submarine buns

Mayonnaise, lettuce leaves, tomato slices, pickle slices

Hot pepper sauce, for serving (optional)

Lemon wedges, for serving (optional)

Prepare a breading station by arranging 3 shallow dishes or pie plates with the following: flour, Cajun seasoning, and salt and pepper to taste in the first; beaten eggs in the second; and cornmeal and panko stirred together in the third.

Add oil to a deep-fryer or pour enough oil into a deep saucepan to come 2 to 3 inches (5 to 8 cm) up side of pan. Heat oil to 350°F (180°C) over medium heat.

Dredge shrimp first in seasoned flour, then in eggs and lastly in the bread crumb mixture, coating well. Working in batches, carefully add shrimp to hot oil. Fry, turning once, until just cooked through and coating is golden brown, about 3 minutes. Drain on paper towels.

Slice sub buns in half horizontally. Assemble sandwiches with shrimp, mayonnaise, lettuce, tomato and pickles. Serve with hot sauce and lemon wedges, if desired.

Grilled Shrimp Tacos

Who doesn't like a good taco? These shrimp tacos are dusted with just the right amount of spice and take only a few minutes on the grill. Fill a warm tortilla with your smoky shrimp, add some fresh toppings and you've got a casual main that'll please everyone. **MAKES 8 SERVINGS**

1 tbsp (15 mL) ancho chili powder

1 tbsp (15 mL) dried oregano

1 tbsp (15 mL) ground cumin

1 tbsp (15 mL) ground coriander

1 tbsp (15 mL) granulated garlic

1 tbsp (15 mL) brown sugar

Salt and freshly ground pepper

24 medium to large shrimp, peeled and deveined, tails removed

Olive oil, for drizzling

8 small flour or corn tortillas or taco shells

Tomatillo salsa or fresh tomato salsa

Shredded lettuce, cilantro leaves and finely chopped green onions

To make the dry rub for the shrimp: In a small bowl, combine ancho powder, oregano, cumin, coriander, garlic, brown sugar, and salt and pepper to taste. Stir well.

Pat shrimp dry with paper towels. Season shrimp with 2 tbsp (30 mL) dry rub or to taste. Drizzle shrimp with a little olive oil. Let marinate for about 15 minutes.

Meanwhile, preheat grill to medium-high. Brush grill with oil.

Add shrimp to grill. Cook shrimp, turning once, until they turn pink, start to curl and are just cooked through, 3 to 5 minutes total.

Meanwhile, heat tortillas over medium heat in a dry hot pan or griddle until warmed and lightly toasted. Wrap tortillas in a clean kitchen towel to keep warm. (Alternatively, wrap tortillas in foil and heat for a few minutes in a 400°F/200°C oven.)

Serve warm tortillas with grilled shrimp and your desired taco toppings.

TIP Use your favourite chili powder if you don't have ancho chili powder. Use leftover rub for grilled chicken or steak.

STEFANO'S DINNER MENUS

RESTAURANT-STYLE CHICKEN DINNER

Roasted BBQ Chicken

When I was a kid, our family would eat out on special "restaurant nights" once a week. I would get so excited about choosing my own dinner from the menu— "Quarter chicken with fries and coleslaw, please!"

You know what this one tastes like—the rotisserie chicken, chunky fries, creamy coleslaw and the addictive finger-licking dipping sauce—it's that classic restaurant-style chicken dinner you crave. Here's how to make it yourself, only this time I'm serving it up with a cheesy baked sweet potato in place of the fries. You don't ever need to go out for chicken again! MAKES 4 TO 6 SERVINGS

ROASTED BBQ CHICKEN

1 chicken (3 lb/1.35 kg)

¼ cup (60 mL) butter, at room temperature

2 to 3 garlic cloves, chopped

1 heaping tbsp (18 mL) paprika

Salt and freshly ground pepper

CHICKEN DIPPING SAUCE

3 tbsp (45 mL) butter

½ onion, minced

1 garlic clove, minced

1 cup (250 mL) ketchup

¼ cup (60 mL) brown sugar

¼ cup (60 mL) maple syrup

2 tbsp (30 mL) bourbon

2 tbsp (30 mL) Worcestershire sauce

1 tbsp (15 mL) chili powder

1 tbsp (15 mL) Dijon mustard

1 tsp (5 mL) dried oregano

2 to 3 cups (500 to 750 mL) chicken stock

¼ to ½ cup (60 to 125 mL) apple cider vinegar

Hot pepper sauce

Salt and freshly ground pepper

Preheat oven to 400°F (200°C).

To make the roasted chicken: Pat chicken dry with paper towels. Remove giblets from cavity. With your fingers, carefully loosen skin from breast meat.

In a small bowl, mash together butter, garlic, paprika, and salt and pepper to taste. Rub butter mixture under skin of chicken breasts, in cavity and then all over chicken. Season chicken and cavity with a little more salt and pepper. Truss chicken with kitchen string. Tuck wings under the bird.

Place chicken on a rack in roasting pan. Roast until skin is golden and crisp and juices run clear, 1 hour to 1 hour 15 minutes, depending on size of chicken.

While chicken is roasting, make the dipping sauce. Melt butter in a medium saucepan over medium heat. When butter has melted, add onions and garlic. Cook, stirring occasionally, until soft, about 5 minutes.

Add ketchup, brown sugar, maple syrup, bourbon, Worcestershire sauce, chili powder, mustard, oregano, 1 cup (250 mL) chicken stock and ¼ cup (60 mL)

cider vinegar. Add up to ¼ cup (60 mL) more vinegar if you prefer a tangy sauce. Season with hot sauce and salt and pepper. Bring to a boil. Reduce heat and simmer, stirring occasionally, until flavours marry and sauce has thickened, 20 to 30 minutes. Set aside.

Transfer chicken to a cutting board and let rest for 10 to 15 minutes before carving.

Deglaze roasting pan with 1 cup (250 mL) chicken stock over medium heat, stirring to incorporate all the pan juices and brown bits from bottom of pan. Bring to a boil, then reduce heat and simmer for 5 to 10 minutes. Add pan juices to dipping sauce. Bring to a boil. Thin sauce with more chicken stock, if desired.

Serve chicken with the sauce.

Cheesy Baked Sweet Potatoes

MAKES 4 SERVINGS

About 1 cup (250 mL) coarse kosher
    or sea salt

2 large sweet potatoes

4 tsp (20 mL) brown sugar

¼ tsp (1 mL) ground allspice

¼ tsp (1 mL) chili powder

Pinch of cayenne pepper, or to taste

Salt and freshly ground pepper

1 cup (250 mL) shredded Jarlsberg
    or aged Cheddar cheese

GARNISHES

Sour cream, crumbled cooked bacon,
    chopped fresh chives

Preheat oven to 400°F (200°C). Spread coarse salt on a small baking sheet.

Pierce each sweet potato all over with a fork. Transfer to baking sheet. Bake until fork-tender, about 1 hour, depending on size.

Cut each potato in half lengthwise.

Preheat broiler.

In a small bowl, stir together brown sugar, allspice, chili powder, cayenne, and salt and pepper to taste. Sprinkle seasoning mixture evenly over cut side of each potato. Fluff potatoes with a fork to incorporate the seasoning. Sprinkle with cheese. Transfer to a clean baking sheet. Broil until cheese melts and bubbles, 3 to 5 minutes. Serve with desired garnishes.

Creamy Cabbage Coleslaw

MAKES 6 SERVINGS

6 cups (1.5 L) thinly sliced or shredded
   savoy cabbage (about ½ head)

½ red onion, thinly sliced

1 large carrot, julienned or grated

¼ cup (60 mL) chopped fresh parsley

DRESSING

⅓ cup (75 mL) sour cream

3 tbsp (45 mL) olive oil

2 to 3 tbsp (30 to 45 mL) mayonnaise

1 tbsp (15 mL) Dijon mustard

1 tbsp (15 mL) apple cider vinegar

1 tbsp (15 mL) liquid honey

1 to 2 tsp (5 to 10 mL) celery seeds

Salt and freshly ground pepper

Combine cabbage, red onion, carrot and parsley in a large bowl. Set aside.

To make the dressing: In a small bowl, combine sour cream, olive oil, 2 tbsp
(30 mL) mayonnaise, mustard, vinegar, honey and celery seeds. Season with salt
and pepper. Whisk to blend. If desired, whisk in 1 tbsp (15 mL) more mayonnaise.

Toss salad with dressing. Taste and adjust seasoning. Let stand for 15 to 20 minutes in fridge before serving to allow flavours to marry.

STEAKHOUSE DINNER

Steak with Peppercorn Brandy Sauce

Sometimes you just want a great big honkin' steak. You don't have one very often, but when you do, you want it to be grilled to perfection. Going out for a big steakhouse dinner can be expensive, so I'm sharing my make-at-home steak menu with you.

My hearty lineup includes thick grilled steaks with a fragrant peppercorn sauce, homemade hand-cut fries with a creamy tarragon aïoli for dipping, and a warm bacony frisée side salad. And since you've saved some money, splurge on a good bottle of red wine. **MAKES 4 SERVINGS**

4 New York strip loin steaks
   (1 to 1 ½ inches/2.5 to 4 cm thick)

3 tbsp (45 mL) black peppercorns, crushed

Coarse kosher salt

1 tbsp (15 mL) grapeseed or peanut oil

2 tbsp (30 mL) butter

2 shallots, finely chopped

1 sprig thyme (optional)

1 tbsp (15 mL) green peppercorns
   in brine, drained

¼ cup (60 mL) brandy

1 cup (250 mL) beef stock

½ cup (125 mL) whipping cream (35%)

1 tbsp (15 mL) grainy Dijon mustard

Season steak on both sides with black peppercorns and salt. Heat oil in a large, heavy skillet over medium-high heat until very hot.

Sear steaks until well browned on both sides and cooked to medium-rare, 3 to 5 minutes per side, depending on thickness. Set aside and keep warm.

Reduce heat to medium. Add butter, shallots and thyme sprig, if desired. Cook, stirring frequently, until shallots are soft, about 2 minutes. Add green peppercorns, brandy and beef stock. Bring to a boil and reduce sauce by half, 4 to 5 minutes. Stir in cream and mustard and reduce until thickened, about 3 minutes. Taste and adjust seasoning. Serve with steak.

Thick-Cut Fries

MAKES 4 SERVINGS

2 to 3 large russet potatoes
(unpeeled), scrubbed

Peanut or vegetable oil, for deep-frying

2 tbsp (30 mL) chopped fresh thyme

Sea salt and freshly ground pepper

Cut potatoes into 4- × ¾-inch (10 × 2 cm) sticks. Soak in water for at least 2 hours. Drain and pat dry.

To make the thyme salt: Combine thyme with salt and pepper to taste. Set aside.

Add oil to a deep-fryer or pour enough oil into a Dutch oven or deep saucepan to come 4 inches (10 cm) up sides of pan. Heat oil to 300°F (150°C).

Add fries in small batches to hot oil. Fry until just cooked through but not browned, 8 to 10 minutes. Drain on paper towels and let cool to room temperature. (This step can be done several hours ahead.)

Before serving, heat oil to 375°F (190°C). Fry potatoes in batches until golden brown and crispy, 2 to 3 minutes. Drain on paper towels. Immediately season fries with the thyme salt. Serve with Tarragon Aïoli (recipe follows), if desired.

Tarragon Aïoli

MAKES ABOUT 1½ CUPS (375 ML)

1 to 2 garlic cloves, chopped

2 large egg yolks or pasteurized egg yolks

2 tbsp (30 mL) white wine vinegar

1 tbsp (15 mL) Dijon mustard

About 1 cup (250 mL) extra-virgin olive oil

2 tbsp (30 mL) chopped fresh tarragon

Salt

In a mini food processor, process garlic and egg yolks on high until mixture thickens slightly. Add vinegar and mustard. While machine is running, slowly drizzle in olive oil. Continue to blend until mixture thickens to the consistency of mayonnaise. (Alternatively, use an electric mixer or whisk by hand.) Stir in tarragon and salt. Refrigerate until ready to use. Use within 2 days.

Frisée Salad with Warm Bacon Dressing

MAKES 4 SERVINGS

4 oz (115 g) thick-cut bacon, diced or sliced

1 shallot, minced

2 tsp (10 mL) honey

¼ cup (60 mL) white wine vinegar

3 tbsp (45 mL) extra-virgin olive oil

Salt and freshly ground pepper

2 bunches frisée, leaves separated

3 oz (85 g) Roquefort cheese, crumbled

2 tbsp (30 mL) chopped fresh chives

In a large skillet over medium-low heat, cook bacon until crisp. Drain on paper towels.

Remove all but ¼ cup (60 mL) bacon fat from pan. Increase heat to medium. Add shallot and cook, stirring frequently, until soft, about 2 minutes. Add honey. Remove pan from heat and whisk in vinegar and olive oil. Season with salt and pepper.

Toss frisée with warm dressing. Serve salad garnished with bacon, blue cheese and chives.

TURKEY AND
ALL THE FIXIN'S

Roast Turkey with Thyme and Rosemary

If there's one menu I'm asked for time and time again, it's a big festive turkey dinner. Everyone wants that ultimate lineup of classic, no-fail dishes that will become a new family tradition during the holidays. Trust me, this is that menu.

The roast turkey with rich herb-infused gravy is the impressive bird that your guests will be talking about until the next gathering. I've put a slightly spicy Italian twist on the stuffing with the addition of sausage and Parmesan cheese. But don't wait for the holidays to enjoy it—this stuffing is great with roast pork or chicken anytime. MAKES 10 TO 12 SERVINGS

1 turkey (15 to 17 lb/6.8 to 7.6 kg), preferably organic or free-range

Salt and freshly ground pepper

1 lemon, cut in half

1 small onion, peeled and quartered

1 small carrot, coarsely chopped

1 celery stalk, coarsely chopped

½ small bunch Italian parsley

4 to 5 sprigs each rosemary and thyme

About ¼ cup (60 mL) olive oil and/or butter, melted

1 onion, 1 celery stalk and 1 carrot, for roasting pan (optional)

Preheat oven to 400°F (200°C).

Remove neck and giblets from the turkey cavity. Place them in a heavy roasting pan.

Pat turkey dry with paper towels. Season cavity with salt and pepper, then stuff cavity with lemon halves, onion quarters, chopped carrot, chopped celery, parsley, and thyme and rosemary sprigs. Tie legs together and tuck wings underneath the bird. Rub turkey with olive oil and/or melted butter. Season with salt and pepper.

Place turkey breast side up on a rack in roasting pan. If you like, add an onion, celery stalk and carrot to roasting pan to add extra flavour to the pan juices.

Roast turkey for 30 minutes. Reduce heat to 350°F (180°C). Roast, basting occasionally, until juices run clear and joints of bird start to loosen, 3 to 4 hours. Total cooking time depends on the following factors: size of turkey, how cold the turkey was before it went in the oven and how many times you open the oven door to baste and check the bird.

Transfer turkey to a cutting board. Loosely tent with foil and let rest for 20 to 30 minutes before carving. Serve turkey with Easy Turkey Gravy (page 314) and Sausage and Parmesan Stuffing (recipe follows).

Sausage and Parmesan Stuffing

MAKES 10 TO 12 SERVINGS

10 to 12 cups (2.4 to 2.8 L) day-old ciabatta bread cut in bite-size pieces (about 1 large loaf)

4 tbsp (60 mL) olive oil

1 lb (450 g) spicy Italian sausages, casings removed, sliced in bite-size pieces (3 to 4 sausages)

1 large onion, chopped

3 celery stalks, chopped

Leaves from 6 to 8 sprigs thyme, chopped

Leaves from 1 to 2 sprigs rosemary, chopped

6 to 8 fresh sage leaves, chopped

Salt and freshly ground pepper

2 large eggs, lightly beaten

1 cup (250 mL) grated Parmesan cheese, plus more for topping

½ cup (125 mL) dried currants

¼ cup (60 mL) chopped fresh Italian parsley, plus a handful more for garnish

1 to 1 ½ cups (250 to 375 mL) chicken stock

Preheat oven to 350°F (180°C). Generously butter or oil a 3-quart (3 L) baking dish.

Place bread pieces in a very large bowl. Set aside.

Heat a large skillet over medium-high heat. Add 1 tbsp (15 mL) olive oil. When oil is hot, add sausage. Cook, stirring occasionally, until meat is browned, 8 to 10 minutes. Using a slotted spoon, transfer sausage to bowl with bread.

Add remaining 3 tbsp (45 mL) olive oil to sausage fat in skillet. (Don't remove any sausage fat from the pan—it will add more flavour and moisture to the stuffing.) When oil is hot, add onions, celery, thyme, rosemary and sage. Season with salt and pepper. Reduce heat to medium. Cook, stirring occasionally, until onions and celery are tender, 5 to 8 minutes. Add mixture to bowl with bread. Stir to combine. Let cool to room temperature.

Once bread mixture is cool, add eggs, Parmesan, currants, ¼ cup (60 mL) parsley, and salt and pepper to taste. Drizzle with enough chicken stock to moisten, tossing gently to combine. (The amount of stock will depend on how dry the bread was. The bread should be moist but not soggy.)

Transfer bread mixture to prepared baking dish, packing gently. Cover with foil and bake until centre of stuffing is hot, 50 minutes to 1 hour. Remove foil and continue to bake until stuffing is golden brown and the edges are a little crispy, 20 to 25 minutes more. If desired, sprinkle with additional Parmesan and chopped parsley.

Easy Turkey Gravy

MAKES 4 CUPS (1 L)

4 cups (1 L) chicken stock or turkey stock

2 sprigs each thyme and rosemary

Roasted turkey neck and giblets from Roast Turkey with Thyme and Rosemary

¼ cup (60 mL) cornstarch

About ½ cup (125 mL) cold water

Salt and freshly ground pepper

Remove neck and giblets from turkey roasting pan; set aside. Remove any excess fat from roasting pan. Transfer roasting pan to stovetop and heat over medium heat. Add chicken stock. Stir and scrape bottom of pan to incorporate pan drippings into stock. Bring to a boil. Add herbs and roasted neck and giblets. Reduce heat and simmer for 5 to 10 minutes.

In a small bowl, make a cornstarch slurry by whisking together cornstarch and just enough water to dissolve the cornstarch.

While whisking, slowly add half the slurry to the gravy. Bring to a boil. (Cornstarch will thicken to full extent when it comes to a boil.) If you prefer a thicker gravy, whisk in remaining slurry, a little at a time, bringing to a boil after each addition, until gravy is desired thickness. Season with salt and pepper. Simmer, stirring occasionally, for 5 more minutes. Strain.

FUN FAMILY DINNER

Stefano's Chicken Fajitas

This chicken fajita menu is a fun way to make dinner as a family on a Saturday night. It's a lineup of colourful Mexican-inspired dishes that has something for everybody. **MAKES 4 SERVINGS**

¼ cup (60 mL) fresh lime juice

2 garlic cloves, chopped

1 tsp (5 mL) chili powder

½ tsp (2 mL) ground cumin

¼ cup (60 mL) vegetable oil

Salt and freshly ground pepper

3 boneless, skinless chicken breasts, thinly sliced on the diagonal

8 small flour tortillas

1 large yellow onion, sliced

1 large sweet red pepper, sliced

1 large sweet green pepper, sliced

1 lime

GARNISHES

Mango-Lime Salsa (recipe follows), Refried Beans with Bacon (page 319), Guacamole (page 51), sour cream, pickled jalapeños, fresh chilies, shredded cheese, shredded lettuce

In a medium bowl, combine lime juice, garlic, chili powder, cumin, 2 tbsp (30 mL) oil, and salt and pepper to taste. Stir to combine. Add chicken slices and turn to coat. Cover and marinate in the fridge for at least 30 minutes or up to 1 hour.

Preheat oven to 350°F (180°C).

Wrap tortillas in foil. Heat in oven until warmed through, about 10 minutes.

Meanwhile, heat remaining 2 tbsp (30 mL) oil in a large cast-iron pan or heavy skillet over medium-high to high heat. Remove chicken from marinade (discarding marinade). Add chicken to hot pan. Sauté until golden brown and chicken is almost cooked through, 3 to 4 minutes. Add onions and peppers. Season with salt and pepper. Sauté until chicken is cooked through and veggies are crisp, 2 to 3 minutes. Add a squeeze of fresh lime juice. Serve chicken fajitas with warm tortillas and desired garnishes.

Mango-Lime Salsa

MAKES ABOUT 2 CUPS (500 ML)

2 large mangoes, peeled and diced

2 tbsp (30 mL) finely chopped red onion

1 fresh chili, chopped, or to taste

2 tbsp (30 mL) chopped fresh cilantro

Juice of 1 to 2 limes

Salt

Pinch of sugar (optional)

In a medium bowl, combine mangoes, onion, chili, cilantro and lime juice to taste. Season with salt. Toss to combine. Add a pinch of sugar if needed. Let stand for 15 minutes before serving to allow flavours to marry.

Refried Beans with Bacon

MAKES 4 SERVINGS

2 slices bacon, chopped

1 tbsp (15 mL) olive oil

½ onion, chopped

1 to 2 garlic cloves, chopped

1 tsp (5 mL) ground cumin

1 tsp (5 mL) dried oregano

Salt and freshly ground pepper

1 can (14 oz/398 mL) black beans, drained and rinsed

½ to 1 cup (125 to 250 mL) water or chicken stock

TOPPINGS

Sour cream, chopped green onions, sliced fresh chilies (optional)

In a small skillet over medium heat, fry bacon until it is just crispy. Remove any excess fat. Add olive oil, onions, garlic, cumin, oregano, and salt and pepper to taste. Cook, stirring occasionally, until onions and garlic are soft, about 3 minutes.

Add beans and ½ cup (125 mL) water. Cook, stirring occasionally, until mixture is simmering and beans are heated through, 8 to 10 minutes. Using a potato masher, mash beans until smooth, adding more water if needed. Cook beans until all the liquid has evaporated, about 5 minutes. Serve beans with desired toppings.

Mexican Chocolate Shake

MAKES 1 SERVING

1 ¼ cups (300 mL) almond milk

1 scoop chocolate ice cream

1 tsp (5 mL) vanilla extract

¼ tsp (1 mL) cinnamon

Pinch of chili powder, such as cayenne, ancho or chipotle

Whipped cream and grated chocolate, for garnish

In a blender, combine almond milk, ice cream, vanilla, cinnamon and chili powder. Purée until smooth. Serve garnished with a dollop of whipped cream and a sprinkle of grated chocolate, if desired.

HEARTY MEATLESS DINNER

Eggplant Parmigiana

We love hearing from our *In the Kitchen* viewers, and so many of you tell me that you're setting aside at least one night a week to eat a meatless dinner. I'm always happy to share inspiring vegetarian options, and I know you'll love this menu. This is one of my family's favourites, even pleasing my little girl, Emilia—and she can be a tough customer! MAKES 6 SERVINGS

5 large eggplants

¼ cup (60 mL) coarse kosher salt

3 tbsp (45 mL) extra-virgin olive oil

2 garlic cloves, minced

1 can (28 oz/796 mL) diced tomatoes

¼ tsp (1 mL) dried oregano

1 bay leaf (optional)

Salt and freshly ground pepper

Handful of chopped fresh basil

Vegetable oil, for frying

2 tbsp (30 mL) butter

1 cup (250 mL) fresh or dry bread crumbs

1 cup (250 mL) freshly grated Parmesan cheese

18 oz (500 g) shredded mozzarella cheese

Peel eggplants and cut lengthwise into ½-inch (1 cm) slices. Arrange eggplant slices on baking sheets. Sprinkle with coarse salt. Let sit for about 30 minutes. (The salt will draw out the bitter juices from the eggplant.)

While the eggplant is draining, make the tomato sauce. Heat olive oil in a medium saucepan over medium heat. When oil is hot, add garlic. Cook, stirring occasionally, until garlic starts to soften, about 2 minutes. Add tomatoes, oregano, bay leaf, and salt and pepper to taste. Bring to a boil, reduce heat and simmer until sauce is slightly thickened, about 15 minutes. Remove from heat and stir in fresh basil.

Wipe excess salt and juices off eggplant slices or rinse eggplant and pat dry well. Heat a large skillet over medium heat. (Use 2 skillets to make the process go faster.) Add enough vegetable oil to come 1 inch (2.5 cm) up the side the pan. When oil is hot, add eggplant slices in batches, being careful not to crowd the pan. Fry eggplant, turning once, until golden brown on both sides. Drain on paper towels.

Preheat oven to 375°F (190°C).

To assemble the dish: Spread a ladleful of sauce in the bottom of a 13- × 9-inch (3 L) baking dish. Add a few knobs of butter. Layer about one-third each of the eggplant slices, sauce, bread crumbs, Parmesan and mozzarella in the baking dish. Repeat to make 3 layers, finishing with the cheeses. Bake until golden brown and bubbling, 25 to 30 minutes. Let stand for 5 minutes before serving.

Stefano's Simple Side Salad

MAKES 4 SERVINGS

1 small bunch watercress, thick
    stems trimmed
6 handfuls of frisée lettuce leaves
¼ cup (60 mL) parsley leaves
⅓ cup (75 mL) olive oil

Juice of 1 lemon
Salt and freshly ground pepper
Lemon slices, for garnish

In a large bowl, combine watercress, frisée and parsley leaves. Drizzle with olive oil and half the lemon juice. Season with salt and pepper. Toss to combine. Taste and add a touch more lemon juice if you prefer more acidity. Garnish with lemon slices, if desired.

Rum Raisin Baked Apples

MAKES 6 SERVINGS

6 Fuji apples
6 to 8 tbsp (90 to 125 mL) brown sugar
6 tbsp (90 mL) butter, at room temperature
1 tbsp (15 mL) cinnamon
Handful of raisins or other dried fruit

Handful of chopped walnuts,
    almonds or pecans
⅓ cup (75 mL) rum
⅓ cup (75 mL) apple juice
⅓ cup (75 mL) maple syrup

Preheat oven to 350°F (180°C).

Core each apple with a melon baller, without going all the way to the bottom of the apple.

Stir together brown sugar to taste, butter, cinnamon, raisins and walnuts. Fill apples evenly with the brown sugar mixture. Place apples in a medium baking dish. Combine rum, apple juice and maple syrup. Pour over and around apples.

Cover and bake, basting occasionally, until apples are tender, 25 to 30 minutes. Serve warm with whipped cream or ice cream, if desired.

EASY ENTERTAINING MENU

Spiced Pork Chops with Pear Sauce

My Spiced Pork Chops take no time to cook, and the Pear Sauce is a delicious change from the usual applesauce. The veggie dish has to be one of the most amazing sides we've made on the show. Squash, pecorino cheese and pumpkin seeds—the combination is incredible. Use some of your reserved Pear Sauce to make a quick-and-easy pear and ginger dessert that will have your guests raving! MAKES 4 SERVINGS

PEAR SAUCE

5 ripe pears, such as Forelle, Bosc or Anjou, peeled and diced

3 tbsp (45 mL) brown sugar

1 tsp (5 mL) cinnamon

Pinch of ground cloves

Juice of ½ lemon

SPICED PORK CHOPS

1 tbsp (15 mL) dried rosemary

1 tbsp (15 mL) coriander seeds

1 tbsp (15 mL) cumin seeds

1 tbsp (15 mL) mustard seeds

1 tbsp (15 mL) peppercorns

Coarse kosher or sea salt

4 thick-cut bone-in pork chops (1 ½ to 2 inches/4 to 5 cm thick), at room temperature

2 tbsp (30 mL) olive or vegetable oil

To make the pear sauce: Combine pears, brown sugar, cinnamon, cloves and lemon juice in a medium saucepan. Add enough water to come halfway up pears. Cover and bring to a boil. Reduce heat and simmer until pears start to soften and break down, 10 to 15 minutes, depending on how ripe the pears are.

Mash sauce with a potato masher or immersion blender until smooth. Continue to cook, uncovered and stirring occasionally, until thickened, about 5 minutes. Let cool to room temperature. Set aside 1½ cups (375 mL) if you are making the Pear and Ginger Fool.

Preheat oven to 400°F (200°C).

To make the spiced pork chops: In a spice grinder, combine rosemary, coriander seeds, cumin seeds, mustard seeds and peppercorns. Pulse to grind. Transfer to a small bowl and stir in coarse salt. Coat pork chops with spice mix.

Heat an extra-large ovenproof skillet over medium-high heat. (Alternatively, use a large skillet and brown pork chops in batches, transferring them as cooked to a baking sheet.) Add oil. When oil is hot, add pork chops and sear, turning once, until browned on both sides, 2 to 3 minutes.

Transfer skillet (or baking sheet) to the oven. Bake pork chops until just a blush of pink remains in the centre, 10 to 15 minutes, depending on thickness of pork chops. Serve chops with pear sauce.

Roasted Butternut Squash with Pecorino and Pumpkin Seeds

MAKES 6 SERVINGS

1 small to medium butternut squash

2 garlic cloves, chopped

3 tbsp (45 mL) olive oil

1 tbsp (15 mL) finely chopped fresh sage

¼ tsp (1 mL) ground allspice

Salt and freshly ground pepper

1 to 2 tbsp (15 to 30 mL) maple syrup

Handful of toasted pumpkin seeds

Shaved pecorino cheese, to taste

Preheat oven to 400°F (200°C).

Cut butternut squash in half lengthwise and then cut into 6 equal pieces. In a large bowl, combine squash, garlic, olive oil, sage, allspice, and salt and pepper to taste. Toss to coat well. Transfer to a baking sheet.

Bake until fork-tender, 20 to 30 minutes. Drizzle with maple syrup, sprinkle with pumpkin seeds and top with pecorino. Serve.

Pear and Ginger Fool

MAKES 4 SERVINGS

1 cup (250 mL) whipping cream (35%)

1 ½ cups (375 mL) Pear Sauce (page 326), cooled completely

½ cup (125 mL) Greek-style plain yogurt

1 tsp (5 mL) vanilla extract

1 tbsp (15 mL) dark rum (optional)

Honey, for drizzling (optional)

Finely chopped preserved or crystallized ginger

Gingersnap cookies, crumbled

Blackberries and mint sprigs, for garnish

In a large bowl, whip cream. Set aside.

In a medium bowl, combine pear sauce, yogurt, vanilla and rum, if desired. Stir to blend. Fold in whipped cream, leaving some streaks.

Spoon into 4 serving dishes. Drizzle with honey, if desired. Top with preserved ginger and gingersnap cookies. Garnish with blackberries and mint.

TAKEOUT AT HOME

General Tao's Chicken

Whenever I eat at a certain Szechuan restaurant in Montréal, I get so inspired by all the delicious sauces, spices and flavour combinations. Since I can't always make my way across town for their Chinese takeout, I've created this ridiculously good lineup of dishes that brings some of those amazing flavours home. This menu cooks up quickly, and you will have dinner on the table before your takeout food would have arrived!

The main act, General Tao's Chicken, is one of my Chinese-inspired favourites, and the garlicky bok choy and herby jasmine rice are the perfect sides.

MAKES 4 SERVINGS

CHICKEN

1 boneless, skinless chicken breast, cut in 1½-inch (4 cm) pieces

2 boneless, skinless chicken thighs, cut in 1½-inch (4 cm) pieces

3 tbsp (45 mL) cornstarch

3 tbsp (45 mL) soy sauce

1 tbsp (15 mL) water

SAUCE

¼ cup (60 mL) sugar

¼ cup (60 mL) rice wine vinegar

¼ to ½ cup (60 to 125 mL) chicken stock

1 tbsp (15 mL) soy sauce

1 tbsp (15 mL) sesame oil

1 tbsp (15 mL) hoisin sauce

2 tsp (10 mL) cornstarch

Pinch of 5-spice powder (optional)

TO ASSEMBLE

Vegetable oil, for frying

Cornstarch, for dredging

6 to 8 small whole dried chilies, or to taste

2 garlic cloves, chopped

1 tbsp (15 mL) chopped fresh ginger

4 green onions, cut in 1½-inch (4 cm) batons

½ bunch broccoli, cut into florets, blanched

Sesame seeds, for garnish

To start the chicken: In a medium bowl, sprinkle chicken with cornstarch. Add soy sauce and water. Stir well. Let sit for 15 to 20 minutes.

Meanwhile, make the sauce: In a small bowl, combine sugar, vinegar, ¼ cup (60 mL) chicken stock, soy sauce, sesame oil, hoisin sauce, cornstarch and 5-spice powder, if desired. Stir until sugar has dissolved. Set aside.

Heat a wok or large, heavy skillet over medium heat. Add enough vegetable oil to come 2 to 3 inches (5 to 8 cm) up the sides of the wok. When oil is hot, working in batches, dredge chicken in cornstarch and fry, turning, until coating is crispy and chicken is cooked through, 3 to 4 minutes. Drain on paper towels.

Remove all but 2 tbsp (30 mL) oil from the wok. Heat oil over medium-high to high heat. When oil is hot, add chilies and stir-fry for 30 seconds. Add garlic, ginger and green onions; stir-fry for 30 seconds more. Add reserved sauce and bring to a boil. If sauce reduces too quickly, add ¼ cup (60 mL) more chicken stock. Add blanched broccoli and cooked chicken, stir-frying to coat in the sauce and heat through.

Garnish with sesame seeds, if desired. Serve with steamed rice.

Garlicky Stir-Fried Baby Bok Choy

MAKES 4 SERVINGS

2 tbsp (30 mL) vegetable oil

2 to 3 garlic cloves, sliced or chopped

8 baby bok choy, sliced in half or quartered

1 sweet red pepper, sliced

1 can (4 oz/113 g) baby corn, drained

1 tbsp (15 mL) soy sauce

1 tbsp (15 mL) oyster sauce

1 tbsp (15 mL) chicken stock

Heat a wok or large skillet over medium-high heat. Add oil. When oil is hot, add garlic. Stir-fry garlic until just tender, about 30 seconds. Add bok choy, red peppers and baby corn; stir-fry for 1 to 2 minutes. Add soy sauce, oyster sauce and chicken stock; stir-fry until veggies are tender-crisp, about 1 minute more. Serve.

Jasmine Rice with Fresh Herbs

MAKES 4 SERVINGS

1 ½ cups (375 mL) vegetable stock or water

1 cup (250 mL) jasmine rice, rinsed

¼-inch (5 mm) slice fresh ginger

Pinch of salt

1 tbsp (15 mL) chopped fresh Thai basil

1 tbsp (15 mL) chopped fresh cilantro

In a small saucepan, combine vegetable stock, rice, ginger and salt. Stir. Bring to a boil over high heat. Reduce heat to low, cover and cook until rice is tender and all the water is absorbed, 18 to 20 minutes. Remove from heat. Let stand, covered, for 5 minutes. Fluff with a fork. Stir in fresh herbs and serve.

BIG ITALIAN SUNDAY DINNER

Osso Buco with Lemon

Being part of an Italian family has its perks, and let me tell you, osso buco is certainly one of them. I still remember asking my mom to make this dish as a gift for my tenth birthday. And my gift to your family is this rustic Italian feast that will make any Sunday night a special one.

The centrepiece of the meal is my version of my mom's ever-popular veal Osso Buco with Lemon, and the side dishes—rich, creamy mashed potatoes with olive oil and Parmesan and a classic tossed green salad—would be a tasty addition to any dinner. Finish it off with my much-requested Easy Tiramisù, and Sunday nights will never be the same at your house! *MAKES 6 SERVINGS*

6 veal shanks

Salt and freshly ground pepper

Flour, for dredging

4 tbsp (60 mL) olive oil

6 tbsp (90 mL) butter

1 large onion, finely chopped

1 garlic clove, minced

2 carrots, diced

2 celery stalks, diced

1 bay leaf

Leaves from 2 sprigs thyme, chopped

Leaves from 1 sprig rosemary, chopped

1 cup (250 mL) dry white wine

Grated zest and juice of 2 lemons

2 ½ to 3 cups (625 to 750 mL) veal or chicken stock

¼ cup (60 mL) chopped fresh Italian parsley

TIP If you prefer a thicker sauce, remove cooked shanks from pot and reduce sauce over medium-high heat until syrupy. Then add the remaining butter and lemon zest and juice. Return shanks to pot and reheat before serving.

Preheat oven to 350°F (180°C).

Season veal shanks with salt and pepper and lightly dredge in flour. Heat a Dutch oven over medium to medium-high heat. Add 2 tbsp (30 mL) oil and 2 tbsp (30 mL) butter. When butter has melted, add shanks and cook until browned on each side, about 5 minutes per side. Remove from pot and set aside.

Reduce heat to medium to medium-low. Add remaining 2 tbsp (30 mL) olive oil and 2 tbsp (30 mL) butter to pot. Add onions, garlic, carrots, celery, bay leaf, thyme and rosemary. Cook, stirring frequently, until vegetables have softened, 5 to 7 minutes. Deglaze with white wine and reduce until most of the liquid has evaporated. Add half the lemon juice and half the zest.

Add 2 ½ cups (625 mL) stock and bring to a boil. Reduce heat to a simmer. Return shanks and any juices to the pot. Cover and transfer to oven. Cook until meat is very tender, about 2 hours, adding more stock if liquid evaporates too quickly.

To finish, stir in the remaining 2 tbsp (30 mL) butter and the remaining lemon zest and juice. Serve garnished with chopped parsley.

Mashed Potatoes with Olive Oil and Parmesan

MAKES 4 SERVINGS

4 medium Yukon Gold potatoes (unpeeled), washed

¼ cup (60 mL) whipping cream (35%), or to taste

2 tbsp (30 mL) extra-virgin olive oil, or to taste

¼ cup (60 mL) freshly grated Parmesan cheese

1 tbsp (15 mL) chopped fresh chives

Pinch of freshly grated nutmeg

Salt and freshly ground pepper

In a medium saucepan, cover potatoes with cold water. Season generously with salt. Bring to a boil. Reduce heat, cover and simmer until potatoes are fork-tender, 20 to 25 minutes. Drain.

While potatoes are still warm, peel off skins. Return potatoes to saucepan or transfer to a large bowl. Mash potatoes until smooth, adding cream and olive oil. Stir in Parmesan and chives. Season with nutmeg, salt and pepper. Serve hot.

Tossed Green Salad with a Classic Olive Oil Vinaigrette

MAKES 4 TO 6 SERVINGS

½ head radicchio

½ head romaine

½ head escarole

½ head Boston or Bibb lettuce

1 small red onion (or ½ large), sliced

1 large field tomato (or 2 smaller), cut in wedges

¼ cup (60 mL) red wine vinegar

½ cup + 1 tbsp (140 mL) extra-virgin olive oil

Salt and freshly ground pepper

Cut or tear all lettuce leaves into bite-size pieces and place in a large bowl. Add red onion and tomatoes. Toss to combine.

In a small bowl or jar, combine red wine vinegar, olive oil, and salt and pepper to taste. Whisk or shake until emulsified. Add vinaigrette to salad greens and toss to combine. Taste and adjust seasoning.

Easy Tiramisù

MAKES 8 TO 10 SERVINGS

2 cups (500 mL) brewed espresso, cooled

½ cup (125 mL) sambuca liqueur

5 large eggs, separated

⅔ cup (150 mL) sugar

1 lb (450 g) mascarpone cheese

1 package (1 lb/450 g) savoiardi biscuits or ladyfingers

¼ cup (60 mL) cocoa powder

TIP If you do not want to use raw eggs in the tiramisù, whisk yolks with sugar in a double boiler over barely simmering water until mixture falls in ribbons when whisk is lifted. Replace the egg whites with 1 cup (250 mL) whipping cream, whipped.

Combine espresso and sambuca in a bowl. Set aside.

In a large bowl, combine egg yolks and sugar. Beat with an electric mixer until thick and lemony in colour. Add mascarpone and beat until smooth.

In a separate large bowl, beat egg whites with cleaned beaters until stiff peaks form. Gently but thoroughly fold egg whites into mascarpone mixture.

One at a time, quickly dip cookies in espresso mixture. (If you immerse the cookies in the espresso mixture, they will get too soggy.) Arrange a single layer of dipped cookies in a 13- × 9-inch (3 L) pan.

Spread half the mascarpone mixture over the cookies. Using a sieve, sprinkle with 2 tbsp (30 mL) cocoa. Top with remaining coffee-dipped cookies, then remaining mascarpone mixture. Sprinkle with remaining 2 tbsp (30 mL) cocoa. Cover and let tiramisù set in refrigerator for 12 to 24 hours.

BIG LAMB DINNER

Roasted Leg of Lamb with Mediterranean Stuffing

Traditionally, Easter is the time that I serve up the great big leg-of-lamb dinner at my house—we graze on the feast over a nice long lunch. I don't always want to wait until Easter for my lamb fix, though. If I have a craving, I pull out this menu anytime of year. **MAKES 6 SERVINGS**

3 potatoes (unpeeled)

3 tbsp (45 mL) olive oil, plus more for rubbing roast

2 medium onions, chopped

2 tbsp (30 mL) capers

2 tbsp (30 mL) chopped fresh parsley

2 garlic cloves, minced

¼ cup (60 mL) pitted black olives, thinly sliced

2 tbsp (30 mL) chopped fresh rosemary

2 tsp (10 mL) chopped fresh thyme

2 small hot peppers, chopped (optional)

1 boneless leg of lamb (3 to 4 lb/ 1.35 to 1.8 kg)

Salt and freshly ground pepper

To make the stuffing: Blanch potatoes, then peel and cut into large chunks. Set aside.

Heat 3 tbsp (45 mL) olive oil in a large skillet over medium heat. When oil is hot, add onions. Cook, stirring occasionally, until soft and transparent, 5 to 7 minutes. Transfer onions to a food processor. Add potatoes, capers and parsley. Pulse until smooth. Transfer to a medium bowl. Add garlic, olives, 1 tbsp (15 mL) rosemary, 1 tsp (5 mL) thyme and hot peppers, if desired. Stir to combine. Set aside.

Preheat oven to 400°F (200°C).

To butterfly the boneless leg of lamb: Without slicing all the way through, cut lamb in half horizontally and open it up like a book into one bigger piece. Spread stuffing over lamb. Roll up lamb and tie with kitchen string. Transfer to a rack in a roasting pan. Season lamb with salt and pepper. Coat with a little olive oil. Sprinkle with the remaining 1 tbsp (15 mL) rosemary and 1 tsp (5 mL) thyme.

Roast lamb until medium-rare, or until internal temperature reaches 140°F (60°C), 40 to 50 minutes. Transfer to a cutting board and tent with foil. Let rest for 10 to 15 minutes before slicing. (While lamb is resting, make the Roasted Broccoli and Cauliflower.) Cut lamb into thick slices and serve.

Roasted Broccoli and Cauliflower

MAKES 6 SERVINGS

1 large bunch broccoli (or 2 small),
    cut into florets

1 large head cauliflower (or 2 small),
    cut into florets

1 to 2 garlic cloves, minced

½ tsp (2 mL) coarsely ground fennel seeds

Salt and freshly ground pepper

⅓ to ½ cup (75 to 125 mL) olive oil

Preheat oven to 425°F (220°C).

In a large bowl, combine broccoli, cauliflower, garlic, fennel seeds, and salt and pepper to taste. Drizzle generously with olive oil and toss to coat well.

Spread veggies in a single layer on 1 or 2 baking sheets. Roast, turning veggies halfway, until golden brown and tender, 12 to 15 minutes. Serve.

Spring Vegetable Salad

MAKES 8 SERVINGS

2 bunches baby beets, such as candy cane,
    yellow or red, scrubbed

Olive oil, for drizzling

Salt and freshly ground pepper

1 bunch baby carrots, scrubbed

1 bunch asparagus

6 baby zucchinis, cut in half lengthwise

5 to 6 oz (140 to 170 g) mixed greens,
    such as watercress, frisée, baby arugula
    and/or mustard greens

Handful of chervil or parsley leaves

SHERRY WALNUT DRESSING

1 shallot, minced

2 tsp (10 mL) Dijon mustard

¼ cup (60 mL) sherry vinegar

1 tbsp (15 mL) honey

3 tbsp (45 mL) walnut oil

3 tbsp (45 mL) extra-virgin olive oil

Salt and freshly ground pepper

Preheat oven to 400°F (200°C).

Place half the beets on a double layer of foil. Drizzle generously with olive oil and season with salt and pepper. Fold foil over beets and tightly seal to create a package. Repeat with remaining beets. Roast beets until tender when pierced with a knife, about 1 hour, depending on size of beets. Unwrap beets and let cool slightly. Peel skins with a paring knife. Cut beets in half or quarters, depending on size. Set aside.

Add carrots to a pot of boiling salted water. Blanch for 3 to 4 minutes. Add asparagus and zucchinis. Cook until all vegetables are tender-crisp, about 2 minutes more. Drain. Transfer to a bowl of ice water. When veggies are cool, drain and pat dry with a kitchen towel.

To make the dressing: In a small bowl, combine shallot and mustard. Whisk in vinegar and honey. Gradually whisk in walnut oil and olive oil, whisking until emulsified. Season with salt and pepper. Taste and adjust seasoning.

In a large bowl, combine mixed greens, chervil or parsley leaves, beets, carrots, asparagus and zucchinis. Toss with dressing right before serving.

SHOW-STOPPING FISH DINNER

Salt-Baked Snapper

When my girlfriend and I have guests over for dinner, we like to make impressive-looking dishes that don't take much effort to prepare. This colourful, show-stopping menu brings three stars to the table, each beautiful in its own way.

The salt crust that surrounds the baked snapper is not only a show when you crack it open at the table, it also helps to keep the fish moist—it's a foolproof technique. The Brussels sprouts side dish is as tasty as it looks, with the combination of tangy sun-dried tomatoes and crunchy toasted pine nuts. The make-ahead French Lemon Tart is the stunning capper to the meal, finishing your night on a sweet, tangy note. MAKES 2 TO 4 SERVINGS

SALT-BAKED SNAPPER

6 to 7 large egg whites

1 ½ lb (675 g) kosher salt

1 tbsp (15) water

1 whole snapper (about 2 lb/900 g), cleaned

Freshly ground pepper

2 to 3 thyme sprigs

2 to 3 parsley sprigs

1 lemon, sliced

SIMPLE TOMATO SALAD

4 cups (1 L) sliced mixed tomatoes, such as heirloom, grape or cherry

1 tbsp (15 mL) chopped fresh parsley

Coarse sea salt and freshly ground pepper

Extra-virgin olive oil

Squeeze of lemon juice

Preheat oven to 400°F (200°C).

To make the salt-baked snapper: In a large bowl, lightly beat 6 egg whites. Add kosher salt and stir to combine, adding 1 more beaten egg white or 1 tbsp (15 mL) water to make a moist mixture. Set aside.

Pat fish dry. Season cavity with pepper. Fill with thyme, parsley and half of the lemon slices.

On a baking sheet, spread a thin layer of salt mixture a little larger than the fish. Place fish on salt. Pour remaining salt mixture over fish to cover completely. With your hands, mould the salt into the shape of the fish, pressing gently. Bake fish until internal temperature reaches 135°F to 140°F (58°C to 60°C), 25 to 30 minutes. Let fish rest in crust for 5 to 10 minutes.

While the fish rests, make the tomato salad: Combine tomato slices and parsley in a bowl. Season with salt and pepper. Drizzle with olive oil to taste and sprinkle with a squeeze of lemon juice. Toss.

Crack crust with the back of a spoon and scrape off crust. Make an incision along the top of the fish and peel off the skin. Gently remove the top fillet from the bones and transfer to a plate. Flip the fish over and repeat to remove the remaining fillet from the bones. Serve fish with the remaining lemon slices and Simple Tomato Salad.

Brussels Sprouts Sautéed with Sun-Dried Tomatoes and Pine Nuts

MAKES 4 TO 6 SERVINGS

1 lb (450 g) Brussels sprouts, trimmed and cut in half

2 tbsp (30 mL) olive oil

1 garlic clove, chopped

2 tbsp (30 mL) chopped sun-dried tomatoes

Salt and freshly ground pepper

¼ cup (60 mL) pine nuts, toasted

Blanch Brussels sprouts in boiling salted water until tender-crisp, 4 to 5 minutes. Drain.

Heat oil in a large skillet over medium-high heat. Add garlic and sauté for 1 minute. Add blanched Brussels sprouts and sun-dried tomatoes. Season with salt and pepper. Sauté until sprouts are just tender, about 5 minutes. Add pine nuts and toss to combine. Serve immediately.

French Lemon Tart

MAKES 8 SERVINGS

LEMON CURD

Grated zest of 2 lemons

1 cup (250 mL) lemon juice

2 cups (500 mL) sugar

7 large eggs

3 large egg yolks

¾ cup (175 mL) unsalted butter, cubed

SWEET TART PASTRY

2 cups (500 mL) all-purpose flour

1 tsp (5 mL) sugar

1 tsp (5 mL) salt

¾ cup (175 mL) cold unsalted butter, cut in small cubes

6 to 8 tbsp (90 to 125 mL) cold milk

1 large egg yolk

continued . . .

TIP You will have leftover curd. It is delicious in trifle or mini tarts, with scones or Lemony Pound Cake (page 407), in Lemon Mascarpone Mousse (page 389) or spooned over fresh berries.

To make the lemon curd: In a non-aluminum saucepan, combine lemon zest, lemon juice, sugar, eggs and egg yolks. Whisk to combine. Heat over medium-low heat, whisking or stirring constantly, until thick enough to coat the back of a spoon, 10 to 15 minutes. Remove from heat.

Add butter cubes, burying them so they melt quickly. Let sit for a minute, then stir until butter is melted and blended into the curd. Strain through a fine sieve into a bowl. Place plastic wrap directly on surface and let cool to room temperature. Cover and refrigerate for 1 to 2 hours. Curd will thicken as it cools.

To make the pastry: In a large bowl, stir together flour, sugar and salt. Cut butter into flour mixture with your fingertips or a pastry blender until mixture resembles coarse meal. Do not overwork.

Whisk together 6 tbsp (90 mL) milk and egg yolk. Stir into flour mixture just until dough comes together, adding a little more milk if mixture is too dry. Form into a ball and flatten into a disc. Wrap in plastic wrap and refrigerate for at least 1 hour.

Preheat the oven to 375°F (190°C).

Lightly flour work surface. Roll out dough into a circle ⅛-inch (3 mm) thick. Fit pastry into a 9-inch (23 cm) tart pan with removable bottom. (This is a generous amount of pastry so that it is easy to work with and roll. You may have a little extra pastry; you could also make a larger tart.) Trim off excess around edges.

Prick bottom of pastry all over with a fork. Line pastry shell with parchment paper or foil. Fill with pie weights or dried beans. Bake until pastry holds its shape and is almost fully cooked, 20 to 25 minutes. Remove weights and parchment and continue to bake until pastry is cooked through, lightly golden and crisp, 10 to 15 minutes more. Let tart shell cool completely on a rack before filling.

Remove sides of tart pan. Scrape curd into tart shell, smoothing top if needed. Refrigerate for at least 4 hours before serving.

CLASSIC COMFORT DINNER

Stefano's Tourtière

Natives of Québec know the tourtière well, and now here is your chance to enjoy it, too! I grew up enjoying this famous meat pie—my friend's mom would make a deep-dish version with chunks of veal and beef. I was shocked when they would eat their pie with a rustic, homemade ketchup on the side, but I soon bought into the idea.

Years later I'm still enjoying tourtière, but now I make a yummy comforting version of my own. Instead of meat chunks, I use a combination of ground beef, veal and pork and serve it with my own Sweet Tomato Ketchup—kind of a play on the sweet-and-savoury thing. Serve it with a mix of seasonal vegetables and, *bien sûr*, you'll feel like an honorary Quebecer! **MAKES 6 SERVINGS**

SHORTCRUST PASTRY

2 ¼ cups (550 mL) all-purpose flour

1 ¼ tsp (6 mL) salt

1 cup (250 mL) cold unsalted butter, cut in cubes

4 to 6 tbsp (60 to 90 mL) ice water

1 egg yolk, beaten, for egg wash

FILLING

1 tbsp (15 mL) olive oil

1 tbsp (15 mL) butter

½ lb (225 g) ground veal

½ lb (225 g) ground beef

½ lb (225 g) ground pork

Salt and freshly ground pepper

4 oz (115 g) cremini mushrooms, finely chopped

1 onion, finely chopped

3 garlic cloves, minced

1 tsp (5 mL) allspice

1 tsp (5 mL) cinnamon

⅛ tsp (0.5 mL) ground cloves

⅛ tsp (0.5 mL) nutmeg

1 small Yukon Gold potato, peeled and grated

½ cup (125 mL) white wine

To make the shortcrust pastry: In a large bowl, stir together flour and salt. Cut butter into flour mixture with your fingertips or a pastry blender until mixture resembles coarse meal. Do not overwork. Stir in enough ice water to make the dough come together. (Alternatively, make pastry in a food processor.)

Divide dough in half, one half slightly larger than the other. Flatten each half into a disc. Wrap in plastic wrap and refrigerate for at least 1 hour.

To make the tourtière filling: Heat a large skillet over medium heat. Add olive oil and butter. When butter has melted, add ground meats. Season with salt and pepper. Cook, stirring frequently, until meat is browned and just cooked through, 8 to 10 minutes. Add mushrooms, onions, garlic, allspice, cinnamon, cloves, nutmeg and grated potatoes. Cook, stirring occasionally, until veggies have softened, 5 to 10 minutes. Add white wine and cook until mixture is dry, 5 to 10 minutes more. Taste and adjust seasoning. Let cool completely.

Preheat oven to 450°F (230°C).

Lightly flour work surface. Roll out the larger pastry round into an 11-inch (28 cm) circle about ⅛-inch (3 mm) thick. (If pastry is soft while rolling, pop it in the freezer for 5 to 10 minutes.) Fit pastry into a 9-inch (23 cm) pie plate. Spoon tourtière filling into pastry shell. Brush edge with a little egg wash. Roll out second pastry round. Cover tourtière with top pastry, pressing edges together to seal. Trim pastry edge and crimp with tines of a fork. Brush pastry with egg wash. Score top of tourtière a few times with a paring knife to allow steam to escape while baking.

Bake tourtière for 15 minutes. Reduce heat to 350°F (180°C) and bake until crust is golden brown and filling is steaming, about 35 minutes, covering loosely with foil if pastry browns too quickly. Let tourtière cool for 10 minutes before slicing. Serve with Sweet Tomato Ketchup (recipe follows), if desired.

Sweet Tomato Ketchup

MAKES 3 CUPS (750 ML)

1 star anise

3 to 4 allspice berries

3 to 4 whole cloves

2 bay leaves

½ cinnamon stick

1 to 2 small dried chilies, or to taste (optional)

3 tbsp (45 mL) olive oil

1 large onion, chopped

1 celery stalk, chopped

1 large sweet red pepper, chopped

1 garlic clove, chopped

2 peaches, peeled and chopped

2 apples, peeled and chopped

1 pear, peeled and chopped

3 canned plum tomatoes, chopped (or 3 fresh plum tomatoes, blanched, peeled and chopped)

3 tbsp (45 mL) tomato paste

1 cup (250 mL) brown sugar

1 cup (250 mL) white vinegar

Salt and freshly ground pepper

Make a bouquet garni: Wrap star anise, allspice berries, cloves, bay leaves, cinnamon stick and dried chilies, if desired, in cheesecloth and tie with kitchen string.

Heat olive oil in a Dutch oven or large skillet over medium heat. Add onions, celery, red pepper, garlic, peaches, apples, pear, tomatoes, tomato paste, brown sugar, vinegar and bouquet garni. Season with salt and pepper. Bring to a gentle boil. Reduce heat and simmer, stirring often, until ketchup is thick, 1 hour to 1 hour 15 minutes. Let cool. Discard bouquet garni. Store in refrigerator for up to 1 week or freeze for up to 1 month.

Medley of Market Vegetables

MAKES 6 SERVINGS

8 cups (2 L) diced vegetables, such as
    butternut squash, celery root, rutabaga,
    green and yellow zucchini, asparagus,
    and French green beans

2 tbsp (30 mL) butter

1 tbsp (15 mL) olive oil

2 tbsp (30 mL) chopped mixed herbs,
    such as chervil, parsley, chives,
    tarragon, and basil

Salt and freshly ground pepper

When dicing vegetables, divide them into quick-cooking (zucchini, asparagus, green beans) and longer-cooking (celery root, rutabaga, butternut squash).

Bring a large pot of water to a boil. Generously salt. Add longer-cooking vegetables to boiling water and cook until firm to the bite, 7 to 10 minutes. Add quick-cooking vegetables and cook until all vegetables are tender-crisp, 3 to 4 minutes. Drain well. Return vegetables to pot. Add butter, olive oil, herbs, and salt and pepper to taste. Toss to combine.

PRIME RIB FEAST

Prime Rib Roast with Red Wine Jus

There's no classier dish at a dinner party or family get-together than prime rib. It's a big, beautiful cut of beef that never goes out of style.

My Prime Rib Feast has a classic complement of dishes, including the special roast itself. Cook it to your liking—I'm a medium-rare guy—and drizzle it with some of the flavourful red wine jus. The horseradish-infused Yorkshire puddings are the perfect side dish, especially when served up with a scoop of my Maple-Mustard Glazed Vegetables. **MAKES 8 TO 10 SERVINGS**

1 bone-in standing prime rib roast (5-rib roast, 8 to 10 lb/3.5 to 4.5 kg)

Coarse kosher salt

Crushed peppercorns

1 onion, cut in half crosswise

1 head garlic, cut in half horizontally

1 carrot, cut in half crosswise

1 celery stalk, cut in half crosswise

RED WINE JUS

1 cup (250 mL) red wine

1 cup (250 mL) beef stock

2 sprigs thyme

2 bay leaves

Salt and freshly ground pepper

Let prime rib roast sit at room temperature for 1 hour before cooking. (The roast will cook more evenly.)

Preheat oven to 425°F (220°C).

Pat roast dry with paper towels and season generously with salt and crushed pepper. Transfer to a rack in a roasting pan. Add onion, garlic, carrot and celery to pan.

Cook roast for 30 minutes. Reduce heat to 300°F (150°C). For a medium-rare roast, cook until internal temperature reaches 130°F to 135°F (55°C to 58°C), 2 to 2 ½ hours, depending on size of roast. Temperature will rise 5°F to 10°F (3°C to 5°C) as meat rests. (If making Yorkshire puddings, make batter while roast cooks.) Transfer roast to a cutting board, loosely tent with foil and let rest for 25 to 30 minutes before slicing. (Bake Yorkshire puddings while roast rests.)

To make the red wine jus: Skim excess fat from roasting pan. Heat pan (with vegetables) over medium heat. Deglaze pan with wine and stock, stirring to incorporate pan drippings. Add thyme and bay leaves. Bring to a boil. Simmer until sauce reduces by half. Season with salt and pepper. Strain through a fine sieve and serve with roast.

Yorkshire Puddings with Horseradish

MAKES 12 SERVINGS

4 large eggs

1 ½ cups (375 mL) milk

2 heaping tsp (12 mL) prepared horseradish

1 ⅓ cups (325 mL) flour, sifted

Pinch of salt

About ⅓ cup (75 mL) peanut oil

In a medium bowl, whisk eggs. Whisk in milk and horseradish. Gradually whisk in flour and salt. Let batter rest in fridge for at least 1 hour before using. Whisk again before using. Batter should be a little thicker than crêpe batter or whipping cream; add 1 to 2 tbsp (15 to 30 mL) water, if needed, to thin batter. Transfer to large measuring cup or pitcher so batter is easy to pour into muffin cups.

Preheat oven to 550°F (290°C).

Add a generous teaspoon (6 mL) oil to each cup of a 12-cup muffin pan. Heat pan until oil is hot and almost smoking, 10 to 12 minutes. The key to Yorkshire puddings rising perfectly is that the oil and pan should be really hot when you add the batter.

Quickly and evenly pour batter into muffin cups. Bake until puddings are golden brown and puffed, 15 to 20 minutes. Do not open the oven door while the puddings are baking—you'll lower the oven temperature and they may fall. Serve immediately; puddings will slowly deflate as they cool.

Maple-Mustard Glazed Vegetables

MAKES 8 SERVINGS

3 large carrots, peeled

1 large bunch asparagus, trimmed

12 small cipollini onions

2 tbsp (30 mL) butter

2 tbsp (30 mL) olive oil

Salt and freshly ground pepper

1 tbsp (15 mL) grainy mustard

3 tbsp (45 mL) chicken stock

2 tbsp (30 mL) maple syrup

2 tbsp (30 mL) chopped mixed fresh herbs, such as basil, chives and parsley

Cut carrots into batons about ¼ inch × ¼ inch × 2 ½ inches (5 mm × 5 mm × 6 cm). Cut asparagus crosswise into thirds. Set aside.

Add cipollini onions to a pot of boiling salted water and cook for 2 to 3 minutes. (This will make it easier to peel them.) Using a slotted spoon, transfer to ice water. (Remove pot from heat but do not drain.) Trim and peel cipollini. Pat dry.

Bring water back to a boil. Add carrots and blanch until crisp, 3 to 4 minutes. Add asparagus and cook for 1 to 2 minutes more. Drain and transfer to ice water to stop the cooking. Drain again and pat dry.

Heat butter and olive oil in a large skillet over medium heat. Add cipollini onions and season with salt and pepper. Sauté until golden and tender, about 10 minutes. Add mustard, stock and maple syrup. Toss to combine. Add carrots and asparagus. Toss to combine. Cook until vegetables are heated through and tender, about 5 minutes. Remove from heat and stir in chopped herbs.

FEED-A-CROWD MENU

Stefano's Oven-Roasted Porchetta

There are always occasions when you need to feed a crowd, like watching the big game, a family reunion or a birthday party. Well, there's no better way to feed all the hungry people at your gathering than an oven-roasted porchetta.

The whole pig shoulder is butterflied, seasoned with a fresh herb mixture, rolled up and roasted until the skin is nice and crisp. Serve a slice with my Classic Caesar Salad and my Decadent Potato and Vegetable Gratin and you'll be hosting a very happy group. And when a moist Cardamom Orange Cake is brought out for dessert, your guests may just never leave! MAKES 8 TO 10 SERVINGS

1 boneless pork shoulder (5 to 6 lb/2.25 to 2.7 kg)

¼ cup (60 mL) chopped fresh Italian parsley

2 tbsp (30 mL) chopped fresh sage

2 tbsp (30 mL) chopped fresh rosemary

1 tbsp (15 mL) fennel seeds, crushed

1 tsp (5 mL) hot pepper flakes, or to taste

5 garlic cloves, chopped, or to taste

6 tbsp (90 mL) olive oil, plus more for rubbing roast

2 tbsp (30 mL) white wine

Salt and freshly ground pepper

Preheat oven to 400°F (200°C).

To make the herb paste: In a small bowl, combine parsley, sage, rosemary, fennel seeds, hot pepper flakes, garlic, 6 tbsp (90 mL) olive oil, white wine, and salt and pepper to taste. Mix well. Set aside.

To butterfly the pork shoulder: Without slicing all the way through, cut pork in half horizontally and open it up like a book into one bigger piece. Massage herb mixture into pork. Roll up pork and tie with kitchen string. Transfer to a roasting pan fat side up. Season with salt and pepper and rub a little oil over the roast.

Roast pork for 15 minutes. Reduce heat to 325°F (160°C) and continue to roast to medium doneness, or until internal temperature reaches 155°F to 160°F (68°C to 70°C), 1½ to 2 hours, depending on thickness of roast. For an extra-crispy skin, broil roast until golden brown, 3 to 5 minutes. Transfer roast to a cutting board, tent with foil and let rest for 15 to 20 minutes before slicing.

Serve as a main dish or serve in sandwiches, using ciabatta buns and topping with mustard, mayonnaise, fontina cheese, arugula, roasted red peppers and/or artichokes.

Classic Caesar Salad

MAKES 6 TO 8 SERVINGS

PARMESAN CROUTONS

About ½ day-old baguette

4 small garlic cloves, peeled and crushed

¼ cup (60 mL) unsalted butter

½ cup (125 mL) grated Parmesan cheese

SALAD

1 large garlic clove, minced

2 to 3 anchovies, mashed with a fork

½ tsp (2 mL) capers, rinsed and minced

2 large fresh egg yolks

2 tbsp (30 mL) lemon juice

¼ tsp (1 mL) dry mustard

½ cup (125 mL) extra-virgin olive oil

Salt and freshly ground pepper

2 heads romaine

½ cup (125 mL) shaved Parmesan cheese

To make the Parmesan croutons: Preheat oven to 350°F (180°C). Cut baguette into ¾-inch (2 cm) cubes. You need about 2 cups (500 mL). Set aside in a large bowl.

Combine garlic and butter in a small saucepan. Heat over medium heat until butter has melted and starts to bubble but not brown. Remove from heat and let stand for 15 minutes. Strain butter and discard garlic cloves.

Toss bread cubes with garlic butter until evenly coated. Transfer to a baking sheet and bake, stirring occasionally, until golden brown and crispy, about 15 minutes. Return croutons to bowl and toss with Parmesan while still hot. Set aside.

To make the dressing: In a small bowl, mix together garlic, anchovies and capers to form a paste. Add egg yolks, lemon juice and dry mustard. Whisk to combine. Continue to whisk while adding olive oil in a slow, steady stream, whisking until all the oil is incorporated and the dressing is thick and smooth. Season with salt and pepper. Refrigerate dressing for 30 minutes to develop extra flavour, if desired.

To finish the salad: Tear romaine leaves into bite-size pieces. Wash and dry leaves well. Place romaine in a large bowl. Pour dressing down the side of the bowl and toss to coat romaine evenly. Add Parmesan croutons and toss again. Garnish salad with shaved Parmesan.

Decadent Potato and Vegetable Gratin

MAKES 8 TO 10 SERVINGS

3 tbsp (45 mL) butter

4 to 5 medium Yukon Gold potatoes, peeled

2 small sweet potatoes, peeled

2 parsnips, peeled

2 carrots, peeled

2 shallots, thinly sliced or diced

Leaves from 1 sprig thyme, finely chopped

Salt and freshly cracked pepper

1 ½ to 2 cups (375 to 500 mL) whipping cream (35%)

1 ½ cups (375 mL) grated Parmesan cheese

Thyme sprigs or chopped fresh parsley, for garnish

TIP The gratin can be made ahead. Reheat, covered, in a 375°F (190°C) oven until steaming and heated through, 30 to 45 minutes.

Preheat oven to 375°F (190°C).

Grease a 9-inch (2.5 L) round baking dish with 1 tbsp (15 mL) butter. (Alternatively, you could use an oval or rectangular baking dish. Increase the amount of vegetables and the baking time as needed.)

Using a mandoline or sharp knife, slice potatoes, sweet potatoes, parsnips and carrots into ⅛-inch (3 mm) slices. Transfer to a large bowl. Add shallots, thyme, and salt and pepper to taste. Toss to combine. Layer vegetables in prepared baking dish, decoratively overlapping vegetables for the top layer.

Add 1 ½ cups (375 mL) cream. Press down on vegetables. You should see the cream come up the sides of the pan, but the vegetables do not need to be submerged. Add more cream, if needed. Sprinkle gratin with Parmesan and dot with the remaining 2 tbsp (30 mL) butter.

Cover tightly with foil. Bake until vegetables are fork-tender, 1 hour 15 minutes to 1 hour 30 minutes, depending on how deep the dish is.

For a golden brown top: Preheat broiler. Uncover gratin and broil until golden brown, 2 to 3 minutes.

Keep warm and let rest for 10 to 15 minutes before slicing. Garnish with thyme sprigs or chopped parsley.

Cardamom Orange Cake

MAKES 6 TO 8 SERVINGS

CAKE

3 ½ cups (875 mL) all-purpose flour

2 tsp (10 mL) ground cardamom

2 tsp (10 mL) baking powder

Pinch of salt

1 cup (250 mL) unsalted butter, at room temperature

½ cup (125 mL) sugar

8 large egg yolks, lightly beaten

2 tbsp (30 mL) grated orange zest

1 tsp (5 mL) vanilla extract

1 cup (250 mL) milk

1 tbsp (15 mL) grated orange zest, for garnish

⅓ cup (75 mL) sliced blanched almonds, for garnish

ICING

½ cup (125 mL) plain yogurt

2 tbsp (30 mL) honey

2 tbsp (30 mL) orange juice

2 tbsp (30 mL) icing sugar

Preheat oven to 350°F (180°C). Grease and flour an 8-inch (1 L) Bundt pan.

In a medium bowl, whisk together flour, cardamom, baking powder and salt. Set aside.

In large bowl, cream butter and sugar with an electric mixer until light and fluffy. Beat in egg yolks a little at a time, then continue to beat until light and fluffy. Beat in orange zest and vanilla. Beat flour mixture into butter mixture alternately with milk, making 2 additions of each and beating until smooth.

Scrape batter into prepared pan and spread evenly. Bake until cake springs back to the touch and a cake tester comes out clean, 40 to 45 minutes. Let cool in pan.

To make the icing: In a small bowl, combine yogurt, honey, orange juice and icing sugar. Stir until smooth.

When cake has cooled, remove from pan. Drizzle icing over cake and garnish with orange zest and almonds.

TIP For a thicker and sweeter icing: Stir together 2 tbsp (30 mL) yogurt, 2 tbsp (30 mL) honey and 2 tbsp (30 mL) orange juice. Stir in 1 ¾ to 2 cups (425 to 500 mL) icing sugar.

DESSERTS

Classic Crème Brûlée

You don't have to go to a fancy French restaurant to enjoy this classic dessert. The smooth, creamy vanilla custard and crunchy sugar topping are a fantastic pairing. It's easy to make and impressive to serve. **MAKES 4 SERVINGS**

2 cups (500 mL) whipping cream (35%)	5 large egg yolks
1 vanilla bean, split lengthwise and seeds scraped	½ cup (125 mL) + 6 tbsp (90 mL) sugar

TIP Use 6-oz (175 mL) round ramekins and increase the cooking time to 30 to 35 minutes.

Preheat oven to 325°F (160°C). Bring a pot of water to a simmer for the water bath.

Combine cream, vanilla bean and seeds in a small saucepan. Heat over medium heat until cream comes just to a simmer.

Meanwhile, whisk egg yolks and ½ cup (125 mL) sugar in a medium bowl until blended. Whisking constantly, slowly add the hot cream mixture. Strain through a sieve into a large measuring cup. Divide evenly among 4 oval crème brûlée dishes (6 inches/15 cm long and 1 inch/2.5 cm deep).

Transfer dishes to a roasting pan. Place on middle rack of oven. Carefully pour hot water into roasting pan to come halfway up the sides of the dishes. Be careful not to get any water in the custard. Bake custards until almost set in the centre when gently shaken, about 20 minutes.

Remove from oven, cover loosely with foil and let stand in water bath for 5 minutes more until custard is set. Carefully remove from water bath. Let cool to room temperature, about 30 minutes. Cover and chill until completely set, 3 to 4 hours before serving.

To serve, sprinkle 1 to 1 ½ tbsp (15 to 20) of the remaining sugar evenly over each custard. Working with one dish at a time, hold a kitchen blowtorch so that the flame is about 2 inches (5 cm) above the surface of the custard. Direct the flame so that the sugar melts and caramelizes evenly. Keep the flame moving so the sugar doesn't burn. (Alternatively, sprinkle a thin layer of brown sugar and place under broiler.)

Easy Cinnamon Rice Pudding

My nonna used to make a pot of warm rice pudding for us when we were kids—there's nothing more comforting than the thought of that creamy rice goodness and the smell of sweet cinnamon. I now make this rice pudding recipe for my little girls, and they love it just as much as I loved my nonna's. I hope you and your kids love it, too! **MAKES 4 SERVINGS**

½ cup (125 mL) arborio rice

3 cups (750 mL) milk

1 cup (250 mL) whipping cream (35%)

¼ cup (60 mL) sugar

1 small cinnamon stick

1 vanilla bean, split lengthwise

GARNISHES

Chopped pistachio nuts, fresh or canned mandarin segments, dried cranberries

In a small, heavy saucepan, combine rice, milk, cream, sugar, cinnamon stick and vanilla bean. Bring to a gentle boil over medium-high heat. Reduce heat and simmer, uncovered and stirring occasionally to prevent rice from sticking to the bottom of the pot, until rice is soft and tender, 30 to 35 minutes. Let stand for 10 minutes before serving. Serve warm or cold with desired garnishes.

Amaretti Cookies

When I was little, I used to save my change so I could buy fresh amaretti cookies at a bakery near our house. Nothing was better than the taste of those sweet almond-flavoured cookies, all moist and chewy inside. This recipe reminds me of those little gems, and the best part is they're so easy to make at home.

MAKES ABOUT 24 COOKIES

2 large egg whites

⅔ cup to 1 cup (150 to 250 mL) sugar

2 cups (500 mL) finely ground almonds or almond flour

1 tsp (5 mL) almond or vanilla extract

Whole blanched almonds, for finishing

Set racks in top and bottom thirds of oven and preheat oven to 350°F (180°C). Line 2 baking sheets with parchment paper.

In a medium bowl, beat egg whites until soft peaks form. Slowly beat in ⅔ cup (150 mL) sugar until stiff, shiny peaks form. If you prefer a sweeter cookie, beat in ⅓ cup (75 mL) more sugar. Gently but thoroughly fold in ground almonds and almond extract.

Using a tablespoon to measure, drop cookies, spacing 1 inch (2.5 cm) apart, onto prepared baking sheets. Gently press a whole almond into top of each cookie.

Bake cookies, rotating and switching baking sheets halfway, until golden and set, about 20 minutes. Let stand on baking sheet for 5 to 10 minutes before transferring to a rack to cool completely. Store in an airtight container.

TIP Replace the almonds in this recipe with pistachio nuts. For a chocolate almond treat, add 2 tbsp (30 mL) cocoa powder. If desired, make sandwich cookies: sandwich chocolate hazelnut spread or jam between 2 cookies.

Shortbread Cookies with Butterscotch Sauce

Whether you need a go-to shortbread recipe for the holidays or a sweet, buttery treat any other time of the year, this easy cookie is the one for you. Its light, crumbly texture will win you over, but dipping it in my homemade butterscotch will take you over the moon! **MAKES ABOUT 2 DOZEN COOKIES**

2 cups (500 mL) all-purpose flour

Pinch of salt

1 cup (250 mL) unsalted butter,
   at room temperature

½ cup (125 mL) icing sugar, sifted

Butterscotch Sauce (page 381)

Set racks in top and bottom thirds of oven and preheat oven to 350°F (180°C). Line 2 baking sheets with parchment paper.

Combine flour and salt. Set aside.

In a large bowl, cream butter and icing sugar with an electric mixer until light and fluffy. Stir flour mixture into butter mixture just until incorporated—do not over-mix. Cover and let rest in fridge for 1 hour.

Roll dough into 1-inch (2.5 cm) balls. Transfer to baking sheets, spacing 2 inches (5 cm) apart. Flatten balls slightly with the back of a fork, making a decorative pattern.

Bake cookies, rotating and switching baking sheets halfway, until top is firm when lightly pressed and bottom is lightly golden, 12 to 15 minutes. Cool on racks. Serve cookies with warm butterscotch sauce.

Kitchen Sink Skillet Cookie

This is definitely a dessert that you can make with the kids. They'll love picking out the tasty fillings for the cookie and helping to press the dough into the skillet. Cram it full of all their favourite candies and treats—anything goes in this one! If desired, decorate or write a message on the cookies with Vanilla Butter Frosting. **MAKES 2 LARGE COOKIES**

2 ¼ cups (550 mL) all-purpose flour

1 tsp (5 mL) baking soda

¼ tsp (1 mL) salt

¾ cup (175 mL) unsalted butter, at room temperature

¾ cup (175 mL) packed brown sugar

½ cup (125 mL) white sugar

1 large egg

1 tsp (5 mL) vanilla extract

¼ cup (60 mL) large-flake rolled oats

¼ cup (60 mL) each peanuts, toffee chocolate pieces, butterscotch chips and chocolate-covered raisins

¼ cup (60 mL) each pretzels and candy-coated chocolate candies

VANILLA BUTTER FROSTING

½ cup (125 mL) unsalted butter, at room temperature

1 ¼ cups (300 mL) icing sugar, sifted

Pinch of salt

2 to 3 tbsp (30 to 45 mL) milk or whipping cream (35%)

1 tbsp (15 mL) vanilla extract

Preheat oven to 350°F (180°C). Line 2 ovenproof 8-inch (20 cm) skillets with parchment paper. (Alternatively, bake cookies one sheet at a time.)

To make the skillet cookies: Stir together flour, baking soda and salt. Set aside.

In a large bowl, cream butter, brown sugar and white sugar with an electric mixer until light and fluffy. Add egg and beat until smooth. Beat in vanilla.

Stir in flour mixture and oats just until combined—do not over-mix. Stir in peanuts, toffee chocolate pieces, butterscotch chips and chocolate-covered raisins.

Divide dough in half and press each half into a skillet. Garnish top of each cookie with pretzels and candy-coated chocolate candies, gently pressing into the dough.

Bake cookies until golden around the edges, 20 to 25 minutes. Let stand for 10 minutes. Remove cookies from skillets, remove parchment paper and cool cookies on a rack.

To make the frosting: In a medium bowl, cream butter with an electric mixer until light and fluffy, about 2 minutes. Using a spatula, stir in 1 cup (250 mL) of the icing sugar and salt until well combined. Stir in 2 tbsp (30 mL) milk and vanilla. Beat to make a spreadable frosting, adding up to ¼ cup (60 mL) remaining icing sugar or 1 tbsp (15 mL) more milk as needed.

Cinnamon Ricotta Cannoli

This is another of those classic Italian desserts that brings us great national pride. The secret to a good cannoli is the shell. In my humble opinion, this is the perfect not-too-sweet version—a crispy tube of pastry filled with rich, creamy ricotta filling and just a hint of cinnamon. Mmmm... **MAKES ABOUT 24 CANNOLI**

CANNOLI SHELLS

1 ½ cups (375 mL) all-purpose flour

2 tbsp (30 mL) sugar

¼ tsp (1 mL) cinnamon

¼ tsp (1 mL) salt

2 tbsp (30 mL) cold unsalted butter, cut in small cubes

6 to 7 tbsp (90 to 110 mL) dry marsala wine

CINNAMON RICOTTA FILLING

2 cups (500 mL) ricotta cheese

½ cup (125 mL) icing sugar, or to taste

½ tsp (2 mL) cinnamon

TO ASSEMBLE

Vegetable oil, for deep-frying

1 egg white, lightly beaten

Ground pistachio nuts and icing sugar, for garnish

To prepare the cannoli shells: In a medium bowl, combine flour, sugar, cinnamon and salt. Whisk to combine. Add butter cubes. Blend with your fingertips until mixture resembles coarse meal. Stir in 6 tbsp (90 mL) marsala just until dough starts to come together, adding more marsala if needed.

Turn mixture out onto a work surface and knead until dough comes together, about 2 minutes. (Dough will be rough, not smooth and elastic.) Flatten into a disc, wrap in plastic wrap and refrigerate for at least 1 hour.

Meanwhile, make the ricotta filling: In a large bowl, beat together ricotta, icing sugar and cinnamon until smooth. Cover and refrigerate for at least 1 hour before filling cannoli.

To assemble the cannoli: Cut dough into 4 pieces. Working with 1 piece of dough at a time, and keeping remaining dough wrapped so it does not dry out, on a lightly floured work surface, roll out dough to about ⅛-inch (3 mm) thickness. Cut out rounds with a 3-inch (8 cm) cookie cutter. Roll each round as thinly as possible. Repeat with remaining 3 pieces of dough. (Chill remaining dough in the fridge if it becomes too soft or warm.) You should be able to get about 24 rounds without re-rolling scraps.

Pour enough oil into a Dutch oven or wide, heavy pot to come halfway up the sides of the pot. Heat oil to 350°F (180°C) over medium heat.

Meanwhile, lightly oil 4 to 8 metal cannoli tubes.

Loosely wrap a round of dough around a cannoli tube, brushing a little beaten egg white between the overlapping edges so the dough sticks together and doesn't slide off the tube while frying. Fry 3 or 4 cannoli shells at a time, turning with tongs, until golden brown, about 1 minute. Drain briefly on paper towels.

Wearing oven mitts and holding the hot cannoli tubes with tongs, carefully slide the hot shells off the tubes. (If you allow the shells to cool, they will stick to the tubes and shatter when you try to remove them.) Transfer shells to paper towels to drain and let cool completely. Cool tubes before reusing. Repeat with remaining dough rounds.

Just before serving, spoon ricotta filling into a pastry bag and pipe some into one end of a shell, filling shell halfway, then pipe into other end to fill completely. Repeat with remaining shells. Garnish cannoli with pistachios and icing sugar.

TIP Don't stuff the shells too far ahead of time or they will get soggy. Feel free to use store-bought cannoli shells. This filling is quite versatile, so add any other ingredients, such as candied orange peel or chocolate chips. You can also use port in place of marsala, if you like.

Stefano's Baci

Baci means kiss in Italian, and this baci is a chocolate kiss from me to you. You'll go head over heels for the layers of hazelnut perfection—a toasted nut, surrounded by crushed hazelnut wafers, enrobed in chocolate and rolled in chopped nuts. Make a batch for the ones you love! **MAKES 24 CHOCOLATES**

8 to 10 oz (225 to 280 g) semisweet chocolate, chopped

1 cup (250 mL) chocolate hazelnut spread

1 cup (250 mL) crushed hazelnut wafer cookies

24 whole hazelnuts

7 oz (200 g) dark chocolate (50 to 70% cocoa), chopped

Pinch of salt

1 to 1 ½ cups (250 to 375 mL) finely ground hazelnuts

Melt semisweet chocolate in top of a double boiler (or in a medium heatproof bowl set over a pan of simmering water), stirring until smooth. Remove from heat and add chocolate hazelnut spread and crushed wafer cookies. Stir until well combined. Refrigerate mixture until firm, about 1 hour.

Roll a tablespoonful of chocolate mixture around a hazelnut and shape into a ball. Repeat with remaining hazelnuts and chocolate mixture. If mixture gets too soft, refrigerate until firm.

Melt dark chocolate with salt in top of a double boiler (or in a heatproof bowl set over a pan of simmering water), stirring until smooth. Let cool slightly. Dip balls in dark chocolate and then roll in ground hazelnuts.

Transfer balls to a baking sheet lined with parchment and refrigerate until chocolate hardens. Store in an airtight container in a cool, dry place.

Salted Chocolate Caramels

Make your own candy at home and try these simple salted chocolate caramels. The pinch of fleur de sel on top of these one-bite wonders enhances the flavour of both the caramel and the chocolate. They're great to give as a hostess gift, so make a big batch during the holidays. **MAKES 20 TO 24 PIECES**

BUTTERSCOTCH SAUCE
¼ cup (60 mL) unsalted butter

1 cup (250 mL) light brown sugar

¾ cup (175 mL) whipping cream (35%)

1 to 2 tsp (5 to 10 mL) vanilla extract

Pinch of salt

TO ASSEMBLE
10 oz (280 g) dark chocolate, finely chopped

Fleur de sel

To make the butterscotch sauce: In a small, heavy saucepan over medium heat, melt butter. Add brown sugar and swirl the pot to combine—do not stir. When brown sugar has dissolved and starts to bubble and thicken, stir in cream. Cook, stirring occasionally, until thick, about 5 minutes more. Stir in vanilla and salt.

Transfer butterscotch sauce to a bowl and let cool completely. Chill in fridge until completely firm, 1 to 2 hours.

To make the caramel centres: Line a small baking sheet with parchment paper. Scoop out butterscotch with a tablespoon and use your hands to shape into rounds. Transfer to baking sheet. Make about 20 to 24 rounds. Chill in fridge or freezer until completely firm.

Melt chocolate in the top of a double boiler (or in a heatproof bowl set over simmering water), stirring until smooth. Dip caramel rounds in chocolate and return to baking sheet. Sprinkle each caramel with a few grains of fleur de sel. Chill in fridge until firm.

TIP The butterscotch sauce is also delicious with apple wedges.

Triple-Chocolate Brownie Explosion

Warning: This recipe is for chocolate lovers only! When we developed this recipe for the show, we added layers of chocolate—dark, milk and white—until it just couldn't hold any more. Serve these brownies with a tall glass of cold milk or use them as the chocolaty base for a decadent ice-cream sundae. **MAKES 9 BROWNIES**

12 oz (340 g) dark chocolate, chopped

¼ cup (60 mL) unsalted butter

1 ½ cups (375 mL) sugar

3 large eggs

¾ cup (175 mL) all-purpose flour

½ tsp (2 mL) salt

1 tsp (5 mL) vanilla extract

1 tsp (5 mL) brewed espresso

2 oz (55 g) milk chocolate chunks

2 oz (55 g) white chocolate chunks

Melted white, milk and dark chocolate, to taste, for drizzling

Preheat oven 325°F (160°C). Butter a 9-inch (2.5 L) square cake pan and line bottom with parchment paper, leaving an overhang to help lift out brownies.

Melt dark chocolate with butter in top of a double boiler (or in a heatproof bowl set over a pan of simmering water), stirring until smooth. Stir in sugar. Let cool slightly. Add eggs one at a time, stirring with a wooden spoon or spatula after each addition until incorporated. Add flour and salt and stir just to combine. Stir in vanilla, espresso and milk chocolate and white chocolate chunks.

Scrape batter into prepared pan, spreading evenly. Bake until a cake tester inserted in centre comes out with just a few moist crumbs clinging to it, 35 to 40 minutes. Let cool completely.

Lift brownies from pan. Drizzle generously with melted white, milk and dark chocolate. Cut into 9 squares.

Chocolate Hazelnut Tartlets

These chocolaty, nutty little tarts are a lifesaver when you're having a crowd over and you need a low-effort dessert. Keep a package of frozen store-bought pastry shells on hand and you're halfway to having them made. Easy to make, easy to serve, and the leftovers make a wicked midnight snack! **MAKES 30 TARTLETS**

30 store-bought mini tart shells (about 2 inches/5 cm), baked and cooled

About ⅔ cup (150 mL) chopped toasted hazelnuts

½ cup (125 mL) whipping cream (35%)

7 oz (200 g) dark chocolate, very finely chopped

2 tbsp (30 mL) unsalted butter, cut in small pieces, at room temperature

1 tsp (5 mL) amaretto liqueur (optional)

Sprinkle about 1 tsp (5 mL) chopped hazelnuts into each baked tart shell.

In a small saucepan over medium heat, bring cream just to a boil. Pour hot cream over chopped chocolate and butter in a bowl. Let stand for 1 minute. Stir until smooth. Stir in amaretto, if desired.

Spoon chocolate mixture into each tart shell. Let set in fridge until chocolate is firm, 1 to 2 hours.

TIP You can make these tarts with milk chocolate instead of dark. Replace the amaretto with orange liqueur.

To freeze: Let tarts set in fridge. Freeze on a baking sheet, then transfer to an airtight container. Freeze for up to 1 month for best results.

Mini Chocolate Chip Ice-Cream Sandwiches

This recipe is a great two-for-one—not only do you get a classic chocolate chip cookie, but you also get a fun dessert to serve at a kid's birthday party. Sandwich a layer of ice cream between two of my tasty cookies and have the kids roll them in their favourite candies or sprinkles. They're as pretty as they are delicious!

MAKES 8 SERVINGS

CHOCOLATE CHIP COOKIES

2 cups (500 mL) all-purpose flour

1 tsp (5 mL) baking soda

¼ tsp (1 mL) salt

¾ cup (175 mL) unsalted butter, at room temperature

¾ cup (175 mL) packed brown sugar

½ cup (125 mL) white sugar

1 large egg

1 tsp (5 mL) vanilla extract

1 ¼ cups (300 mL) milk chocolate chips

TO ASSEMBLE

Vanilla ice cream

Melted chocolate, for dipping (optional)

Sprinkles, candies and/or mini chocolate chips

Set racks in top and bottom thirds of oven and preheat oven to 350°F (180°C). Line 2 baking sheets with parchment paper.

To make the cookies: Stir together flour, baking soda and salt. Set aside.

In a large bowl, cream butter, brown sugar and white sugar with an electric mixer until light and fluffy. Add egg and beat until smooth. Beat in vanilla.

Stir in flour mixture just until combined—don't over-mix. Stir in chocolate chips.

Using your hands, roll dough into 16 balls about the size of a golf ball. (You can vary the size to make mini, regular or jumbo cookies, adjusting the baking time as needed.) Transfer cookies to baking sheets, spacing 2 inches (5 cm) apart. Press down on balls to flatten.

Bake cookies, rotating and switching baking sheets halfway, until golden around the edges, 10 to 12 minutes. Let cookies stand for 10 minutes on baking sheets. Transfer to racks and let cool completely.

To assemble the ice-cream sandwiches: Sandwich a scoop of ice cream between 2 cookies. Dip sandwiches in melted chocolate, if desired, or roll in sprinkles, candies and/or mini chocolate chips. Serve immediately or make ahead and freeze.

Whoopie Pies

I first tried this dessert when our family was on vacation in Maine—who knew that the whoopie pie is the state's official treat? It's nearly impossible to pass up that fluffy whipped marshmallow filling sandwiched between layers of rich chocolate-cake-like cookies. **MAKES 12 SERVINGS**

WHOOPIE PIES
1 ¾ cups (425 mL) all-purpose flour
¾ cup (175 mL) cocoa powder
1 tsp (5 mL) baking powder
½ tsp (2 mL) baking soda
Pinch of salt (optional)
⅔ cup (150 mL) unsalted butter

1 ¼ cups (300 mL) sugar
1 large egg
1 cup (250 mL) buttermilk

MARSHMALLOW FILLING
2 cups (500 mL) marshmallow spread
½ cup (125 mL) unsalted butter,
    at room temperature

TIP If you don't have buttermilk, stir 1 tbsp (15 mL) vinegar or lemon juice into 1 cup (250 mL) milk.

Set racks in top and bottom thirds of oven and preheat oven to 350°F (180°C). Line 2 baking sheets with parchment paper.

To make the whoopie pies: In a medium bowl, combine flour, cocoa powder, baking powder, baking soda and salt, if desired. Whisk to combine. Set aside.

In a large bowl, cream butter and sugar with an electric mixer until light and fluffy, about 3 minutes. Add egg and beat until light and fluffy. Beat flour mixture into butter mixture alternately with buttermilk, making 2 additions of each and beating until just combined.

Spoon 24 heaping tablespoonfuls of batter onto prepared baking sheets, spacing 2 inches (5 cm) apart. Bake until a cake tester inserted into centre of cakes comes out clean, 10 to 12 minutes. Transfer to racks and let cool completely.

To make the marshmallow filling: In a large bowl, beat marshmallow spread and butter with an electric mixer until light and fluffy.

Sandwich marshmallow filling between 2 whoopie pie halves. Store pies in an airtight container at room temperature.

S'more Pie

This is my over-the-top take on the classic campfire combination of chocolate, toasted marshmallow and graham wafers. Drizzle a piece with loads of caramel sauce and get ready for the pie of your dreams! **MAKES 8 TO 10 SERVINGS**

GRAHAM CRACKER CRUST

1 ⅓ cups (325 mL) graham cracker crumbs

¼ cup (60 mL) sugar

⅓ cup (75 mL) unsalted butter, melted

CHOCOLATE FILLING

¾ cup (175 mL) whipping cream (35%)

1 cup (250 mL) finely chopped milk or dark chocolate or chocolate chips

¼ cup (60 mL) unsalted butter

Pinch of salt

TO ASSEMBLE

30 to 35 marshmallows

Caramel sauce (homemade or store-bought; optional)

Preheat oven to 350°F (180°C).

To make the graham cracker crust: Stir together graham cracker crumbs, sugar and melted butter until well combined. Press mixture firmly into the bottom and up the sides of a 9-inch (23 cm) pie plate. Bake until golden and crisp, 12 to 15 minutes. Let cool completely on a rack.

To make the chocolate filling: In a small saucepan over medium heat, bring cream just to a boil. (If you prefer a less dense filling, use 1 cup/250 mL cream.) Pour hot cream over chopped chocolate and butter in a bowl. Add a pinch of salt. Let stand for 1 minute. Stir until smooth.

Scrape chocolate filling into pie shell. Let set in fridge until chocolate is firm, 1 to 2 hours.

Preheat broiler.

Top chocolate filling with a layer of marshmallows. Put pie under broiler until marshmallows are golden brown, 1 to 2 minutes, depending on heat of broiler. Serve with caramel sauce, if desired.

Ricotta Espresso Mousse

Ricotta cheese is one of my favourite ingredients—I use it in so many dishes, both sweet and savoury. It's a versatile ingredient that lends itself to pairing with almost any flavour, so I infused it with a little espresso and the result is this decadent dessert. Ricotta Espresso Mousse is the perfect finish to any meal. And the best part is, you can make it in less than 10 minutes. **MAKES 4 SERVINGS**

½ cup (125 mL) cold brewed espresso

1 tbsp (15 mL) amaretto liqueur

1 tsp (5 mL) vanilla extract

14 oz (400 g) ricotta cheese

⅓ cup (75 mL) sugar

1 cup (250 mL) whipping cream (35%)

4 large egg whites or pasteurized egg whites

Chocolate shavings, for garnish

TIP Make sure you beat the ricotta long enough to remove the lumps. You can pass the ricotta mixture through a sieve to make it as smooth as possible.

Stir together espresso, amaretto and vanilla. Set aside.

In a large bowl, beat together ricotta, sugar and ½ cup (125 mL) cream until very smooth.

In another bowl, beat egg whites until soft peaks form. Fold egg whites into ricotta mixture. Fold in espresso mixture a little at a time. You want the mixture to be as smooth and airy as possible. Divide among 4 glass cappuccino cups or serving dishes.

Whip remaining ½ cup (125 mL) cream until soft peaks form. Garnish each serving of mousse with a dollop of whipped cream and chocolate shavings. Serve.

Lemon Mascarpone Mousse

This light and airy mousse is a great dessert for any night of the week or when unexpected guests drop in. The combination of creamy mascarpone cheese and tangy lemon curd is sure to please. Serve this mousse in a glass topped with some fresh berries or spoon a hefty dollop over a slice of my Lemony Pound Cake (page 407). **MAKES ABOUT 5 CUPS (1.25 L)**

1 lb (450 g) mascarpone cheese

½ cup (125 mL) icing sugar, or to taste, sifted

1 to 2 tbsp (15 to 30 mL) limoncello or orange liqueur

1 tsp (5 mL) vanilla extract

2 cups (500 mL) Lemon Curd (page 347)

1 cup (250 mL) whipping cream (35%), whipped

In a large bowl, whip mascarpone, icing sugar, limoncello and vanilla with an electric mixer until lightly and fluffy. Add lemon curd and whip until combined. Fold in whipped cream. Spoon into serving dishes. Garnish with fresh berries and mint sprigs, if desired.

TIP Serve a dollop of this mousse as a rich topping for French toast or use it to stuff doughnuts.

Brioche Gelato Bites

This Sicilian street food is an Italian take on the ice-cream sandwich. Nothing tastes quite like a fresh, buttery brioche stuffed with creamy gelato, then rolled in crushed nuts. It doesn't get any easier than using just two ingredients, so make sure your brioche and gelato are as fresh and good quality as possible.

MAKES 6 SERVINGS

6 scoops raspberry, vanilla or
    pistachio gelato

6 small brioche buns, cut in half horizontally

Handful of chopped pistachio nuts, sliced
    almonds or fresh raspberries, for garnish

Sandwich a scoop of gelato in each bun. Garnish as desired.

Warm Maple Pudding

This traditional Québécois dessert, called *pouding chômeur à l'érable*, has got to be one of my all-time favourites. Essentially a cake baked in maple syrup, it has a warm pudding-like texture that is simply irresistible. Add a scoop of vanilla ice cream on top, let it melt just a little, and it will make you crazy! **MAKES 8 TO 10 SERVINGS**

2 cups (500 mL) all-purpose flour

2 tsp (10 mL) baking powder

Pinch of salt

½ cup (125 mL) unsalted butter, at room temperature

1 cup (250 mL) sugar

2 large eggs, lightly beaten

2 cups (500 mL) whipping cream (35%)

1 cup (250 mL) maple syrup

Preheat oven to 450°F (230°C).

Combine flour, baking powder and salt in a bowl. Whisk to combine. Set aside.

In a large bowl, cream butter and sugar with an electric mixer until light and fluffy. Beat in eggs a little at a time, beating until light and fluffy. Stir in flour mixture just until combined.

In a large saucepan, bring cream and maple syrup to a boil over medium heat.

Using an ice-cream scoop or 2 spoons, scoop batter into individual ramekins or ovenproof bowls. (Alternatively, spread batter in a 13- × 9-inch/3.5 L baking dish.) Place ramekins on a baking sheet lined with parchment paper. Pour maple syrup mixture over batter.

Bake until cake sets and a tester comes out clean, 12 to 15 minutes. Serve puddings warm with ice cream or a dollop of crème fraîche, if desired.

TIP When it's berry season, add some extra goodness to this dessert by incorporating 1 cup (250 mL) of your favourite berries into the cake batter.

Maple-Glazed Doughnuts

What could be more Canadian than a maple-glazed doughnut? Well, you don't need to hit the doughnut shop to buy a dozen—just make these fun and tasty pastries at home. They're made using store-bought pizza dough, and the glaze couldn't be easier. Make a batch on the weekend and let the kids decorate them! **MAKES 9 TO 12 DOUGHNUTS**

DOUGHNUTS

1 lb (450 g) pizza dough

Vegetable oil, for-frying

Maple sugar, chocolate sprinkles and/or crumbled cooked bacon, for garnish

MAPLE GLAZE

3 cups (750 mL) icing sugar

½ cup (125 mL) pure maple syrup

⅓ cup (75 mL) milk

1 tbsp (15 mL) vanilla extract

2 tsp (10 mL) maple extract (optional)

Pinch of salt

To make the doughnuts: Bring pizza dough to room temperature. Let dough rise, covered, at room temperature for 20 to 30 minutes.

On a lightly floured work surface, roll out dough to ¼-inch (5 mm) thickness. Using a 3 ½-inch (9 cm) round cookie cutter, cut out doughnuts. Using 1-inch (2.5 cm) round cookie cutter, cut centres out of each doughnut for doughnut holes. Let dough rest for 5 minutes, then re-roll scraps and cut out more doughnuts.

If you fry the doughnuts immediately, their texture will have a slight chew. For a lighter and fluffier doughnut, let the doughnuts rise, covered, until doubled, 20 to 30 minutes.

Meanwhile, make the maple glaze: In a medium bowl, combine icing sugar, maple syrup, milk, vanilla, maple extract (if desired) and salt. Stir until smooth. For a thicker glaze, add more icing sugar; for a thinner glaze, add more milk.

Pour oil into a saucepan to reach 3 inches (8 cm) up the sides. Heat oil to 375°F (190°C) over medium heat.

Working in batches, carefully add doughnuts and doughnut holes to hot oil. Fry doughnuts, turning once, until golden brown, 1 to 2 minutes on each side. Drain on paper towels.

Dip warm doughnuts in maple glaze. Garnish as desired. Serve warm.

One-Bowl Chocolate Yogurt Cake

It's no lie—you only need one bowl to make this cake! If you're looking for a simple chocolate cake that's rich without a lot of added fat, this is the one. There's a double hit of yogurt in this recipe—it's not just the secret ingredient that makes the cake moist and tender, but it also serves as the thick, decadent topping.

MAKES 8 TO 9 SERVINGS

1 ¾ cups (425 mL) all-purpose flour

1 ⅓ cups (325 mL) brown sugar

¼ cup (60 mL) cocoa powder

1 tsp (5 mL) baking powder

1 tsp (5 mL) baking soda

½ tsp (2 mL) salt

1 cup (250 mL) plain whole milk yogurt, at room temperature

½ cup (125 mL) vegetable oil

2 large eggs, at room temperature

3 oz (85 g) dark chocolate, preferably 70% cocoa, melted and cooled slightly

1 tbsp (15 mL) vanilla extract

TOPPING

Drained yogurt or Greek-style plain yogurt

Icing sugar

Pomegranate seeds, for garnish

Icing sugar or cocoa powder, for garnish

Preheat oven to 350°F (180°C). Grease a 9-inch (2.5 L) square cake pan.

In a large bowl, combine flour, brown sugar, cocoa powder, baking powder, baking soda, salt, yogurt, oil, eggs, melted chocolate and vanilla. Beat until smooth and fluffy, scraping down sides of bowl as needed, 3 to 5 minutes.

Scrape batter into prepared pan. Bake until a cake tester comes out clean, 30 to 40 minutes. Let cool completely in pan before turning out.

Sweeten yogurt with icing sugar to taste. Serve cake with a dollop of sweetened yogurt. Garnish with pomegranate seeds and a dusting of icing sugar or cocoa powder.

Hazelnut Cake

This is honestly one of the most delicious cakes I've ever tasted—I could eat it morning, noon and night. It's a light and extremely moist flourless cake made with ground toasted hazelnuts. Top it with a pretty combination of orange zest and pistachios, and a bit of my yogurt icing, and your guests will be asking for the recipe. Use gluten-free baking powder for a gluten-free cake. **MAKES 6 TO 8 SERVINGS**

HAZELNUT CAKE

2 ½ cups (625 mL) hazelnuts

6 large eggs

1 cup + 2 tbsp (250 + 30 mL) sugar

½ cup (125 mL) unsalted butter, melted

2 tsp (10 mL) baking powder

1 tsp (5 mL) vanilla extract

Pinch of salt

YOGURT ICING

1 cup (250 mL) full-fat plain yogurt

2 tbsp (30 mL) honey

TIP This cake can also be made with ground almonds or ground walnuts.

Preheat oven to 350°F (180°C). Line bottom of an 8-inch (2 L) springform pan with parchment paper.

To make the hazelnut cake: In a food processor, pulse hazelnuts until finely chopped. Set aside.

Separate eggs, placing whites in a medium bowl and yolks in a large bowl.

Add sugar to yolks and beat until pale. Beat in melted butter. Fold hazelnuts, baking powder, vanilla and salt into yolk mixture. Set aside.

Beat egg whites until stiff peaks form. Gently but thoroughly fold egg whites into yolk mixture.

Scrape batter into prepared pan. Bake until a cake tester comes out clean, about 45 minutes. Let cake cool completely in pan before removing sides.

To make the yogurt icing: Stir together yogurt and honey until smooth.

Dust cake with icing sugar or serve with yogurt icing and garnish with chopped pistachios and grated orange zest, if desired.

Quinoa Carrot Cake with Whipped Coconut Topping

Quinoa is such a healthy ingredient—I use it in salads and side dishes all the time. Viewers challenged me to come up with a dessert recipe using this super-food. This moist and delicious cake is made from quinoa flour, and both the cake and the icing are gluten-free. Try the whipped coconut milk topping on any cake— you'll love it! MAKES 9 SERVINGS

QUINOA CARROT CAKE

1 ¼ cups (300 mL) quinoa flour

1 tsp (5 mL) gluten-free baking powder

½ tsp (2 mL) baking soda

½ tsp (2 mL) salt

2 tsp (10 mL) cinnamon

½ tsp (2 mL) nutmeg

¼ tsp (1 mL) ground cloves

2 large eggs

½ cup (125 mL) sugar

2 tbsp (30 mL) molasses

½ cup (125 mL) pumpkin purée

2 tsp (10 mL) vanilla extract

⅓ cup (75 mL) peanut, grapeseed or other vegetable oil

1 ½ cups (375 mL) shredded carrots

½ cup (125 mL) chopped raisins

½ cup (125 mL) finely chopped walnuts

Toasted coconut, for garnish

WHIPPED COCONUT TOPPING

1 can (14 oz/400 mL) coconut milk (not low-fat) or coconut cream, chilled overnight

Icing sugar

Preheat oven to 350°F (180°C). Grease an 8-inch (2 L) square cake pan and line bottom with parchment paper.

To make the carrot cake: In a medium bowl, combine quinoa flour, baking powder, baking soda, salt, cinnamon, nutmeg and cloves. Whisk to combine, and then sift. Set aside.

In a large bowl, beat eggs and sugar with an electric mixer until light, fluffy and pale yellow. Beat in molasses until light and fluffy. Beat in pumpkin purée and vanilla until incorporated. Beat in oil until light and fluffy. Stir in flour mixture just until combined. Fold in carrots, raisins and walnuts.

Scrape batter into prepared pan. Bake until cake springs back when touched and a cake tester comes out clean, 25 to 30 minutes. Let cake cool in pan on a rack for 10 minutes. Invert onto rack and cool completely.

While the cake cools, make the whipped coconut topping: Open the can of coconut milk. There should be a firm, hardened layer on top. Carefully spoon the

solidified cream into a bowl. (Reserve the liquid for other uses.) Whisk or beat cream with an electric mixer until light and fluffy. Sweeten to taste with icing sugar.

Serve cake with a dollop of whipped coconut topping and a sprinkle of toasted coconut.

Vary the topping with a Cream Cheese Frosting: With an electric mixer, whip 8 oz (225 g) cream cheese with 3 tbsp (45 mL) softened butter until fluffy and smooth. Add 1 cup (250 mL) icing sugar, ½ tsp (2 mL) vanilla and a pinch of salt. Beat until smooth.

TIP Some brands of coconut milk don't separate when they're chilled. Make sure you buy a brand free of stabilizing agents such as guar gum.

Olive Oil Cake with Plum Compote

Made with olive oil instead of butter, this cake is unbelievably moist with a lovely, soft crumb. It's topped with a plum compote that's infused with a little rosemary—a terrific flavour combination that's perfect for people who like a dessert that's not too sweet. This one's great for afternoon tea or a dinner party with friends.

MAKES 8 SERVINGS

OLIVE OIL CAKE

2 cups (500 mL) all-purpose flour

½ tsp (2 mL) baking powder

½ tsp (2 mL) baking soda

Pinch of salt

3 large eggs

2 cups (500 mL) sugar

1 cup (250 mL) extra-virgin olive oil

1 ½ cups (375 mL) milk

1 tbsp (15 mL) vanilla extract

Grated zest of 1 orange or 1 lemon

PLUM COMPOTE

2 tbsp (30 mL) extra-virgin olive oil

8 plums, such as Santa Rosa, prune and/or yellow, sliced

1 tiny sprig rosemary

Juice of 1 orange

¼ cup (60 mL) honey, or to taste

1 tsp (5 mL) vanilla extract

Pinch of cinnamon

Preheat oven to 350°F (180°C). Line a 10-inch (2.5 L) round cake pan with parchment paper. Grease sides of pan with butter.

To make the olive oil cake: In a bowl, combine flour, baking powder, baking soda and salt. Whisk to combine. Set aside.

In a large bowl, beat eggs with sugar until well combined. Add oil, milk, vanilla and zest. Beat just until combined. Add flour mixture. Stir just until combined—don't over-mix.

Scrape batter into prepared pan. Bake until a cake tester inserted in centre of cake comes out clean, about 1 hour. Let cool in pan, then turn out.

While cake bakes, make the plum compote: Heat olive oil in a skillet over medium heat. When oil is hot, add plums, rosemary, orange juice, honey, vanilla and cinnamon. Cook, stirring occasionally, until plums are warm and soft and juices are syrupy, about 5 minutes. Serve warm.

Serve cake warm or cooled completely with plum compote. Serve garnished with a dusting of icing sugar, a dollop of Greek yogurt and a drizzle of olive oil, if desired.

TIP Be creative with the fruity topping and replace the plums with peaches or figs.

Pineapple Upside-Down Cake

This retro-inspired dessert is timeless because it has it all: moist cake, fresh fruity goodness and a sweet brown sugar syrup. My version is made in a heavy skillet, which makes it easy to throw together and bake up quickly, even on a week-night. MAKES 6 TO 8 SERVINGS

1 ½ cups (375 mL) all-purpose flour

2 tsp (10 mL) baking powder

Pinch of salt

⅔ cup (150 mL) unsalted butter, at room temperature

1 cup (250 mL) brown sugar

8 fresh pineapple slices, about ½ inch (1 cm) thick

1 cup (250 mL) white sugar

1 large egg

1 tsp (5 mL) vanilla extract

1 cup (250 mL) milk

Preheat oven to 350°F (180°C).

In a bowl, combine flour, baking powder and salt. Whisk to combine. Set aside.

Heat ⅓ cup (75 mL) butter and brown sugar in an 8-inch (20 cm) heavy, oven-proof skillet over medium heat. When brown sugar has melted and starts to bubble, remove from heat. Arrange pineapple rings over sugar in a decorative pattern. Set aside.

In a large bowl, cream remaining ⅓ cup (75 mL) butter and white sugar with an electric mixer until light and fluffy, about 2 minutes. Add egg and vanilla. Beat until light and fluffy. Beat flour mixture into butter mixture alternately with milk, making 3 additions of flour mixture and 2 of milk. Beat until just combined.

Scrape batter over pineapple rings, spreading with a spatula to cover. Bake until a cake tester inserted into centre comes out clean, 25 to 30 minutes. Let cake stand in pan for 5 minutes, then invert onto a cake plate. Serve warm or cooled.

Grandma's Apple Cake

I remember the smell of my grandma's house when she would make this cake—the sweet scent of apples and cinnamon spreading through every room. This old-fashioned cake is packed with hearty ingredients and is perfect for snacks, dessert or even breakfast. Grab a piece to go with a frothy cappuccino!

MAKES 6 SERVINGS

2 tbsp (30 mL) dry bread crumbs

2 cups (500 mL) all-purpose flour

1 tbsp (15 mL) cinnamon

1 tsp (5 mL) baking powder

½ cup (125 mL) unsalted butter, at room temperature

¾ cup (175 mL) packed brown sugar

2 extra-large eggs

½ cup (125 mL) plain yogurt

¼ cup (60 mL) orange juice

Grated zest of ½ lemon

2 large apples, peeled and diced

⅔ cup (150 mL) raisins

⅔ cup (150 mL) chopped almonds or hazelnuts

TIP You can replace the almonds in this recipe with whatever nuts you have in the pantry.

Preheat oven to 350°F (180°C). Butter an 8-inch (20 cm) round cake pan and coat the bottom and sides of pan with bread crumbs. Set aside.

In a bowl, combine flour, cinnamon and baking powder. Whisk to combine. Set aside.

In a large bowl, beat butter and brown sugar with an electric mixer until light and fluffy. Add eggs one at a time, beating until smooth after each addition. Add yogurt, orange juice and lemon zest. Beat until smooth. Stir flour mixture into wet mixture a little at a time until batter is smooth. Do not over-mix. Gently fold in apples, raisins and almonds.

Scrape batter into prepared pan. Bake until cake springs back when touched and a cake tester comes out clean, 40 to 45 minutes. Let cool in pan, then turn out.

Serve cake with butterscotch sauce (page 381) and vanilla ice cream, if desired. Alternatively, dust with icing sugar.

Lemony Pound Cake

A good old-fashioned pound cake has to be one of the most versatile desserts around. My Lemony Pound Cake has a moist, dense texture and a fresh hit of lemon. For a really beautiful presentation, layer on lots of tangy lemon glaze and a sprinkle of zest. **MAKES 12 SERVINGS**

POUND CAKE

1 ½ cups (375 mL) all-purpose flour, sifted (½ lb/225 g)

Pinch of salt

1 cup (250 mL) unsalted butter, at room temperature (½ lb/225 g)

1 cup + 2 tbsp (250 + 30 mL) sugar (½ lb/225 g)

4 large eggs, at room temperature (½ lb/225 g)

1 tbsp (15 mL) vanilla extract

Grated zest of 2 lemons

GLAZE

1 ½ to 2 cups (375 to 500 mL) icing sugar, sifted

Juice of 2 lemons

Preheat oven to 325°F (160°C). Grease and flour a standard loaf pan.

To make the pound cake: Stir together flour and salt. Set aside.

In a large bowl, cream butter and sugar with an electric mixer until light and fluffy. Add eggs one at a time, beating well after each addition. Add vanilla and lemon zest. Beat to combine. On low speed, add flour just until combined.

Scrape batter into prepared loaf pan. Bake until cake springs back when gently pressed and a cake tester comes out clean, 60 to 70 minutes. Let cool in pan for 10 to 12 minutes. Turn out of pan and let cool completely on a rack.

To make the glaze: In a small bowl, stir together icing sugar and lemon juice until smooth. Adjust sweetness and consistency with more icing sugar or lemon juice to taste.

Pour glaze over pound cake and let set. Garnish with lemon zest, if desired.

TIP This cake is perfect on its own, but you can use it (unglazed) in recipes like strawberry shortcake or trifle.

Strawberry Tall Cake

We all know the strawberry shortcake—petite packages of sweet strawberry and creamy deliciousness. This is my take on the shortcake, but, of course, I don't like to do anything small. My Strawberry TALL Cake is the granddaddy of strawberry desserts—eight layers of creamy, fruity fun, stacked sky-high. The next time you need a show-stopping dessert, think BIG! **MAKES 16 TO 20 SERVINGS**

SPONGE CAKE

1 ½ cups (375 mL) almond flour or finely ground almonds

1 cup (250 mL) all-purpose flour

2 tsp (10 mL) baking powder

Pinch of salt

6 large eggs, at room temperature

1 cup + 2 tbsp (250 + 30 mL) sugar

½ cup (125 mL) unsalted butter, melted

1 tsp (5 mL) vanilla or almond extract

TO ASSEMBLE

1 pint (500 mL) strawberries

¼ cup (60 mL) white sugar, or to taste

2 cups (500 mL) whipping cream (35%)

3 tbsp (45 mL) icing sugar, or to taste

3 cups (750 mL) good-quality strawberry jam

Preheat oven to 350°F (180°C). Line bottoms of two 9-inch (1.5 L) round cake pans with parchment paper.

Sift together almond flour, all-purpose flour, baking powder and salt. Sift again. Set aside.

In a large bowl, whip eggs and sugar with an electric mixer until tripled in volume, thick, and mixture falls in ribbons when whisk is lifted, about 5 minutes. Gently fold in flour mixture. Gently fold in melted butter and vanilla.

Scrape batter into prepared pans. Bake cakes until tops spring back when gently pressed and a cake tester comes out clean, 20 to 25 minutes. Cool in pans for 5 to 10 minutes, then invert onto racks and let cool completely.

Bake another batch of the sponge cake to make 4 cakes in total.

To assemble the cake: Slice strawberries, leaving a few of the best ones whole for garnishing the top of the cake. Toss strawberries with white sugar and set aside.

Whip cream until soft peaks form. Beat in icing sugar.

Using a serrated knife, cut each cake in half horizontally to make 8 cake layers. Arrange a bottom cake layer on a serving plate. Spread with ¾ cup (175 mL) of the jam. Top with a cake layer. Spread with one-quarter of the whipped cream. Top with another cake layer and spread with ¾ cup (175 mL) jam. Top with a cake layer, one-quarter of the whipped cream, and half of the sliced strawberries.

Repeat layers, ending with whipped cream and sliced strawberries. Garnish with reserved whole strawberries. Slice cake with a serrated knife.

TIP Use the sponge cake in other recipes, such as trifle. Replace the strawberries with any fresh berry of your choosing.

Cherry Clafouti

Clafouti may sound complicated and look fancy, but it's not at all difficult. This classic French dessert is basically a simple sweet custard with fresh fruit. That's it! Serve this impressive dish to family and friends, but don't tell anyone how easy it was to make. **MAKES 6 TO 8 SERVINGS**

1 lb (450 g) pitted sweet cherries

3 large eggs

½ cup (125 mL) icing sugar,
    plus more for dusting

½ cup (125 mL) all-purpose flour

1 cup (250 mL) milk

½ cup (125 mL) whipping cream (35%)

1 tsp (5 mL) vanilla or almond extract

Grated zest of 1 lemon

Pinch of salt

Preheat oven to 400°F (200°C). Butter a 10-inch (2.5 L) round baking dish. Spread cherries in dish.

In a large bowl, whisk together eggs and ½ cup (125 mL) icing sugar until combined. Whisk in flour. Whisk in milk and cream a little at a time until batter is smooth. Add vanilla, lemon zest and salt. Whisk just to combine. The consistency of the batter should be a little thicker than whipping cream. Let batter rest for 10 minutes.

Pour batter over cherries. Bake until set and puffy, 40 to 50 minutes. Serve warm with a dusting of icing sugar.

TIP Cherries are the traditional choice for this dessert, but change the fruit depending on the season. Try pears, plums or raspberries.

Peach Cobbler

Get your hands on some fresh peaches, guys! This is one of the tastiest fruit desserts ever. If you want to use frozen peaches, let them thaw before baking. Serve a generous scoop of cobbler while it's still warm. I like it with a little drizzle of maple syrup and some ice cream. Who's counting calories?! **MAKES 6 SERVINGS**

PEACH FILLING

7 cups (1.75 L) sliced unpeeled peaches (7 to 9 fresh or use frozen)

Juice of ½ lime

3 tbsp (45 mL) brown sugar

2 tbsp (30 mL) unsalted butter, cut in small pieces, at room temperature

2 tbsp (30 mL) amaretto liqueur (optional)

1 tsp (5 mL) vanilla extract

½ tsp (2 mL) cinnamon, or to taste

COBBLER TOPPING

¾ cup (175 mL) all-purpose flour

3 tbsp (45 mL) white sugar

2 tsp (10 mL) baking powder

1 tsp (5 mL) grated lime zest

¼ tsp (1 mL) salt

¼ cup (60 mL) cold unsalted butter, cut in cubes

½ cup (125 mL) half-and-half cream (10%)

2 tbsp (30 mL) brown sugar

Preheat oven to 375°F (190°C). Generously butter a 13- × 9-inch (3.5 L) baking dish.

To make the peach filling: In a large bowl, combine peaches, lime juice, brown sugar, butter, amaretto (if desired), vanilla and cinnamon. Toss until well combined. Spread mixture in baking dish. Set aside.

To make the cobbler topping: In a large bowl, combine flour, sugar, baking powder, lime zest and salt. Stir with a whisk to thoroughly combine. Cut in butter with your fingertips or a pastry blender until mixture resembles coarse crumbs. Try not to overwork the mixture, or the butter will melt and the topping won't be as fluffy. Add cream to flour mixture. Stir until just combined—don't over-mix.

Top fruit mixture with large spoonfuls of batter to create a "cobblestone" finish. Sprinkle with brown sugar.

Bake cobbler until peaches are soft and tender, fruit mixture bubbles, and topping is golden brown, 35 to 40 minutes, depending on ripeness of peaches.

Serve cobbler warm with ice cream and a drizzle of maple syrup, if desired.

TIP Make this cobbler with a mixture of fresh berries in place of peaches.

Apple Pecan Crisp

Everyone needs a good crisp recipe, and I'm sharing mine with you. Crispin apples are perfect for baking in pies and crisps, but you can also use Spy, Cortland, Golden Delicious or Pink Lady varieties. Be sure to add pecans to your topping—they add great texture and a nice nutty flavour. **MAKES 4 TO 6 SERVINGS**

CRISP TOPPING

½ cup (125 mL) large-flake rolled oats
½ cup (125 mL) all-purpose flour
½ cup (125 mL) chopped pecans
½ cup (125 mL) brown sugar
½ cup (125 mL) unsalted butter, melted

APPLE FILLING

6 cups (1.5 L) sliced peeled Crispin apples
Juice of ½ lemon
¼ cup (60 mL) brown sugar
¼ cup (60 mL) unsalted butter, cut in cubes
1 tsp (5 mL) cinnamon
1 tsp (5 mL) vanilla extract

Preheat oven to 350°F (180°C). Butter a 9-inch (2.5 L) square baking dish.

To make the crisp topping: In a bowl, combine oats, flour, pecans and brown sugar. Stir to mix. Add melted butter and stir until well combined. Set aside.

To make the apple filling: In a large bowl, combine apple slices, lemon juice, brown sugar, cubed butter, cinnamon and vanilla. Toss to coat apples well.

Spread apple filling in baking dish. Sprinkle with crisp topping. Bake until topping is golden brown, filling is bubbling and juices are thick, 30 to 40 minutes.

Serve warm with whipped cream or vanilla ice cream, if desired.

Easy Blueberry Frozen Yogurt

This may just be the easiest recipe in this book, yet the results are so delicious. Make your own fruity frozen yogurt in just minutes—all you need is blueberries, Greek yogurt and a touch of maple syrup to make magic in your food processor. It's the perfect thing to make on busy weeknights when the kids ask, "What's for dessert?" **MAKES 4 SERVINGS**

4 cups (1 L) frozen blueberries

2 cups (500 mL) Greek-style vanilla
   or plain yogurt

¼ cup (60 mL) maple syrup, or to taste

In a food processor, combine frozen blueberries, yogurt and maple syrup. Pulse to combine. Serve immediately or put in freezer for 10 minutes for a firmer texture, if desired. Garnish with fresh blueberries and a sprig of mint, if desired.

TIP This instant dessert is just as delicious made with frozen raspberries, mangoes or peaches.

Layered Blueberry Pie

This layered blueberry dessert is a perfect cross between pie and cheesecake. The simple homemade pastry is filled with a tangy layer of cream cheese and a jammy blueberry filling, then only made better when topped with some fresh whipped cream and lemon zest. **MAKES 6 TO 8 SERVINGS**

PASTRY

2 cups (500 mL) all-purpose flour

1 tsp (5 mL) sugar

1 tsp (5 mL) salt

¾ cup (175 mL) unsalted butter, at room temperature, cut into small cubes

¼ cup (60 mL) milk, at room temperature

1 large egg yolk

LAYERED FILLING

8 cups (2 L) fresh blueberries

2 ½ cups (625 mL) sugar

2 cups (500 mL) whipping cream (35%)

1 tsp (5 mL) vanilla extract

8 oz (225 g) cream cheese, at room temperature

Lemon zest, for garnish

To make the pastry: In a large bowl, mix together flour, sugar and salt. Cut butter into flour mixture with your fingertips or a pastry blender until mixture resembles coarse meal. Beat together milk and egg yolk. Stir into flour mixture just until dough comes together. Form dough into a ball and flatten into a disc. Wrap in plastic wrap and refrigerate for at least 1 hour.

Preheat oven to 375°F (190°C).

Lightly flour work surface. Roll out pastry to ¼-inch (5 mm) thickness. Fit pastry into a 9-inch (23 cm) tart pan with removable bottom. Trim off excess around edges. (You will have lots of leftover pastry.)

Prick bottom of pastry all over with a fork. Line pastry shell with parchment paper or foil. Fill pie with pie weights or dried beans. Bake for 15 minutes. Remove weights and parchment and continue to bake until pastry is cooked through, lightly golden and crisp, 5 to 10 minutes more. Let cool.

To make the blueberry filling: Combine 7 cups (1.75 L) of the blueberries and 2 cups (500 mL) of the sugar in a large, heavy saucepan. Bring to a boil over medium-high heat. Reduce heat to medium and simmer, stirring occasionally, until mixture reaches a jam-like consistency, 20 to 25 minutes. Set aside to cool.

In a large bowl, combine cream, vanilla and the remaining ½ cup (125 mL) sugar. Whip until soft peaks form.

To assemble the pie: Remove sides of tart pan. Stir the remaining 1 cup (250 mL) blueberries into the cooled filling. Spread cream cheese over bottom of tart shell. Then spread blueberry filling over the cream cheese layer. Top pie with whipped cream. Let set in refrigerator for at least 1 hour before serving. Garnish with lemon zest, if desired.

DRINKS

Classic Cosmopolitan

This slightly sweet, slightly tangy cranberry drink is one of the most popular vodka cocktails around. It's a must at any fancy party. Just shake it up, pour it into a martini glass and top it with a curl of lime zest. Voilà, instant cocktail chic!

MAKES 2 SERVINGS

2 oz (60 mL) vodka

½ oz (15 mL) orange liqueur, such as Cointreau

Juice of 1 lime

3 oz (90 mL) cranberry juice cocktail

2 strips lime zest, for garnish

Pour vodka, orange liqueur, lime juice and cranberry juice into a cocktail shaker with ice. Shake well and strain into 2 martini glasses. Garnish with lime zest.

Classic Margarita

Make a great big pitcher of this classic crowd-pleaser the next time you're having friends over. Nothing goes better with my Grilled Shrimp Tacos (page 295) or Chicken Fajitas (page 318) than a glass of this lime and tequila cocktail. Don't forget to add a hit of peppery heat to the salted rim of the glass! **MAKES 2 SERVINGS**

Coarse salt, for rimming glass

Chili powder (optional)

Lime wedge, for rimming glass

¼ cup (60 mL) tequila

1 to 2 tbsp (15 to 30 mL) orange liqueur

¼ cup (60 mL) freshly squeezed lime juice

2 tbsp (30 mL) simple syrup, or to taste

Lime slices, for garnish

Place ¼ to ½ inch (5 mm to 1 cm) coarse salt in a shallow bowl or a side plate. For a spicy salt, stir in a little chili powder (such as cayenne, ancho or chipotle). Moisten the rim of each martini glass with lime wedge. Dip rim of glass in salt mixture. Set aside.

Pour tequila, orange liqueur to taste, lime juice and simple syrup into a cocktail shaker with ice. Shake well and strain into 2 martini glasses. Garnish with a slice of lime, if desired.

TIP To make a simple syrup, combine equal parts sugar and water in a saucepan. Bring to a boil until sugar dissolves. Let cool before using. Keeps in the fridge for several weeks.

Classic Piña Colada

It's like a trip to the islands in a drink. Who can resist a tall glass of this coconuty, pineappley, rummy goodness? Not me! A little umbrella, a pineapple wedge and a maraschino cherry are all you need to send your taste buds to the tropics.

MAKES 2 SERVINGS

½ cup (125 mL) white or dark rum

Juice of 1 lime

1 cup (250 mL) canned sweetened
    cream of coconut

½ cup (125 mL) chopped fresh pineapple

2 cups (500 mL) crushed ice

Pineapple wedges, maraschino cherries and
    cocktail umbrellas, for garnish

In a blender, purée rum, lime juice, cream of coconut, pineapple and crushed ice until smooth. Pour into 2 glasses. Garnish each drink with a wedge of pineapple, a maraschino cherry and a cocktail umbrella.

White Sangria with Raspberries

When you make a pitcher of this Spanish-inspired drink, everyone is happy. I love a good red wine sangria, but this sangria blanca, made with white wine and loads of raspberries and citrus fruit, is a beautiful, refreshing choice to serve with a spicy dinner. **MAKES 4 SERVINGS**

¼ cup (60 mL) orange liqueur

1 pint (500 mL) raspberries

1 tbsp (15 mL) sugar

1 lemon, thinly sliced

1 orange, thinly sliced

Juice of 1 orange

1 bottle (750 mL) dry white wine, such as sauvignon blanc, pinot grigio or vinho verde

Sparkling water (optional)

In a pitcher, combine orange liqueur, raspberries, sugar, lemon slices, orange slices, orange juice and wine. Pour into glasses with ice. If desired, finish with a splash of sparkling water.

Pineapple Rum Punch

This simple Caribbean cocktail can be made in big batches for a party and customized to your taste. Pineapple juice is the base of this drink, but feel free to add dark or light rum (or any rum you like) and make it carbonated (or not!) with some sparkling water. MAKES **6 SERVINGS**

1 ½ cups (375 mL) rum, or to taste

2 cups (500 mL) pineapple juice

1 cup (250 mL) simple syrup (page 421)

½ cup (125 mL) lime juice

4 cups (1 L) sparkling water (optional)

Pineapple wedges, for garnish

In a pitcher, combine rum, pineapple juice, simple syrup, lime juice and ice. Stir to combine. Pour into glasses. Top up with sparkling water, if desired, and garnish with pineapple wedges.

Fresh Mint Iced Tea

Nothing says summer like iced tea, and this mint-infused version is one of the best ways to cool off a hot day. Mint grows like crazy in my garden, and this is a delicious way to make use of its flavour. Throw a handful of fresh, minty goodness in with the super-simple mix of water, lemon and sugar and you have a great way to beat the heat. **MAKES 4 SERVINGS**

1 cup (250 mL) packed fresh mint leaves

2 tbsp (30 mL) sugar

1 piece lemon peel (about 2 inches ×
   ½ inch/5 × 1 cm)

2 cups (500 mL) boiling water

2 cups (500 mL) cold water

Mint leaves and lemon slices, for garnish

Fresh squeezed lemon juice,
   to taste (optional)

Place mint leaves, sugar and lemon peel in a large measuring cup or pitcher. Add boiling water. Stir and let steep for 10 minutes. Add cold water. Chill in fridge for 1 hour. Strain.

To serve, pour into glasses with ice and garnish with fresh mint and lemon slices. If desired, add a squeeze of fresh lemon.

Iced Green Tea with Lychee

I could drink green tea any time of day—morning, afternoon or night. This iced green tea got me really excited, because not only does it have the fresh, fantastic flavours of ginger and mint, but you also get the health benefits of the tea itself. The frozen lychee does double duty: it is a sweet surprise at the bottom of the glass, and it's also an ice cube! MAKES 4 SERVINGS

1 can (19 oz/540 mL) lychee fruit in syrup

4 cups (1 L) boiling water

2 green tea bags

1 tbsp (15 mL) grated fresh ginger

1 lime, cut in thin slices

Handful of fresh mint leaves

Handful of raspberries

Strain lychee fruit, reserving syrup. Freeze lychee fruit on small tray.

Pour boiling water over tea bags and steep for about 4 minutes. Remove tea bags. Let tea cool completely.

In a pitcher, combine cooled green tea, lychee syrup and ginger. Stir. Add frozen lychee fruit, lime slices, mint leaves, raspberries and ice. Serve.

Prosecco Cranberry Ice Pops

Think of this as the adult version of a kids' ice pop—the perfect finishing touch to an outdoor party. It combines a cocktail with a frozen dessert and it's a real conversation-starter. Your guests will love the tangy hit of fresh fruit and slight sweetness of the sparkling wine, all served on a stick! **MAKES 18 TO 20 SERVINGS**

3 cups (750 mL) Prosecco or sparkling wine

3 cups (750 mL) white cranberry juice
    cocktail

¼ cup (60 mL) chopped frozen cranberries

Combine Prosecco and cranberry juice in a large measuring cup. Stir to combine. Pour about ⅓ cup (75 mL) into each ice pop mould. Add cranberries to each mould. Freeze until firm, at least 6 hours.

Lemongrass Soda

This fizzy non-alcoholic drink will add a fresh citrus-infused flavour to your next summer barbecue. The unique flavour of lemongrass and the natural sweetness of the honey pair up to make magic in a highball glass in this lovely soda.

MAKES 4 SERVINGS

3 stalks lemongrass
1 cup (250 mL) water
⅓ cup (75 mL) honey

Juice of 2 limes
2 limes, thinly sliced
Small handful of fresh mint leaves
4 cups (1 L) sparkling water

Cut off the bottom 4 inches (10 cm) of each lemongrass stalk reserving the remaining stalk for garnish, if desired. With the side of a knife, smash and bruise the lemongrass bottoms, then finely chop.

Combine chopped lemongrass, water and honey in a small saucepan. Bring to a boil over medium heat. Let cool completely, 1 to 2 hours. Strain through a fine sieve, discarding lemongrass. (Infusion can be made ahead and stored in the fridge for up to 5 days.)

To serve, combine lemongrass infusion, lime juice, lime slices and mint in a pitcher. Top with sparkling water. Pour into glasses with ice and garnish with lemongrass stalks, if desired.

Spiced Apple Cider

A mug of warm apple cider is the perfect way to thaw out on a cold day. There's something about the smell of cinnamon and cloves simmering away on the stove that makes you all warm and fuzzy inside. My advice is to make a big batch for your next skating party or holiday open house. **MAKES 8 SERVINGS**

8 cups (2 L) apple cider

2 cinnamon sticks

8 whole cloves

Peel of 1 orange

½ cup (125 mL) apple brandy,
    or to taste (optional)

Combine apple cider, cinnamon sticks, cloves and orange peel in a large saucepan. Warm over medium heat until piping hot. Let cider mull over low heat until fragrant, 10 to 15 minutes. Add apple brandy, if desired.

Affogato

This Italian classic is half coffee, half ice cream... and 100% delicious. It couldn't be easier to make this après-dinner coffee treat, the perfect way to end a big dinner party when everyone's too stuffed for dessert. **MAKES 1 SERVING**

1 scoop vanilla ice cream

½ oz (15 mL) grappa

1 shot freshly brewed espresso

Grated chocolate, to garnish

Biscotti cookie, for serving (optional)

Place a scoop of ice cream in an espresso cup or serving glass. Pour grappa and espresso over ice cream. Garnish with grated chocolate. Serve with a biscotti cookie on the side, if desired.

ACKNOWLEDGMENTS

THANK YOU!

Making TV shows and cookbooks takes a lot of support. A lot of great people provided it.

My thanks to . . .

. . . the four most important ladies in my life: my partner, Isabelle, and princesses Emilia and Anna, for their patience while Daddy went to Toronto every week to shoot *In the Kitchen*; and my mother, Elena, for passing on her culinary know-how and giving me my first shot at pasta-making when I was five!

. . . my Executive Producer and cookbook co-author, Krista Look, and her husband, David Childerhose, for their unwavering belief in all I do.

. . . the "big cheese," Executive Director, Studio and Unscripted Programming, CBC Television, Julie Bristow, and Factual Entertainment executives Jennifer Dettman, Sandra Kleinfeld, Grazyna Krupa and Marc Thompson. Thanks for giving viewers an opportunity to visit me In the Kitchen every day.

. . . CBC Licensing Division's Karen Bower, for finding us a wonderful publishing partner in Penguin Canada. To Penguin publishing director Andrea Magyar, who gave us all the freedom in the world, and copy editor Shaun Oakey, who ensured all the recipes were the best they could be.

. . . the cookbook creative team: food producer and developer Josie Malevich, food photographer Leila Ashtari, chef Jonah Snitman, food stylist Michael Elliott, prop stylist Nikole Rutherford and production assistants Julia Bakker, James Lourenço and Brandon Ventresca.

. . . the amazing production team of *In the Kitchen*: Senior Producer Portia Corman ("the gorgeous blonde in my ear"), Unit Manager Thérèse Attard who keeps us on track, Josie Malevich, Recipe Developer Audrey Lessard, Associate Producer Zoë Kazakos, Producer Angela Economopoulos, set decorators Danielle Hunter and Nikole Rutherford, PAs James and Brandon, and our audience booking and warm-up team.

. . . the best kitchen team in TV: the unflappable Jonah Snitman, jack-of-all-food-trades Flo Leung, my "bald-is-beautiful brother" Jason Skrobar, Michael Elliott, and production assistants Grace Volpe, Yun Yu (Charlene) Lin and Ashshita Hossein.

. . . our Digital Producer Yasmin Seneviratne, Associate Producer Jessica Brooks and website designer Amanda York.

. . . our fabulous directors—Heather Jenken, Dave Russell and Jane Wilson—and the CBC studio team, including Technical Producer Dinu Cebzan, Project Manager Erin Rubenstein and set designer Mario Vecchi.

. . . our outstanding studio crew and editors Ilan Doitch, Neil MacNaughton and Alicia Lee, who make us look good.

Finally, to the amazing audiences who watch us on-air and visit our live tapings, we would be nothing without you.

IN THE KITCHEN

WITH

STEFANO FAITA

INDEX